DOROTHEA DIX

Dorothea Dix
From an oil portrait in the New Jersey State Hospital in Trenton; taken
from a daguerreotype made about 1840.

Dorothea Dix

FORGOTTEN SAMARITAN

By

HELEN E. MARSHALL

NEW YORK / RUSSELL & RUSSELL

FIRST PUBLISHED IN 1937 BY
THE UNIVERSITY OF NORTH CAROLINA PRESS
REISSUED, 1967, BY RUSSELL & RUSSELL
A DIVISION OF ATHENEUM PUBLISHERS, INC.
BY ARRANGEMENT WITH HELEN E. MARSHALL
L. C. CATALOG CARD NO: 66-24729
ISBN: 0-8462-0945-4
PRINTED IN THE UNITED STATES OF AMERICA

TO THE MEMORY OF

My Father

DAVID CONWELL MARSHALL

PREFACE

THIS STUDY which began as an inquiry into the movement for reform in the care and treatment of the mentally ill, has resolved itself into a biography of Dorothea Lynde Dix, humanitarian and reformer. To separate the woman and the movement has been impossible. In the woman the movement had its greatest inspiration and impetus; in the movement the woman lived and had her being. To tell of one is to tell of the other, but the story is one that is not frequently told. The present age has come to take its institutions for the mentally ill for granted and does not inquire of the days preceding the modern psychopathic hospital. In this tendency to accept institutional care without question, the name of Dorothea Dix has been all but lost to posterity. *descendants.*

Rather than emblazoned on monuments of stone her name was written deep in the hearts of the generations that knew her, and with their passing, her place in social history has been overlooked. Yet her career is "a romance in philanthropy that the world can ill afford to forget." Although she was engaged throughout her long life in humanitarian activities of various kinds, she is best remembered for her work in behalf of the indigent psychotic. As a result of her untiring efforts thousands of demented souls were released from dungeons, caves, and prisons, and placed in hospitals where they were given care and treatment befitting the sick and unfortunate of humanity. She popularized institutional treatment for mental diseases and aroused a social conscience; and through her personal activities thirty-two hospitals were established in America, and several in Europe as well. Also at least two in Japan may be traced to the inspiration which she gave Jugio Arinori Mori while he was the Japanese charge d'affaires in Washington.

When Miss Dix died in 1887, Dr. Charles Nichols wrote to his friend Dr. D. Hack Tuke, of York, England, saying, "Thus has died and been laid to rest in the most quiet and unostentatious way the most useful and distinguished woman that America has produced." Five years before, Dr. Tuke, in speaking of her, had written, "Saintship is not the exclusive property of the church, medicine has also her annals."

[vii]

For Miss Dix the author makes no extravagant claims. Her character was enriched by sacrifice and remained unsullied by success. Her letters to Ann Heath, George Emerson, and Mrs. Rathbone chronicle more than the progress of the movement in behalf of the unfortunate of earth; they reveal the triumphant upward march of her own soul.

Very early her friends began pressing her for some account by her own hand of her work in the interest of the mentally ill and of prison reform. Among these friends Luther V. Bell of McLean Hospital, General John A. Dix of New York, Hon. Alexander Randall of Annapolis, Maryland, and the Rev. Mr. William Greenleaf Eliot of St. Louis, were most persistent. Always she pleaded that she was too busy. Moreover there was so much sadness and disappointment in her life that the thought of a biography was not a pleasant one. In 1867, when Mrs. Sarah Josepha Hale, editor of *Godey's Lady's Book* appealed for information to include in her *Lives and Characters of Distinguished Women,* Miss Dix made the acrid reply,

I am not ambitious of nominal distinctions, and notoriety is my special aversion. My reputation and my services belong to my country. My history and my affections are consecrated to my friends. . . . I confess that giving unnecessary publicity to women while they are yet alive seems to me singularly at variance with the delicacy and modesty which are the most attractive ornaments of their sex.

Late in life she yielded to the solicitations of her friends and tried to reduce her papers to order, but she was very weak and the work was tiresome. "I regret thee has never kept a diary," wrote John Greenleaf Whittier. At last she turned her papers over to Horace A. Lamb, of Boston, to be used after her death as he saw fit, in the preparation of a memoir of her life and work. She talked over with him certain details which she preferred to be omitted as well as those things which she desired might be emphasized. She wished her Civil War experience to be only slightly mentioned, saying it was a work by which she did not want her life judged. She suggested that either William Greenleaf Eliot, or James Freeman Clarke be entrusted with the task; Dr. Eliot's death, however, occurred a few months before her own, and the Rev. Mr. Clarke was growing so feeble that he did not know whether he would be able to complete his own memoirs. The work was finally given to Francis Tiffany, likewise a Unitarian preacher.

The Rev. Mr. Tiffany performed an invaluable service in gathering up many of Miss Dix's letters and in securing from friends and pupils personal anecdotes and testimonials which would otherwise have been lost. Mr. Tiffany returned the larger collections of Miss Dix's letters to their respective owners, and these have been consulted by the author of this biography; but much miscellaneous material was turned back to Mr. Lamb in whose keeping it remained until his death. This is still extant but not available, which circumstance has further indebted the author to Mr. Tiffany for numerous letters quoted in his memoir of Miss Dix.

In the present study an attempt has been made to clear up and explain certain misconceptions regarding Dorothea Dix's unhappy childhood, her relations with her Grandmother Dix, and her Civil War work, as well as to give the general background of the movement for reform, and a survey of the evolution of methods in caring for mental patients.

The fourth chapter, "Psychosis: Superstition and Science," has been written as a parenthetical chapter dealing with the historical background of the therapeutics of mental diseases and may be omitted at the discretion of the reader without impairing the narrative of Miss Dix's activities.

To those who have assisted in the preparation of this biography through the loan of materials, and the giving of counsel and encouragement, the author acknowledges great obligation. Especial gratitude is due Professor Reginald C. McGrane, Cincinnati University, who suggested the possibilities of Dorothea Lynde Dix as the subject of a doctoral dissertation, and to Professor Richard H. Shryock, Duke University, who has generously given of his advice in the research and preparation of the manuscript. Others to whom an expression of appreciation is due are Professor W. K. Boyd, Duke University, for his interest and encouragement; Mrs. W. H. White, Wellesley Hills, Massachusetts; Miss Elizabeth Bond, Cambridge, Massachusetts; Mrs. Hugh Rathbone, Greenbank, Liverpool, England; the Rev. Mr. Thomas Lamb Eliot, Portland, Oregon; Major Julia C. Stimson, Chief of the United States Army Nursing Corps, Washington, D. C.; Colonel Fred A. Olds, Raleigh, North Carolina; Dr. William A. White, Superintendent of St. Elizabeth's Hospital,

Washington, D. C., for the loan of manuscript material; Dr. Robert G. Stone, New Jersey State Hospital, Trenton; and my brother, Leon S. Marshall, for laborious transcripts of the Rathbone Manuscripts. My former teacher, Miss Laura A. Meier, Professor of English, College of Emporia, Emporia, Kansas, has painstakingly read the entire manuscript and made valuable suggestions as to style.

Superintendents of various psychopathic hospitals have responded graciously to requests for data regarding their respective institutions.

The staffs of the following libraries have been most helpful in aiding and facilitating research: Duke University Library; Duke University Medical School Library; University of Chicago Library; Harvard College Library; John Crerar Library, Chicago; Massachusetts Historical Society Library; Boston Public Library; North Carolina Historical Commission Library; University of Kansas Library; University of North Carolina Library; Chicago Public Library; Los Angeles Public Library; Henry E. Huntington Memorial Library, San Marino, California; the Library of Congress; the Library of the Boston Athenaeum; the Library of the Unitarian Association, Boston; and the archives of the Surgeon-General and the Adjutant-General, United States Army, Washington, D. C.

Without the kind assistance of these and other persons whose numbers preclude acknowledgment, this biography could not have been prepared.

HELEN E. MARSHALL

Normal, Illinois
April, 1936

CONTENTS

DOROTHEA DIX

Chapter I

FROM HAMPDEN TO BOSTON

When Elijah Dix's son, Joseph, married against the wishes of the family and was compelled to leave Harvard, the stern old doctor resolved to settle the young man on a distant farm on the outskirts of Hampden, six miles below Bangor. At the close of the American Revolution that part of the country which is now Maine was the frontier of Massachusetts. It was wild, unbroken, and uninhabited; but rich in fine timber and amply provided with swift waterways, it afforded an opportunity for speculation. Of this Elijah Dix, as a shrewd young doctor in Worcester, had early taken advantage; he had realized that shipbuilding and lumbering were still in their infancy, and had acquired vast acres of heavily wooded land along the Penobscot River. These increased in value, and in 1795, Dr. Dix, grown prosperous from the returns of his profession and sundry ventures in trade and real estate, had moved to Boston and was devising schemes for settling the two towns of Dixfield and Dixmont.

It was Dr. Dix's plan to bring settlers into the country, sell farms outright or on long terms, set up saw-mills, and make his profits out of lumber and the increase in land values as the region became populated. Dixfield and Dixmont were about a hundred miles apart, and travel was extremely difficult. There were no roads or bridges; in order to reach Dixmont it was necessary to go up the river and slowly make one's way through the dense forest by means of a blazed trail. Weeks were often required to make the journey, and Dr. Dix could ill afford to spend so much time away from home, his medical practice, the apothecary shop, and the chemical works which he had recently established in South Boston. He decided to make his son agent for the Maine lands and entrust him with the business of securing settlers for Dixmont.

This, thought Dr. Dix, would provide a home and a livelihood, and it would also remove the young couple from Boston where members of the Dix family had already taken a strong dislike to Mary. It might be that Joseph would mend his intemperate ways, settle down to something and make a respectable living; if he did not, no one could ever say that the old doctor had not done his part. He had sent the boy to college, had even consented to his studying for the ministry; but before completing his degree the son had broken faith, married a woman much older than he, and one of whom his parents did not approve. Harvard's doors were now closed to him as to other married men; it was plain that Joseph Dix would have to shift for himself. The outlook was none too promising.

Hampden was a settlement of about one hundred and fifty people. The settlers were "come-outers" for one reason or another; most of them had emigrated from Cape Cod.[1] Like Joseph Dix and Mary Bigelow, they were all poor. They lived in crude log houses chinked with plaster; the floors were of puncheon, the windows were small and in many homes oiled paper, not glass, served to let in light, and there were heavy shutters to keep out the cold in winter. The average home in those early years at Hampden consisted of a single room with an attic or perhaps a "lean-to." A fireplace in the center or one at either end of the structure afforded facilities for heating, cooking, ventilation, and lighting. The furniture was as a rule home-made and at first consisted of only such necessary articles as beds, chests, tables, chairs, and benches. Older children slept in the attics on feather beds and straw ticks, the younger ones, in cradles and trundle-beds.

Settlers on the Massachusetts frontier lived a simple, frugal life; they came to know much of hardship and privation, and little of ease and comfort. Both men and women were compelled to toil long and hard to provide even the necessities for their growing families. In winter when the ground was frozen, the men felled trees, trapped, or worked in the saw-mill; in spring and summer they cleared their fields of stumps, and cultivated a few acres of corn, pumpkins, and potatoes. At odd times they mended harness and made the family shoes. For the women there was an endless round of household tasks, the bearing and rearing of children, the spinning and weaving and dyeing of cloth, the fashioning of garments, knitting, soap-making, the drying of fruits and vegetables, and the making of butter and cheese. Even little children had work to do; boys were taught to knit their own stockings, to make nails, mend shoes, care for stock, and as soon as they were large enough "made hands" or worked beside their fathers in the field or forest; little girls were taught to card and knit and sew, and seldom did one find a girl who had not pieced at least one quilt before she was eight. They took turns at caring for the younger children, helping with the lighter chores, bringing water from the spring, churning, gathering herbs, nuts, and wild fruit. There was little time for play, and the Calvinistic morals of their parents forbade much hilarity. As frontier children they were deprived of the joyous freedom of youth, and all too often they matured before their time.

Such was the environment into which Dorothea Lynde Dix was born on April 4, 1802. On her father's side she was descended from an honorable and substantial family; of the Bigelows little is known. Dorothea's grandfather, Elijah Dix, came from a "poor but upright" family in Watertown. He was born on August 27, 1747. His people could not afford to send him to Harvard so he became apprenticed to Dr. John Green in Worcester. After studying the "institutes and practices of medicine" for three years he went to Boston and took up pharmacy under Dr. William Greenleaf. By 1770 he had sufficiently mastered the rudiments of medicine to feel ready to establish himself as a physician. He returned to Worcester and went into partnership with Dr. Sylvester Gardner. For sixteen years they practiced medicine together and speculated in Maine lands. Dr. Dix had a keen sense for money-making, and in a few years he had not only speculated in real estate and manufacturing, but he had a fleet of vessels plying back and forth between New England and the West Indies. It was because Boston afforded a wider field for his professional and money-making enterprises that he had moved there in 1795.

On October 1, 1771, Elijah Dix was married to Dorothy Lynde, the daughter of Joseph Lynde and Mary Lemmon. She was the eighth of seventeen children, and was such a beautiful and charming young woman that she was spoken of as the "belle of Worcester." Dorothy Lynde's mother came from Charlestown; her father was a graduate of Harvard and a man of means. Dorothy Lynde was born in May 1746. The Lynde children were given the best training and education that Worcester afforded; three of the daughters married into its most substantial families, the Bangs, the Wheelers, and the Duncans.

To Elijah Dix and Dorothy Lynde were born seven sons and one daughter.[2] Joseph Dix, the third son, was born on March 26, 1778. Dorothy Dix, or Madam Dix as she was later known, was very fond of her children, and was especially devoted to her daughter, Mary, and to her son, Joseph, who was always a delicate youth. Elijah Dix was a stern parent; he had little patience, and his violent temper and unbridled tongue brought him into constant difficulty with his sons. On his wife fell the burden of adjudicating family differences, softening harsh judgments, and calming ruffled feelings. The task became a harder one as the doctor grew older; his temper seemed to increase as his prosperity declined. But for the little granddaughter born to Joseph and Mary at Hampden, he always had an indulgent affection, and his love for the little blue-eyed girl on the frontier often made him more lenient with his wayward son and hapless daughter-in-law.

Few facts are known of the life of Mary Bigelow. In the register of Sudbury Church is recorded the christening of Mary Bigelow on May 4, 1760. According to this date, Mary Bigelow Dix was eighteen years older than her husband.[3] She was married to Joseph Dix in Sudbury but the date of their marriage is not known. There was a sharp contrast between the social standing of the two families. Members of the Dix family regarded Mary Bigelow as poor, ignorant, and uncouth, without training either social or domestic; and there are various other traditions as to her general unfitness to become a member of the Dix household.

Neither Joseph Dix nor his wife was prepared to meet the arduous demands of the frontier. Frail in body and nervous in temperament, the young husband soon lost enthusiasm both for farming and the land business. He began to look about for some other means of making a livelihood. While at Harvard he had studied theology; later he had experienced "conversion" in a revival meeting conducted by an itinerant Methodist preacher, and recently he had felt a "call" to preach. He diligently searched the scriptures, prepared some sermons, packed his saddlebags, told his wife and child good-bye and then started out, as he said, "to carry the gospel to the farthest settlements."

For the new work the young man had a singular aptitude. He had a better education than the average Methodist minister of his time; he had a pleasing personality and he spoke with deep conviction. It was not long until Joseph Dix earned the reputation of being a preacher of great ability; however, the remuneration for frontier evangelism was scant and soon the little family began to suffer. The crude home, uncomfortable at best, came to show glaring evidences of neglect and shiftlessness. As Mary Dix realized her own incapacity and her husband's lack of interest in the upkeep of the farm and in providing for the family's needs, she became weary, fretful, unhappy, and discouraged. The state of affairs preyed upon Joseph too, and he fell back into his youthful habits of intemperance; things seemed to go from bad to worse as he shifted about from one occupation to another, and the family moved from village to village. For a while they lived in Bernard, Vermont, near the meetinghouse, where Joseph kept a shop, and advertised for sale "a handsome and useful assortment of miscellaneous books, also schoolbooks, singly or by the dozen, at Boston prices. Cash or produce taken in payment."[4] In Boston, the old father and mother were wont to shake their heads at "the miserable and loveless home which their son's own weakness and folly had created."[5]

Of the little blue-eyed Dorothea, both grandparents were very fond. She reminded them of their own little Mary, now grown and married to the Rev. Thaddeus Mason Harris, pastor of the Old Meeting House Hill Church in Dorchester. In her first years Dorothea was an eager, responsive child; loving by nature, she craved affection in others. Her father was away much of the time, and her mother, tired, unhappy, and often sick, failed to give the child the tender attention that she desired. She came to look forward to the occasional visits of her grandfather and hailed them with great joy. Grandfather Dix always found time to laugh and play with her, and his pockets were sure to be bulging with surprises; sometimes there were trinkets that his ships had brought from the Indies or that some sailor had found in far off China. He told her about her grandmother and Boston and Worcester, and what Aunt Mary did when she was a little girl. There were promises of what Dorothea might see and do when she came to Boston.

The return visits of the child to the city opened up new vistas for her already fertile imagination, and her hungry little heart thrilled to the strange scene. Grandfather Dix lived in a great red brick house in Orange Court. It had fine glass windows, and inside were many beautiful chairs, tables, desks, bureaus, poster beds, and tall old silver candlesticks. There were pictures on the walls and carpets on the floors. When she grew older she learned that many of the graceful old chairs, tables, and desks had been brought from England by Grandfather Dix at the close of the Revolution and bore the names of Heppelwhite, Chippendale, and Sheraton.

Grandmother's flower garden with its trim shell borders, and neat beds of phlox, marigolds, asters, mignonette, tiger lilies, prim hollyhocks, and spicy pinks delighted the child. There were wild flowers in the woods near Hampden but none so beautiful, so fragrant as these. Grandfather often walked with her, telling her the names of the flowers and inspiring an interest in botany that was to give her pleasure as long as she lived. He was especially proud of his fine pear trees and told her how he grafted and crossed one tree with another until he had produced one of the best tasting pears in the country.

Dr. Dix died on June 7, 1809, while on a visit to his Maine lands, and was buried at Dixmont Centre. Dorothea was only seven but she never forgot her visits to him in Orange Court. In after years she liked to recall how he had taken her to the stable, showed her the carriage and the fine horses that he kept, and how he had held her over the manger so that she might stroke their velvet-like noses, and how she was sometimes permitted to feed a lump of sugar to the doctor's favorite mare. She loved the stories that he told and she begged him to tell them over and over again. Because he was quick-witted and quick-tempered old Dr. Dix had made many enemies. Once a plan was made by some of them to drive him out of town or at least to subject him to personal violence and humiliation, but he detected the scheme. Quite simply he evaded the trap set by his enemies when one evening a man called and asked him to visit a sick man several miles out in the country. Dr. Dix expressed a willingness to go, then stepping to the window called very loudly to his stable-boy, "Bring around my horse at once, see that the pistols are double-shotted; then give the bulldog a piece of raw meat and turn him loose to go along." At this point in the story Dorothea always laughed with great delight. Before the doctor had time to gather up his saddlebags and put on his coat and hat, the man had disappeared.[6]

Occasionally he took her for drives in his cart as he jogged about over the cobble streets of Boston, making his calls or attending to business in various parts of the town. He told her stories of Faneuil Hall, the Boston Tea Party, and the battle of Lexington. He told her how the Redcoats had paraded on Boston Common, and how one night when the British had planned to capture some powder magazines, the scheme was discovered, lanterns were hung in the Old North Church, and how Paul Revere, the master silver craftsman, and some of his friends had galloped through Middlesex and awakened all the people. How excited everyone had been when the news reached Worcester. He well recalled the time—Aunt Mary Harris was then a tiny baby less than a week old.

Dorothea remembered how she and her grandfather had jogged along Milk Street and past the intersection where seventy years later, out of her love and compassion for dumb animals, she was to erect a large watering fountain. As they passed the boyhood home of Benjamin Franklin the old doctor often quoted maxims from *Poor Richard's Almanac.* "Never put off until tomorrow what you can do today." "God helps them that help themselves." "A penny saved is a penny earned."

Sometimes he took her into his strange-smelling apothecary shop. The long rows of dark bottles with their mysterious contents of minerals, bitters and pills, the heavy jars of ointment with faded handwritten labels, together with great bunches of queer-looking herbs, mortars, measures, and scales, and the ponderous pharmacopoeia were awe-inspiring to the child. She never tired of looking at the leeches that the doctor kept on hand for use in certain kinds of sickness. She wrinkled up her nose and whiffed the air as she watched her grandfather fill prescriptions. He moved about the shop taking a tiny measure of liquid from one bottle and then another, a bit of powder from a third, and so on, and mixing them with an ease and deftness that even a child would notice. Grandfather Dix was surely a wonderful man, thought the little girl as she drew her quilted petticoat farther down over her pantalettes while they journeyed through the crisp autumn air back to Orange Court. To Dorothea he was always gentle and kind, never gruff or sharp. She saw only the nobler side of his nature and he became for her an ideal.

Even as a very little girl she had been impressed too with Grandmother Dix's neatness, order, and punctuality. The big house was always clean and tidy; the curtains were fresh and crisp, and the meals were served on time. Grandmother Dix was one of the most active women that Dorothea had ever seen. She was always busy, supervising the household, entertaining company, or sewing. In her sewing with its well cut lines, its straight narrow seams and tiny stitches, Madam Dix took much pride. Benevolent by nature, she was always doing something for others. Not all of the family had prospered as had Elijah Dix and usually a number of poor relations were quartered in the Dix home until better fortune should appear. Madam Dix's hospitality was well known; many availed themselves and took shelter under her roof. Occupied as she was with the administration of her household and the entertaining of many guests, she did not have much time to amuse her young granddaughter but she was none the less interested in her welfare and always saw that the child went home well-clothed and supplied with warm underwear, shoes, and stockings for months to come.

What child would ever want to go back to Hampden after having been to Orange Court? How dull and drear the little village of Hampden would be after seeing Boston. How hard it would be to forget the thick carpets, the polished furniture, the shining silver, the sparkling glassware, and the good food at Grandfather Dix's, and to content one's self with the meager fare at home. "Some day," thought the child, "I shall live in Boston."

Until the birth of her brother, Joseph, when she was four, Dorothea was the only child. With no brothers or sisters, or nearby children for companionship, and with apparently little direction from her parents, she became extremely self-centered. She played alone, thought alone, and became the heroine of her own childish dreams. It was not unnatural that she should develop an absorbing self-interest. In early womanhood she became aware of this unfortunate tendency and made such an effort to master it that by the time she was fifty, her friends were urging her to have a care for herself, her health, and her means. The years at Hampden, however, were not without lasting marks upon her character, and even in old age, one could trace many traits and tendencies in her nature to the circumstances and experiences of the childhood that she tried so hard to forget.

The visits to Boston contributed to the pride which was her natural inheritance from her Grandmother Dix. They made her dissatisfied with her life at home, and she came to have little respect for her shiftless parents—her mother, careless and indifferent, her father, fanatical and intemperate. Apparently she had no particular affection for either, and her letters are strangely free from references to her parents. In later years her friends learned that she preferred not to discuss either her family or her childhood. As a young woman she fulfilled a certain obligation to provide for her mother after her father's death, but even then the impelling motive seems to have been a sense of duty rather than love.[7]

The coming of a baby brother undermined the little girl's position in the family circle, and the sensitive Dorothea soon experienced a keen feeling of neglect. With the advent of a second brother, Charles Wesley,[8] she developed what today would be termed a "martyr complex." The two younger children deprived her of much that she had formerly enjoyed; tasks and daily chores took the place of the attention and caresses that she craved. Mary Dix's health, never vigorous, was so greatly impaired after the birth of her second son that she became a semi-invalid for the rest of her life. On Dorothea fell the care of her young brothers as well as such housework as she was old enough to perform. It was irksome to the high-strung girl who was beginning to read and to dream of living in a fine house in Boston and of having servants to do the dishwashing and such other tasks as little girls disliked to do.

Of the early education of Dorothea Dix, nothing is known. It is probable that she was taught to read and write by her father or mother, or she may have been sent to the village school in Hampden. An academy had been founded there in 1803.[9] It is not known how long the family lived in Hampden. Most of the settlers fled from the village before it was taken by the British in the War of 1812, and took refuge in Worcester. It is probable that Joseph Dix and his family were among them. During the Civil War, Miss Dix once remarked that she had not been in Hampden since she was ten.

Meanwhile the fame and reputation of Joseph Dix as an itinerant Methodist preacher spread. He made long journeys away from his home and family, and held meetings that lasted several days and even weeks. Preaching paid poorly, and in order to eke out his slender income, he had his sermons or tracts printed and sold them as he went about the country after the manner of many wandering evangelists of his time. Very often tracts and sermons might be exchanged for lodging at some inn, or for maple sugar, cider, or yarn at some remote farmhouse, and many of the early preachers availed themselves of this means of spreading the gospel and supplementing the family earnings. The expense of publication was considerably reduced by limiting the printer's work to the bare necessities of setting type and striking copy, and by doing the folding, cutting, and stitching at home. It was not hard work except when the tracts were long and made it difficult to push the needle through so many thicknesses of paper, but it was slow and soon became monotonous. Joseph Dix brought home large bundles of sermons and taught his small daughter how to fold and stitch them.

The tracts seem to have sold well at first, and Joseph Dix was encouraged to write more of them. While Dorothea and her mother stitched, Joseph wrote. His quill pen could be heard scratching across page after page as they stitched tract after tract, sermon after sermon. It seemed an endless task. From month to month finances grew worse and poverty was always staring at the little family. To the sensitive child of twelve, the outlook was hopeless. The life was irksome and one day she rebelled. She hated to stitch tracts; she never wanted to stitch another; she would like to go where she would never see another. Of the difficulties or scenes that ensued, there is no record. Whether Joseph Dix gave up in despair of managing his willful daughter and consented to her going to his mother's home in Orange Court, or whether she stole away and secured transportation on the stage or with some relative or friend who was traveling that way is not known.

She is next heard of in Boston appealing to her grandmother and begging permission to remain with her and go to school. Madam Dix was sixty-eight years old; she had raised a large family and all of her children were now grown and away from home except her youngest son, Henry Elijah, who had graduated from Harvard the year before and was now studying medicine under Dr. J. C. Warren. It seemed rather late in life to be taking on the responsibility of a twelve-year-old child. Madam Dix had been a widow five years and time had weighed heavily upon her. Elijah Dix, with all his ability, civic pride, and daring enterprise, had made many enemies; his fortunes had begun to wane long before his death. His sons had squandered as much of his money as they could lay their hands on and were continually asking their mother for more funds to get them out of various difficulties. Three of the sons, victims of their own vices, and alienated by their father's irascible temper, had come to early and tragic deaths. William, the eldest, died in Dominique, West Indies, in 1799; three months before Dr. Dix's death, Alexander, the sixth son, was killed in Canada; two years later, Clarendon, the fourth son, lost his life in Kentucky.[10] Their families and numerous other unfortunates continued to come to Madam Dix for aid so that her house was always filled with needy persons of one character or another. Grandmother Dix and her daughter, Mrs. Harris, were astonished to see Dorothea and to hear her touching appeal. Such a courageous, determined child was certainly deserving of help, and it was decided that she was to have it regardless of the added responsibility that it might bring to the grandmother and aunt.

In fact Madam Dix had been thinking about this grandchild and wondering what would become of her, and what opportunities she would have to learn to do the things that every good housewife should be able to do. Madam Dix had never approved of Mary Bigelow, and her son's marriage was one of the unhappy events of her life. As a wife and mother, Mary had turned out just as her mother-in-law had predicted; the years had proved her physical and domestic incapacities. Joseph, who had departed from the Congregational faith of the family and espoused what she called "fanatical" Methodism, had neglected his business and become a ne'er-do-well. All these facts hurt her pride and she resolved to take a hand. Word was sent to Joseph and Mary that henceforth Dorothea would remain in Boston.

The girl's enthusiasm ran high upon being received into her grandmother's home. It was wonderful to live in a great red brick house surmounted by a cupola.[11] The mansion contained such interesting things, beautiful furniture, bits of storied coral and conch shells, rare old shawls, Smyrna silks, Canton crepes, brasses from the Orient, and queer old hatchments that were hung outside the door in time of death. Dix Mansion was to the young girl a symbol of glorious emancipation, a place of refuge and of opportunity. She recalled the pleasant visits here before her grandfather died, how he had humored her, how pleased and amused he had been to fulfill her childish demands and how free she had been of restraint. It was pleasant to be in Boston again, to be relieved of tract stitching and home responsibilities.

Dorothea observed something of a change in her grandmother since her grandfather's death. She seemed to have become much older and more serious. The girl often paused before the portrait of Madam Dix that had been painted by a Swedish artist one summer in Worcester. She was then a vivacious, attractive woman of forty, dressed in the height of fashion, with huge sleeves, tight blue satin basque, and vast lace headdress. She seemed to be a model of charm and poise; the clear eyes and the fine features which smiled down from the canvas looked as though they had known as yet little of sorrow and tragedy.[12] Madam Dix was still generous and kind but her expression was more pensive and sad.

If the child expected indulgence and absence of discipline in her grandmother's home, she soon discovered her mistake. Although Madam Dix loved her granddaughter, she placed duty above affection and courageously applied herself to the task of training and developing the neglected girl into the kind of a young woman that she believed would be a credit to the name of Dix.

The poor equipment of the child was a source of anxiety to the accomplished and capable grandmother. She resolved to make her neat, orderly, punctual, respectful, obedient. The child, unaccustomed to careful regimen, found the strict discipline irritating. Soon there was a clash of wills, a conflict of personalities. The grandmother could not understand this girl who seemed to be so willful and ungrateful, and the child in turn could not comprehend why her grandmother was so resolute, so meticulous, so exacting. Did she have no sympathy for little girls? Would she never realize that they sometimes had ideas of their own and liked to be left to work them out alone? Aunt Mary Harris might have been a different kind of little girl; but that was so long ago Grandmother had probably forgotten.

Dorothea was soon indulging in self-pity. Her life at home had not been happy; she had known too much of poverty. She longed for affection but it was something that she did not know how to return—it would be late in life before she fully understood. Her life in Orange Court was not much happier than it had been in Hampden. Personalities continued to clash and the child concluded that her grandmother did not love her. Madam Dix had not liked Mary Bigelow, and she did not like Mary Bigelow's child. Dorothea's father and mother had not been demonstrative or lavish in their affection toward her, and she had long ago decided that they did not love her. She never had intimate friends, or even playmates. Hers, she thought, was always a loveless life; no one cared. This orphan complex persisted for years, and the writings of her mature life indicate that she never quite overcame the thought.[18]

The problem of training the girl became more complicated and fatiguing to the grandmother as time went on, and as the child developed more and more initiative. At school Dorothea made rapid strides. She had a quick mind and an almost insatiable desire for knowledge; very soon she expressed a wish to become a teacher. Teaching was regarded as a very "genteel" occupation for a young lady, and Madam Dix approved the idea although it is quite probable that she would have been content to have had her granddaughter master the arts of keeping a home, then marry and "settle down" as her own daughter, Mary, had done at the age of seventeen. The girl's interest in books and school, commendable in itself, did not make her any more tractable or submissive at home. After two years Madam Dix decided that "reforming" the child was quite beyond her strength and arranged to send her back to Worcester, this time to her sister, Sarah, and to her sister's daughter, Mrs. Sarah Fiske. Sarah Lynde had married William Duncan and lived upon the hill above the old Bliss mansion. It was here that Dorothea boarded.[14] Sarah Lynde Duncan's daughter, the wife of Dr. Oliver Fiske, had the reputation of being unusually successful in the management of young people. To these two women Madam Dix entrusted her problem.

Aunt Sarah was a woman of rare tact and sympathy, and it was a "charming home that welcomed Dorothea."[15] The girl was happier here than she had been in Orange Court. She found Aunt Fiske, a much younger woman, to be far more understanding and more discerning than her grandmother had been. Dorothea soon began to take a new attitude toward the duties she was asked to perform, and to assume a poise and charm of manners for which the first Dorothy Lynde was justly famed. There was also more youthful companionship in Worcester to fill the need in the girl's social experience. Her grandmother had many relatives living in and about Worcester, and many of them had children or grandchildren near her own age. She became quite fond of her Worcester cousins and frequently visited in the homes of her other great-aunts and uncles. Especially did she enjoy going to the home of old Judge Bangs where she soon developed a strong attachment for Edward Dillingham Bangs who was her second cousin, and fourteen years her senior.

Educational opportunities, even for very small children, were limited in 1816, and when Dorothea suggested that she be allowed to start a school for little children, Great-aunt Sarah and Mrs. Fiske concluded the experiment worth trying.[16] Dorothea was barely fourteen but she was beginning to be somewhat mature for her years and it was thought that she might profit by the experience. Pupils were solicited and for a time she conducted her classes in an otherwise unoccupied room in the public schoolhouse near the corner of Maine and Central. Later a vacant store building near George Trumbull's book store was secured. It had been a printing office, perhaps that of the *National Aegis;* now it was cleaned and scrubbed, and some benches and a desk for the little teacher were installed.

She was keenly aware of her youth and so anxious was she to impress her small pupils with her maturity and to inspire their respect and obedience that she lengthened her skirts and affected the fashions and hairdress of a grown woman. Her discipline was stern, inflexible, almost extreme, but perhaps no more rigid than in any other well ordered school of that time. There is a tradition to the effect that she "believed implicitly in the wisdom of Solomon and she apparently feared lest some of the Worcester children might be spoiled through her sparing of the rod." It is said that William Lincoln, the mischievous son of the future governor and himself destined to become a distinguished general, never missed a day without birch-rod punishment. "No," said General Lincoln in discussing the matter many years later, "I don't know that she had any special grudge against me but it was her nature to use the whip and use it, she did." Another pupil alleged that William Lincoln was never still and a whipping a day was a sort of necessity. Little girls were not whipped so much; they were more easily disciplined by other means. Humiliation was known to bring positive results in making little girls submissive and obedient, and regardless of the far-reaching ill effects of such discipline, this method was constantly applied in most American schools in the nineteenth century. One little girl in Dorothea Dix's Worcester school was compelled to go through the streets during court week, wearing on her back a placard with the legend, "A very bad girl, indeed."[17] To her own brother, who by this time had been brought to Worcester, Dorothea was especially severe lest she be accused of partiality or favoritism.

Nevertheless the school was well thought of, and it is reported to have had as many as twenty pupils at one time. Among the number were children from the best families in Worcester. There were the two Lincoln boys, William and Levi, sons of Levi Lincoln, Jr., governor of Massachusetts from 1825 to 1834, the Blake children, Francis Chandler and Elizabeth Chandler, and the sisters, Mettiah and Elizabeth Green. The Wheelers, distant cousins of Dorothea Dix, sent their daughters, Nancy and Frances, and William Eaton sent his son, Joseph. Anne Bancroft[18] and Lucy Green, for many years a prominent teacher in New York, were also among her first pupils.

The children were taught the rudiments of reading and writing, manners, customs, and sewing. Years afterward when Dorothea Dix had become a famous woman, many samplers were proudly traced by their owners to the days when she kept her first school in Worcester. Nor were morals and religion neglected in her school; according to tradition every child was required to memorize a chapter from the Bible each week. On Mondays the pupils marched to the front of the room and standing with their toes on a line, arms folded and faces upturned, recited the memory passage for the week.[19]

For nearly three years she kept the school. In 1819 she returned to her grandmother's home in Boston "very much improved in manners and habits of neatness" as a relative described the effect of Dorothea's sojourn in Worcester. Certain traits, however, were too deeply implanted in her character to be uprooted or altered by any one, and they remained unchanged throughout her life; some of these, such as her stubbornness and headstrong faculty, were not admirable in their youthful manifestations but combined with other factors and environment gave her in later years a forcefulness, a stability, and a passion for thoroughness that were secrets of her power. She had left Boston an impetuous, willful child; she returned an eager, ambitious young woman, a trifle dictatorial but with a growing personal magnetism and modest charm. Dorothea Dix would always have her way in life, but in the schoolroom at

Worcester she had acquired something of a technique by which she obtained her end without becoming obnoxious. Some one described her at this time as being "tall, erect, slight, good looking; neither very light nor very dark; with a round face and a very stern decided expression." Less enthusiastic persons saw in her make-up too many of the characteristics of her grandfather, old Dr. Dix. William Lincoln, whom she punished with such regularity, said that he for one never considered her especially pretty.

Madam Dix was seventy-one when Dorothea returned to Boston. She felt very much alone and longed for the companionship of her granddaughter. Dorothea was older now, perhaps she would have more understanding and be a help rather than an added burden to the aging woman who was finding life a little sadder and lonelier each year. The girl might now be a comfort instead of a source of anxiety. Schools were being improved in Boston and there were more opportunities for girls, so that it was now possible for Dorothea to complete her education and eventually open a school of her own.

She returned to Boston to study, but Edward Bangs was not forgotten, nor did he forget his brilliant young cousin. Letters were to be exchanged and the visits back and forth long anticipated and long remembered.

"Can it be that we are in love?" Dorothea asked herself one day.

CHAPTER II

THE DAME SCHOOL IN ORANGE COURT

IN 1821 Dorothea Dix opened her first school in Orange Court. In the years following her return from Worcester she had been very busy studying and preparing for her work as a teacher. At that time opportunity for "female education" was limited. Beyond the grammar school, private instruction in languages, music, and the arts, or perhaps a course of lectures on literature, history, or astronomy, ambitious young women were self-educated.[1] Girls were not permitted to attend any of the public schools in Boston before 1790, and until 1822 they were admitted only during the summer, from April 20 to October 20 when there were not enough boys to fill them. In 1822 certain grammar schools were set aside for girls.[2]

Madam Dix took pride in her talented granddaughter and gave her the best instruction that could be obtained in Boston. When Dorothea had finished her training in the public schools, she took private instruction. She also subscribed to public lecture courses which at that time were given by Harvard professors who were anxious to augment the slender incomes derived from teaching. Her grandfather Dix had acquired a great many books, and so had her uncle, Thaddeus Mason Harris, of Dorchester; of these and of the other library facilities about the town she made good use. The Boston Library, over the arch in Franklin Place and incorporated in 1794, contained five thousand volumes. There were also the Library of the American Academy with fourteen hundred volumes principally on science, and the Boston Athenaeum with ten thousand volumes, where one might go and read if a stockholder or if introduced by a proprietor. Among the circulating libraries were the Union Library on Water Street, the Shakespeare Library on School Street, the Franklin Library on Court Street, and the Boylston Library on Newbury Street.[3] History, science, and literature were the subjects which appealed to the young woman. Years afterward she confided to Daniel Tuke, the English alienist, that until she was nearly twenty, she had determined to live to herself and to enjoy only literature and art.[4]

Her father died on April 2, 1821, and her mother was left dependent upon the bounty of Madam Dix and other relatives. Meanwhile Dorothea's brothers, Joseph and Charles Wesley, had also come to live with their grandmother in Orange Court. Mary Bigelow had never met with the approval of her mother-in-law or her sister-in-law, Mrs. Harris, but in a financial way they were ever coming to her rescue. Although Dorothea never manifested any particular affection for her mother, the girl no doubt winced at the criticisms which were made of her shortcomings by her grandmother and Aunt Mary. She now decided to open a school. Dorothea's school teaching days in Worcester having been successful despite her youth, she entered upon her new work with confidence and enthusiasm. Whether she desired to earn money and contribute to the support of her mother and brothers, or whether she simply wished to assert her independence was long a matter for family conjecture, for regardless of Dorothea's assistance, Mary Dix continued to receive help from Madam Dix and Mrs. Harris as long as she lived.

The educational system in Boston was such that it gave much opportunity for private teaching. By law the public schools were free but the statute specified that "no youth shall be sent to the grammar school unless they shall have learned in some other way to read the English language by spelling the same."[5] This preliminary instruction was obtained in the so-called "dame" or "marm" schools privately taught by women in various parts of the city. There were a number of these schools in Boston between 1820 and 1835. Some of these were quite permanent in character, others transient. Some of the teachers taught many years, even teaching the second generation of pupils; others only "kept" their schools for one, two, or three years, and then married or moved away. Classes were occasionally conducted in vacant store buildings but usually a room was set aside in the teacher's home. Often the dining room was used and the children grouped themselves around the bare table-top and "did their sums" or copied exercises from the Scriptures in their copy books. Pupils were admitted to these primary schools at four, and to the grammar schools at seven if "they were acquainted with the common stops and abbreviations in the spelling book and able to tell chapters and verses and read fluently in the New Testament." Not all children were prepared for the grammar school at seven; moreover, many parents preferred to pay tuition and send their children to the marm's schools for an additional year or two because of the character of the public schools.

The element that attended the public schools was often rough and the discipline harsh. Edward Everett Hale, who attended Miss Susan Whitley's school, said, "There was no thought of sending us to the regular grammar schools of Boston. They were simply dens of cruelty kept by tyrannical men who were proud of their different switches, rattans, and rawhides, and regarded them as the only real instruments of education. . . ." He and his brothers were sent to the Latin school as soon as they were nine and were simply to be occupied until that time. It was to meet such a need that Dorothea Dix established her school.[6]

Madam Dix did not favor the school. There was no need of it, she stoutly maintained. Although the family fortunes had been somewhat dissipated by her reckless sons, there was still enough to keep them in comparative ease. There was no necessity, she said, for a granddaughter of Elijah Dix to wear her life away teaching school. There were other women in Boston who really needed to teach; and again there was Dorothea's health to consider. From her parents she had inherited a physique that was far from strong, and she manifested very early a tendency toward throat and pulmonary disorders. The strain of teaching would only aggravate those delicate conditions. Long hours in the schoolroom would deprive Madam Dix of the companionship of her granddaughter, and there were many other reasons why she felt that Dorothea should not undertake the school. Furthermore, it would disrupt the household. Little feet tramping across the carpets, the scraping of chairs, and the dropping of books, slates, and pencils would all be very annoying to the proud grandmother. But there was nothing that could be done about it. Even Mary Harris, with her gift of tact and diplomacy, could not dissuade this child of Joseph Dix once her mind was set upon an undertaking.

Grandmother Dix finally gave in to her granddaughter because she loved her and had not the strength or the gift of argument to oppose her. Dorothea developed a unique capacity for management and organization, and it was not long before she was ably directing both the affairs of the household and of the school. Secretly Madam Dix and her daughter admired the girl for her determination, her courage, and thoroughness; they were pleased to hear of the general approval with which the school met, and of the strict discipline and the utmost propriety which were enforced.[7]

As for Dorothea Dix, she experienced a pleasure and a satisfaction which she had never known before. Her whole nature seemed to unfold in the schoolroom. An enthusiastic student herself, she delighted in teaching and inspiring the same zeal in younger minds. She thrilled to the opportunity that lay about her; she toiled early and late, looking after the household, preparing lessons, gaining new knowledge, and imparting that which she already knew. She loved being a teacher. Early in the twenties she confided in a letter written to a friend one Sunday evening:

To me the avocation of a teacher has something elevating and exciting. While surrounded by the young, one may always be doing good. How delightful to feel that even the humblest efforts to advance the feeble in their path of toil will be like seed sown in good ground . . . all soils are not equally fertile but I have long been of the opinion that however sterile may appear the ground it will in time become fruitful and though it may not yield luxuriantly it may be made to supply the common necessaries of life. I love to watch the progress of a young being just emerging from infancy, when thoughts first spring into existence and infant fancy is excited by every passing occurrence.[8]

Reflecting again of a Sunday evening, she wrote:

What greater bliss than to look back on days spent in usefulness, in doing good to those around us, in fitting young spirits for their native skies; the duties of a teacher are neither few nor small but they elevate the mind and give energy to the character. They shed light like religion on the darkest hours and like faith they lead us to realms on high.

Thea.[9]

Quaint as such sentiments may sound to the modern reader, they were entirely genuine; success could scarcely fail to reward the efforts of one who brought to the task such vision and spirit. The pupils in the school increased and the young teacher tried daily to enrich the quality of her teaching and to interest her pupils beyond the field of the average curriculum. In most of the schools instruction included only reading, writing, and number 'work as far as "vulgar" and decimal fractions, in addition to manners and such handicrafts as sewing and lace-making. Frequently boys as well as girls brought their knitting from home and had certain "stints" to do. Miss Dix, already interested in astronomy and the natural sciences, brought illustrations from these fields to her classes.

No sooner was this private school well launched in the Dix Mansion than she became interested in providing similar facilities for the poor. A "Society for the Moral and Religious Instruction of the Poor" had been formed in Boston, and in 1816 Sunday Schools were established for the purpose of teaching morals and instruction in reading so that the poor might at least be able to read the Scriptures. Of the 336 children admitted to the Mason Street Sunday School, all over five years of age, it was reported that one-fourth could not read words of one syllable.[10] With only one meeting each week progress was slow and there was current a conviction that some other plan should be devised to provide this training. So much of the lesson period had to be given over to secular instruction that the religious was neglected. There were a few charity schools in Boston but they were mainly for girls. Dorothea Dix longed to take over the instruction of some of these poor children but she knew what a protest would come from her grandmother and Aunt Mary if she undertook this teaching in addition to her other work. There were many reasons why they should object. It was disconcerting enough to have a dozen or two children from the best families in town "traipsing" through the house every morning, but to extend the privilege to the "rough and tumble" element in the afternoons would be asking too much.

Nevertheless these were the children that she wanted to help most of all. Finally she thought of the room over the carriage house back of the stable in Orange Court. It was no longer used and would be an ideal location for a charity school. With very little effort and expense it could be converted into a serviceable schoolroom. She hesitated about approaching her grandmother. Madam Dix was charitable enough; she was a subscriber to the Widows Society, a member of the Bible Society, and personally saw to it that every young married couple in the two villages of Dixfield and Dixmont was provided with a Bible. She had given the land on which the meeting-house at Dixmont stood. She was always helping the needy in her own way, but this was an instance where Dorothea was confident that only opposition would be given.

Still she resolved to try the experiment. Afraid that an interview with her grandmother would be cut short by a flat refusal, she decided to appeal to her in a letter.

My dear Grandmother,

Had I the saint-like eloquence of our minister, I would employ it in explaining all the motives and dwelling on all the good, good to the poor, the miserable, the idle, and the ignorant, which would follow your giving me permission to use the barn chamber for a school-room for charitable and religious purposes. You have read Hannah More's life, you approve of her labors for the most degraded of England's paupers; why not, when it can be done without exposure or expense, let *me* rescue some of America's miserable children from vice and guilt? . . . Do, my dear grandmother, yield to my request, and witness next summer the reward of your benevolent and Christian compliance.

Your affectionate Granddaughter,
D. L. Dix.[11]

Such an appeal could not be denied and in a short time the charity school was opened. From this barn-loft school with its earnest young teacher came Dr. Barnard's inspiration for the Warren Street Chapel School where some ten years later he established the first evening school in New England.[12]

In addition to her classes in the Dix Mansion and charity schools, lectures, church and home work, Dorothea Dix plunged into the study of natural science and planned a book for children. This book she hoped would answer many of the questions that children were continually asking, and at the same time put before them new and useful information about plants, animals, and the manufacture of objects in daily use; it was to be a "book of knowledge," a veritable children's encyclopedia in one volume. Similar works had been attempted before but either the content was not adapted to the interests of children or the style had been too difficult. The preparation of such a book required much and varied reading, discrimination, and careful couching of detail. It was an ambitious task but Dorothea Dix was never to be deterred by the magnitude of an enterprise or the labor required to complete it. She took little thought for herself and of how she might be undermining her strength. Her days were spent in teaching and household cares, and her nights in study, reading, and writing. Not everything came to her easily, as a letter to Ann Heath testifies:

Madame Dorothy Lynde Dix, grandmother of Dorothea Dix.
From an oil painting made about 1780.

I did not learn oratory from Francis Bassett, Esq., lady Anne, but I learned feeling from my nurse, stern rugged nurse, Nature, notwithstanding the seeming paradox. I am not quite so well tonight but will not sleep till I have said a few words to you. You do not know that Webber's Mathematics have this evening turned my poor brain, and I have just laid aside the slate (not in despair but hope that after saying a little to you I shall find my perceptions clearer and accomplish a sum that now defies my ingenuity and I had almost said my patience). Charles is sitting by me and begged that he might try but has just interrupted me as I expected, to say, "It does not come right." It shall come right though if I try all night. . . .[13]

Letters to friends were often dated after midnight. Aunt Mary and Uncle Thaddeus marvelled at her endurance.

Dorothea Dix had in Ann Heath a devoted friend and confidante. As a little girl Dorothea did not have the companionship of an older sister, and as she grew up she did not find her cousins congenial. She longed for some one in whom she could trust, some one to whom she might pour forth her soul, her inmost thoughts and secret ambitions, some one who would understand and with whom she might share her joys, triumphs, and sorrows. Ann Heath was such a person; she was gentle, sympathetic, and possessed of a fine intellect and a spiritual nature not unlike Dorothea's own. There was only enough difference in their ages to inspire the confidence of the younger woman.

The Heaths lived in a large white house at the top of the hill overlooking the valley that is now Reservoir Park, Brookline. They were a happy family and Dorothea loved to visit in their home. "I always leave your house with regret," she wrote, "and feel that there I might always be happy." She enjoyed talking to Mr. and Mrs. Heath who gave the lonely girl such a gracious welcome. Hannah was married, but the other children were still at home, Abby, Susan, Ann, Elizabeth, Mary, and the two boys, Charles and Fred. There was also the orphan, Eleanor, for whom Dorothea felt a kinship and of whom she always spoke as the "good Eleanor."

Dorothea was busy with her school, her studies and writing; Ann had many cares at home so that the young women did not see each other as often as they wished, and a correspondence was begun in 1823 which continued over a period of fifty years. In these letters each set down exactly what she was doing, and what she was thinking. Both had come under the influence of Channing and each was determined to pursue a course of intellectual, moral, and spiritual improvement. In their letters they hoped to record the progress made and thus stimulate and assist one another to greater achievement. They discussed the respective sermons that they heard on Sunday, assiduously memorizing the text, and repeating the substance of the discourse if it were particularly striking. At other times they wrote of the books that they were reading and recommended to the other's perusal various volumes of poetry or sermons. They were delighted with the verses of Laetitia Landon. Dorothea shed tears over her *Improvasitrice* and predicted that sometime she would be ranked as one of England's "noblest poets." Ann too was fond of poetry, and each week the poems in the *Christian Register* came in for their share of praise and criticism. A little later Dorothea would be contributing to its column and Ann would thrill to see her friend's verses in print.

There was usually a member of the family passing back and forth between Brookline and Boston, and so the early letters were sent by messenger instead of by mail. Curious little folded notes they were—finely written on three sides of a double sheet of pale blue or white note paper, then carefully folded and addressed; instead of sealing wax to keep the contents inviolate, the edges were neatly buttonholed together with needle and thread. The minute one of these notes was received, it was spirited away to some secret place, the stitches quickly snipped with sharp scissors, and the precious message read. Sometime the letters contained bits of gossip as well as philosophy and admonition regarding the other's health. Dorothea's letters frequently embodied effusive declarations of affection for her friend, and ended with the caution, "Do not show or read any one this note." She sometimes signed herself, "Thea," and Ann in addressing her friend often reversed the name and called her, "Theodora."

The sympathy of one so gentle and generous as Ann Heath helped to take the sting out of the disappointment in which her romance with Edward Bangs was to end, and for a time Dorothea's regard for Ann became almost an adoration. She cherished the memory of her visits to Brookline. "Annie," she wrote, "we have enjoyed many delightful hours together. We have exchanged many notes."

These moments are hallowed by smiles and by tears
The first look of love and the last parting given
   As the sun in the dawn of his glory appears
   And the cloud weeps and glows with the rainbow in heaven.

These are the hours, these are minutes which memory brings
Like blossoms of Eden, to twine round the heart,
   And as time rushes by on the might of his wings
   They may darken awhile but they never depart.[14]

Again she addressed her friend in verse:

To A. E. H.

In the sad hour of anguish and distress
To thee for sympathy will I repair
Thy soothings sure will make my sorrows less
And what thou canst not soothe, thou wilt share.

Though many are to me both good and kind
And grateful still my heart shall ever be
Yet thou are to me a more congenial mind
More than a sister's love binds thee to me.
                                   Thea.[15]

Ann Heath treasured the letters of her devoted friend. Fifty years later she left a small chest containing several hundred of these dim and faded missives. Scattered among them were bits of pressed flowers, heartsease, verbena, sprigs of evergreen, and now and then a carefully tied and labeled wisp of Dorothea's own hair. Pieced together one by one they give the story of a beautiful friendship, the pageant of a soul's progress, and the personal history of a great humanitarian. Ann Heath's friend traveled far and wide; she met great and mighty men, and across those yellowed pages troop some of the best and noblest minds of the nineteenth century, William Ellery Channing, Samuel Gridley Howe, Lincoln, Whittier, Samuel Tuke, Pius IX. In their twenties, friends teased the girls about their correspondence, but they persisted; sometimes there was one letter a week, sometimes two, and again three or four. Later Dorothea Dix had many correspondents who valued and kept her letters, among them Francis Lieber, Thomas Lamb Eliot, George Emerson, John Greenleaf Whittier, and the Rathbones in Liverpool but it is due to the diligence of Ann Heath that an intimate portrait has been preserved of her earlier years.

In the 1820's it seemed as though everyone in Boston were studying, plunging into some new field of thought and endeavor; but it was not until the late thirties and forties that this intellectual unrest came to full fruition in such minds as Emerson, Hawthorne, Ripley, Theodore Parker, Henry Hedges, Margaret Fuller, Elizabeth Peabody, and Thoreau, and manifested itself in such movements as perfectionism, transcendentalism, and abolition. Harvard professors continued to give popular lectures and they were patronized more extensively than ever. Professor Chickering gave a series of lectures in the winter of 1823-1824, and these Dorothea Dix attended despite her ill health. She wrote Ann Heath:

> You will be glad to know I found myself well enough to attend an evening lecture. The Misses Hayward very politely sent me a ticket for Mr. Chickering's Astronomical Lectures, and though I had not ventured to breathe the night air for many weeks thought I ought not to neglect so good an opportunity of perfecting my acquaintance with the subject above named.[16]

In the middle twenties the lyceum movement with its object "the diffusion of knowledge," was begun under the guidance and inspiration of Josiah Holbrook, and a new interest was aroused in making botanical, geological, and mineral collections. Homemade apparatus was set up and interesting scientific experiments were performed. Communities became civic-conscious, circulating libraries were established, town histories and local statistics were compiled; the lecture platform and private "conversations" grew in popularity.[17] Soon the young mistress of the Dix Mansion school found another call for her services.

> In addition to my usual employment, my pupils of the two highest classes come two or three evenings in the week to astronomical lectures and I am preparing to give up two afternoons in the week to a class in mineralogy. As regards the latter I had some hesitation as to the expedience of undertaking it. It will require much time and you will know that even now I have little unoccupied but it has been proposed and urged by a gentleman who has three daughters and I think I shall make the attempt. There are hours when I feel equal to almost every undertaking and again times are singularly changed, and I find every energy enfeebled.[18]

In religion, too, there were signs of unrest. English Arianism and French liberalism had crept into Congregational theology during the Revolution,[19] and there was an almost unconscious shift of emphasis from the doctrines of the Old Testament to the New Testament, and a new belief in the parental character of God, and a fresh evaluation of humanity. "Man," said Channing, "must be sacred in man's sight." Unitarianism taught essential goodness. It held that "an enlightened disinterested human being morally strong and exerting a wide influence by the power of virtues was the clearest reflection of the divine splendor on earth; and that man glorified God as he fashioned himself and others after that model."[20]

Dorothea Dix, the young teacher in her early twenties, was fascinated by it all. This gospel of Dr. Channing and the Unitarians was so different from the Methodist doctrines that her father had proclaimed, and from the conservative Congregational beliefs that her uncle, the Reverend Thaddeus Mason Harris, preached in Dorchester. Unitarianism laid no stress on excitements; it did not "judge the bent of men's minds by their raptures."[21] To Dorothea, the flowering of whose fine spiritual nature had been retarded and repressed by the cold unequivocal theology of the fathers with its vigorous commands and ascetic inhibitions, these new teachings came as a joyous release and an abundant promise. Love supplanted fear and mysticism took the place of dogmatism. To her grandmother's disapproval she now frequently absented herself from the family pew in the Hollis Street Church and attended Dr. Channing's services in the church on Federal Street. Later when her health declined and her mind became troubled, she sought in religion not only comfort and inspiration but healing.

During all of her educational activities in Boston Dorothea corresponded quite regularly with her cousin, Edward Bangs. He frequently came to Boston and occasionally she visited his family in Worcester. They became engaged and were to have been married but for some reason, now unknown, they became estranged and the engagement was broken. It was a hard blow to the twenty-four year old teacher. In the chaste imagery of youth she had idealized love; it was a glorious symbol, something almost ethereal, sacred. Disillusionment came hard to a person of her sentimental, trusting nature. Perhaps Dorothea Dix had loved as much for love's sake as for Edward Bangs; but it mattered not, she had loved deeply and beautifully, and now the dream was shattered. She did not wish to talk, and no one knows what became of the letters they had exchanged, whether they were returned or destroyed. Much of her other correspondence has been preserved, but only family tradition has kept alive the story of her blighted romance. She carried this sorrow close to her heart, a secret shrine, but the fact that she guarded it so closely may also indicate the frequency with which she worshipped there. In Dorothea's letters to her friend, Ann Heath, who was likewise adjusting herself to a life of New England spinsterhood, no specific reference was ever made to this disappointment, but her letters to the George Emersons, written in the late vigil of the night often revealed the musings of a broken heart. One sees her ever trying to rise above its pain, never entirely forgetting, ever trying to sublimate, yet never quite succeeding. At first this unhappy experience gave her an air of retiring melancholy, but later when the conquest over self was more complete and wider interests were aroused, it seemed to have only mellowed and enriched her personality.[22]

In religion Dorothea Dix searched for compensation. Unconsciously she built up a great spiritual reserve. In young womanhood her study of the Bible brought her hope, in old age consolation. Through the Scriptures and through self-culture, she hoped to attain the highest moral and spiritual development. Had not Dr. Channing taught that "the supreme good of an intelligent and moral being is the perfection of its nature," and that "religion is the spring of peace and joy, and the inspirer of universal virtue."[23]

Society she scorned. This seemed strange to the grandmother who had been the "belle of Worcester." Dorothea attended the meetings of the Fragment Society[24] and the Orphan Sewing Society and helped to make garments for the poor, but purely social affairs she avoided. "I have little taste," she wrote, "for fashionable dissipations, cards, and dancing; the theatre and tea parties are my aversion and I look with little envy on those who find their enjoyment in such transitory delights, if delights they must be called."[25] She made calls and seemed to enjoy them. In her letters to Ann Heath numerous references are made to visits at Mrs. Hayward's, Mrs. Worthington's, the Channing's, and the Howes'. She wanted friends but she seemed reticent about mingling with people in large gatherings. In the schoolroom she realized her superiority and maintained poise and dignity, but at parties where older and more brilliant minds were present, she felt less confident and was ill at

ease. On the occasion on an informal reception in honor of Lafayette, she confessed:

> This evening I am to be presented to the Marquis and dare not think
> what I shall appear like but fear like a simpleton. I half dread going
> but I may never enjoy the opportunity again so shall summon all my
> courage and confidence to meet the emergency of the case.[26]

Regardless of her misgivings about attending the affair, she enjoyed
the evening, and it became the inspiration for a poem dedicated to
the famous general and three effusive and detailed letters to her
friend in Brookline. She was, no doubt, too self-conscious and
modest about her social charm. After a party in 1823 where Dr.
Ezra Stiles Gannett and the Emersons, Ralph Waldo and Edward,
were present, a friend wrote that Dorothea Dix was also there and
"looked sweet and was very much admired."[27] She was tall, slight
but well-proportioned, comely with regular features, and a bright,
intelligent expression. She had a fine shapely head with an abundance of red brown hair which was always dressed very simply.
After she became famous there were many reports of her great
beauty, her striking personality, and her peculiar ability to influence
men and convince them of the significance of the projects which she
sponsored.

The effect of her youthful love affair was to make her reserved
and in a sense unapproachable. She evolved a rigid standard of
values as a "defense mechanism for her social timidity." "You
know well," she told Ann, "that the measure of my days is filled
with constant business, teaching, and learning, reading, and writing; sewing and mark(et)ing seem to leave me little leisure for
amusements of any kind."[28]

To her cousins in Dorchester, Dorothea's conduct seemed unusual. They could not understand why a girl so attractive and
gifted as Dolly Dix should want to shut herself up in a schoolroom
for the rest of her life. Marriage had brought to Madam Dix a
succession of tragedies and disappointments but she had piously accepted them as her earthly lot, and she wondered why her granddaughter set up such a barrier between herself and the men who
would gladly have paid her court. There was, for instance, Mr.
Wentz, who gave Dorothea lessons in French. He liked to linger
in the comfortable sitting room of the Dix Mansion and visit with
his brilliant pupil and her agreeable and interesting old grand-

mother. For a long time the younger woman did not consider his attentions as serious; then one day she was compelled to admit to Ann, "Your suspicions concerning L. W. are not unfounded and I must learn patiently to endure all things." Some time later she flatly denied rumors of an engagement.

I . . . should like to have been present at Miss Stebbins an invisible guest. Oh, Anne, is it not vexing to be so ridiculously spoken of. Miss Bellows and I are acquaintances but not intimates, never exchanged half a dozen letters with her in my life. Mr. Wentz, my former French master, never had a line of my writing except my grammatical exercises and a note to request his discontinuance at my study, alias grandmother's parlor, while I was out of town for my health. They, my correspondents. Never. It is not wise to think much of this matter. I rather think I am to thank Eliza Bellows for the report of my being engaged to Mr. Wentz. She charged me with it when she and the Haywards were taking lessons, merely because he spoke of me to them, knowing our acquaintance, in rather favorable terms. . . . Thank you for changing the conversation as soon as possible.[29]

Dorothea Dix had set herself to a rigorous schedule and it is little wonder that she began to show the strain. In summer she rose at four, in winter at five. She always read her Bible for an hour before breakfast. After breakfast there were long hours of teaching, study, and writing. Long after midnight she continued her work. It would have been a test for a strong physique. She was determined to complete the little textbook—*Conversations on Common Things* —which she had begun. Much of the material which she wished to use involved research, and she had to go through many books before she found just what she wanted, and then it often took hours to reduce it to language within the grasp and comprehension of children to whom the information was addressed. By the spring of 1824 it looked as though she would not be able to complete the task she had begun.

A huskiness appeared in her voice, her shoulders began to sag, and she grew very pale. The pain in her chest became more and more intense. She was threatened with tuberculosis, or "rheumatism of the lungs" as Dr. Hayward diagnosed her illness. At this time she was teaching in Mr. Fowle's Monitorial School as well as keeping a school of her own. She often had to stop at her cousin's and rest on the way to and from school. "Dear Anne," she wrote, "that has been the re-echoed song for months; yes, it is nearly three months since I have been able to attend school and fulfill its duties for a whole day."

For the next few years the correspondence was colored by ill health and unattained ambitions; nevertheless *Conversations on Common Things* was made ready for the press. It appeared in 1824. The *United States Literary Gazette,* in a favorable review, described this new book as a compendium of information "covering nearly three hundred topics more or less interesting." "We are gratified," the review continued, "with finding an American writer who duly estimates the importance of giving to American children knowledge as will be actually useful to them, instead of filling their minds with vague, and therefore useless, notions of subjects not accomodated to their age."[30]

The introduction and preface of the modest little volume revealed the fluttering hopes of the self-conscious young author:

If parents and teachers shall on examination approve and adopt this for their children and pupils, I shall feel a degree of satisfaction and the hours employed in writing whether redeemed from sleep or appropriated after the fatigues of daily school duty were fulfilled, have not been profitless, and that I have attained the object of my highest ambition, the improvement of children, and their advancement in the pathway of learning.[31]

It was piously dedicated by the "affectionate teacher" to her "young pupils with the fervent wish that it might inform their minds and excite them to seek after such knowledge as would be useful to them through life and fit them to lay up treasures which would not like the riches of this world take to themselves wings nor yet by moth or rust be corrupted."

The book was well received. It was highly instructive, intelligent, simple, and easy to read. In places it was somewhat saccharine, after the manner of children's books of the period, but the research was thorough and the information was sound. A third edition was brought out in 1828 and by 1869 it had gone through its sixtieth edition. The remarkable success of the book meant much to the young teacher; it delighted her to know that the hours spent in preparation had not been wasted. It gave her school prestige and she was encouraged to begin other literary ventures.

The teacher's health, however, was broken and it was recommended that she give up teaching for the next two or three years. It was a hard judgment for the young woman to accept.

Dr. Hayward thinks I must be very careful, that I shall be well soon, but that it is most likely that some time will pass before I feel quite strong. He told Mrs. H—— that "unless she takes great care, she will be where none of us can help her." So you see I have an incentive offered to prize myself very highly. I hope I shall not become selfish, but seriously I shall neglect no practicable means of resting and keeping my health.[32]

It was not long before "Thea" was lamenting the weariness of her room and longing to get back to her teaching. "Nothing seems to me so likely to make people unhappy in themselves and at variance with others as the habit of killing time." She tried to resume her schoolwork but after a few weeks was compelled to give it up again.

Meanwhile she was compiling a book of *Hymns for Children* to be published in 1825. It was not such an ambitious undertaking as *Conversations on Common Things* but the author was as deeply convinced of the need it would fill in the education of youth. It was the custom of many families to require their children to devote a portion of the Sabbath to reading and memorizing the Scriptures or other religious poetry. There were no such collections prepared and parents were often at a loss to make selections. Dorothea Dix believed that there was a certain charm to poetry that fastened itself on the memory and impressed the heart. "Children," she said, "rarely if ever forget hymns which they have been taught in infancy but when arrived at years of reflection, retain and repeat with delight those sublime and beautiful lessons acquired in their earlier and more leisure hours."[33] The little book contained texts of scripture appropriate to each hymn in the hope that the memory would impress the reader and stimulate him to a more extensive acquaintance with the Bible which she believed was the "only sure guide to a future and immortal life of perfect blessedness."[34]

Dorothea Dix was not sure of the impression that her second book would make, and it was with a genuine thrill that she reported to Ann how she had encountered Mr. Pierpont at Dr. Lowell's Thursday evening lecture and how he, to her "utter astonishment" poured forth a most "flattering eulogium" on the little hymn book. That she was pleased is evident from the way in which she naively goes on to say, "It would be indecorous to doubt the sincerity of his commendations so I quietly took it all for granted that he spoke the truth of his mind in all sincerity."[35] Dorothea Dix, like Lucy Larcom, had learned to forget sorrow in the joy of a hymn, and to the end of her long and useful life, she too made a habit of repeating them and writing songs appropriate to certain texts from the Bible. Her first hymn, printed in the *Christian Register,* was written, she said, "in a moment of excitement, without premeditation, and without thought, and in less than ten minutes."[36]

The authors' names were not cited in *Hymns for Children;* some of the poems are in quotation marks, and others are not. The authorship of only nine out of nearly two hundred can be determined through Julian's *Dictionary of Hymnology.* Miss Dix stated in her preface that many of the poems might not be classed as hymns. The fact that it was published not under her own name but that of the "Author of *Conversations on Common Things,*" and the fact that she was unduly excited over its reception suggests the possibility that she may have incorporated her own poems in the little hymn book. It is also interesting to note that a number of the unidentified poems are similar in sentiment, verse form, and phraseology to the devotional passages and poems in *Meditations for Private Hours* which she published in 1828.[37] The hymns reflect the Unitarian ideal; the idea of a god of good is continually apparent.

In 1825 Dorothea Dix also published a small volume of devotional studies entitled *Evening Hours.* She seemed never to rest; even when ill and compelled to stay in her room her mind was occupied with elaborate plans for the work she hoped to accomplish when she had regained her strength. Her poems were often composed when she was too ill to write them down; she repeated them over and over until she was able to copy them or dictate to a friend. "Verse writing," she often remarked, "helps to assuage the pain."[38]

During her years of teaching her vacations were likewise filled with wide and varied activity. She wrote Ann from Weston where she was spending a holiday in January 1826:

Our time is divided between books and needle-work, walking and riding when favorable, affords variety and vigor to enjoy our fireside pursuits. Cowper, Montgomery, Wordsworth, and Percival daily contribute to our social intercourse. We have read Swinburne's travels in the Sicilies and Spain, Hasselquist's journey through Egypt and Palestine, and are now engaged in Robertson's *Scotland*. Of novels we are not fond but have read *The Pilot* which does the author little credit.[39]

After 1826 she left the severe New England climate in winter and spent several months each year either in Philadelphia or Alexandria, Virginia, with relatives of her father. There too her leisure hours were study hours, and she indulged her love for books of travel, poetry, history, botany, and science. Fond of plants and flowers of all kinds, she made valuable collections or herbariums and sent them back to northern friends. Rest she refused; at home again, her grandmother and aunt found it impossible to restrain her. Dr. Channing who had become interested in the earnest young woman was distressed at the way she overtaxed herself. Was she trying to submerge some disappointment in her life by throwing all her energies so wantonly into her work? On one occasion he addressed her frankly:

I look forward to your future life not altogether without solicitude, but with a prevailing hope. Your infirm health seems to darken your prospects of usefulness. But I believe your constitution will yet be built up, if you give it a fair chance. You must learn to give up your plans of usefulness, as much as those of gratification, to the will of God. We may make *these* the occasion of self-will, vanity, and pride as much as anything else. May not one of your dangers lie there? . . . The infirmity which I warn you of though one of good minds, is an infirmity. . . . It is said that our faults and virtues are sometimes so strangely interwoven that we must spare the first for the sake of the last. If I thought so in your case, I would withhold my counsel, for your virtues are too precious to be put to hazard for such faults as I might detect.[40]

So sincere was Dr. Channing's appreciation of Dorothea Dix's abilities that he invited her in the spring of 1827 to accompany his family to "Oakland," their summer home on Narraganset Bay and act as tutor to his children. She accepted and remained in the Channing household until October. Mary Channing Eustis, daughter of Dr. Channing, described Miss Dix at that time as being "tall and dignified but stooped somewhat, very shy in manners, and colored extremely when addressed."

This may surprise you who knew her only in later life, when she was completely self-possessed and reliant. . . . She was strict and inflexible in her discipline, which we her pupils disliked extremely at the time, but for which I have been grateful as I have grown older and found how much I am indebted to that iron will from which it was hopeless to appeal, but which I suppose was not unreasonable, as I find my father expressing great satisfaction with her tuition of her pupils. . . . I think she was a very accomplished teacher, active and diligent herself, very fond of natural history and botany. She enjoyed long rambles, always calling our attention to what was of interest in the world around us. I hear that some of her pupils speak of her as irascible. I have no such remembrance. Fixed as fate we considered her.[41]

Six months in the Channing home gave the young teacher an opportunity to know more intimately the great man she had so long admired from afar. His fine intellect and noble character had already made a deep impression upon her. He had stimulated her to beautiful, abundant living. Now it was her privilege to live in his home, to sit at his table, and to teach his children. As Elizabeth Peabody, who was Channing's amanuensis during 1825 and 1826 afterward remarked, such an experience might be set down as the first year of one's intellectual life.[42] Daily companionship with one who believed so devoutly in the potential divinity of every child could not but challenge her to broader, better teaching and nobler thought. No other person revealed to Dorothea Dix her own imperfections and inspired her to rise above them as did Dr. Channing. She wrote to Ann from Oakland, June 23, 1827:

Do you know that I think the duty of self-examination one of the most difficult which we are called to perform as Christians. It is so flattering to our pride and it ministers so agreeably to our vanity to assign praiseworthy reasons for our conduct that the investigations we ought to make into our motives and rules of action is far from bringing us to a knowledge of ourselves. . . . Life is truly a state of discipline and of hourly trial that it is wonderful so little progress is made in the attainment of religious perfection. . . . It is dangerous to be neither hot nor cold.[43]

No one could ever accuse Dorothea Dix of being "neither hot nor cold." She was always positive; as Emerson once said of Margaret Fuller, conviction always sat upon her lips. The teaching responsibilities at Oakland were not heavy and there was much time for reading from the books in Dr. Channing's excellent library, and for long walks along the beach. She made collections of flowers, shells, and marine life. At the close of the summer she rejoiced that the

Channings had approved her teaching, and had invited her to return to Oakland the following summer.

Her spare time during the next two years was given over to writing. During 1827 and 1828 there appeared ten short stories which were later collected and published under the title, *American Moral Tales for Young Persons*. *Meditations for Private Hours* was published in 1828, *Garland of Flora* in 1829, and *Pearl or Affection's Gift* in 1829. The ten short stories were truly moral tales, intended to entertain, instruct, and mold. They were designed to inculcate habits of thrift, neatness, charity, courage, and industry. Dorothea Dix lived in an age that was beginning to talk and think perfectionism, and it was only natural that it should creep into her writings. The little boys and girls in her *Moral Tales* were affected by it. Her heroes are model "little men," punctual, studious, and tidy to the point of discomfort; the little girls most worthy of emulation are neat, orderly, cheerful, and their chief delight is in helping their mothers and in doing deeds of kindness. There were a few "naughty" children in Miss Dix's stories but they were put there not because they had any spark of individuality in themselves or because they were human and interesting; their purpose was to show that even the worst might reform and become good little boys and girls. Their presence provided contrast and the author made the moral so obvious that fair-minded children should have only the utmost contempt for boys who lied, cheated, and played marbles for keeps, and for girls who forgot their manners and whispered in church, "a thing highly irreverent and sinful in the sight of God."[44]

How typical the *Moral Tales* are of early nineteenth century literature for children is evident from a few of her characters. There was George Danforth who opened the door with too much bustle and noise,[45] and William Montague, "the dainty boy," who complained about his food, "cutting up three times as much as he consumed, saying one thing was fat, another was gristle, this was dry, and that was sour; and was indeed both dainty and ungrateful; he did not reflect that there were many miserable beings suffering for as much as he cast away in disgust . . . he did not realize that the eye of his father in heaven is upon him." George Mills was a boy who did not like to study. Marrion Wilder was "the passionate little girl" of five who had a pretty face, curls, rosy cheeks, and sparkling eyes but a very selfish and ungrateful disposition, and an ugly temper; however, it is only fair to say that little Marrion did mend her ways and at the age of seven engaged in the unselfish business of making pocket handkerchiefs for her brothers. "Happiness," the wise young author wrote, "depends on being good and correcting our faults." In another tale we read how one sister, Ruth, worked till quite late, cheerfully singing the hymns she had learned at Sabbath school hoping to divert her mother's mind from the anxiety which weighed upon it. Sad indeed the heart must be, said Miss Dix, which could not be comforted by the sweet tones of Ruth's voice as she sang:

> The Lord, my shepherd is
> No sorrows will I fear.[46]

"Alice," we regret to learn, "was much less interested in the delightful service of prayer and thanksgiving, and consequently lost much of the good influence which might have affected her and produced a change in her character." The explanation is simple; Alice had forgotten "that the fear of the Lord is the beginning of wisdom and He taketh pleasure in them who serve him."[47]

In this child world the good were always handsomely rewarded for their virtue while the guilty paid the price of their sin; and if the children of the *Moral Tales* are often "tatlers" it is not because they wish to accuse their playmates but because they have been taught to love truth more. Queer little wooden puppets were these children of Miss Dix's imagination.

On religious subjects Dorothea Dix wrote best. In *Meditations for Private Hours* she reflects the finest flower of Unitarianism, the ideals of duty, perfection, and Christian piety.[48] Between the lines one may read the epitome of her own religious experience, the incessant conquest over things of earth, and the triumphant upward march of her soul. In this series of devotional paragraphs to be read on arising and retiring, before and after weekly services, one may glimpse the high purpose, the earnestness, and the depth of feeling which dominated her own life and motivated her writings. To her as to Channing, religion was the spring of peace and joy, the inspiration of virtue.

> Blessed are the souls that hear and know
> The Gospel's joyful sound

> Peace shall attend the paths they go
> And light their steps surround.
>
> The Lord, our glory and defence
> Strength and salvation gives;
> Christian. Thy maker reigns
> And Christ, thy savior lives.[49]

For Sunday morning contemplation she wrote:

On this day, Sabbath of the Soul, I would especially avail myself of the benefits to be derived from devoutly contemplating the life and character of Jesus Christ. I would remember that impressive lesson which He taught his disciple, "Be ye therefore perfect, even as your father in heaven is perfect." Above all, may I remember how beautifully this precept was illustrated in his own practice.

His life viewed through its whole course presents a pattern of excellence which I can never hope to equal but must daily strive to imitate. I must not be dispirited because I can not at once attain or be on earth, perfect, but rather animated that I have such aids,

> "To help me on to heaven."

It is as intimate and personal as though the woman were searching her soul, and talking alone in the night.

Jesus did the whole will of his Father and our Father, of his God, and our God; and shall I, one of those for whom so much was done, so much endured, shall I shrink from sustaining the ills of mortal life? Shall I decline to overcome the obstacles that obstruct my path? Shall I refuse to engage in the Christian warfare?

> No, I must fight, if I would reign
> Increase my courage, Lord.
> I'll bear the cross, endure the pain
> Supported by thy word.

The Pearl or Affection's Gift: A Christmas and New Year's Present was a little book of sentiment such as might have been exchanged among friends.[50] The *Garland of Flora* was privately printed in Boston in 1829.[51] It was a sort of floral compendium with appropriate passages from the ancient and modern poets in which references were made to the respective flowers, and it had little intrinsic value. Both were typical of the sentimentalism of the romantic era in which she lived.

Aside from the poems published in the *Christian Register* and the memorials to state legislatures, these constitute the bulk of Miss Dix's published works. The memorials in which she approached almost a Ciceronian eloquence and clarity were her highest literary achievement. Her religious verses, though often exalted in theme, were faulty in execution, and few of them can really be classed as poetry. It was thought, however, in her youth that she had considerable literary ability. She loved to write and the suggestion that she become an editor of a new magazine was a flattering one and she hastened to confide in Ann Heath that "Miss Frances and myself have lately received a handsome offer if we would jointly edit a monthly publication. After some deliberation we both declined; in truth I must had I engaged have done all the writing in the night for my days are filled with teaching and learning."[52] Although most of Miss Dix's purely creative writing dates before 1835, she always maintained a lively interest in things literary, and counted among her friends many authors of note. There was Fredrika Bremer, the Swedish novelist, with whom she traveled through the South; John Greenleaf Whittier, the Quaker poet, with whom she corresponded for many years; James Freeman Clarke and William Greenleaf Eliot, to whom alone she felt she could entrust the sacred task of writing her biography. Among others were Lydia Child, Elizabeth Peabody, and Julia Ward Howe and her famous husband, Samuel Gridley Howe.

The autumn of 1830 brought new experiences to Miss Dix. She was invited to accompany Dr. Channing and his family, as a governess for his children to St. Croix, where Dr. Channing hoped to regain his health. St. Croix, one of the Virgin Islands, at that time belonging to Denmark, is a delightful tropical island, twenty-three miles long and six miles wide; its climate was considered especially beneficial to persons of delicate health and tubercular tendencies. Dorothea was elated over the opportunity to travel with the Channings, and to visit the tropics with their distinct change of scenery, and infinite variety of vines, trees, flowers, and birds. On November 20, 1830, the party set sail from Boston in the schooner, *Rice Plant*. After a short, restful and uneventful voyage they reached the island.

Miss Dix's enthusiasm for study and first hand collection of data on the flora and fauna of the tropics received a distinct shock in the languor which almost invariably attacks any one making a radical change of climate from the north to the south at that particular time of year. She was much disturbed over this lack of energy and the fact that she was in a physical environment over which she had no mastery. For the first time in her life she could make no substitution, no compromise, and still continue active. Before, if her voice failed and she could not teach she could always turn to books, letters, writing; but now she had no desire to do any of these things, and for once she really rested. After a few weeks she began to be her natural self again; she delighted in reading and in gathering strange plants for herbariums to be presented to scientist friends—Benjamin Silliman, John James Audubon, and her cousin, William Harris. According to the Rev. Mr. Tiffany, who had the privilege of examining Miss Dix's papers shortly after her death, she brought back to New England numerous notebooks containing copious excerpts from the great religious thinkers of all the ages, which she had compiled while on the island of St. Croix.[53]

She was much impressed by the Negroes that she saw in the tropics and contrasted them with the Negroes in the United States. At first she thought them the happiest creatures she had ever seen and feared that enlightening them on the injustice of slavery might demoralize their care-free joyous natures. After a few months' observation her New England conscience stirred itself and in a letter to Mrs. Samuel Torrey, in Boston, she cried out against the institution of slavery and declared that retribution would surely fall upon the slave merchants, the slaveholders, even to the second generation.[54]

Miss Dix returned to Boston late in the spring of 1831 and immediately formulated plans for a new school. Since she opened her first school in Boston in 1821, she had read widely on the subject of education. The experience in her own school and in Mr. Fowle's Monitorial School had been valuable, and her association with Dr. Channing helped her to anticipate a new day in the intellectual life of New England. Dorothea Dix had definite ideas on what children should be taught and the methods that should be employed in teaching. She hoped to make her new school the embodiment of an ideal.

More interest was being manifested in "female" education in 1831 than ever before, and Miss Dix's school found much competition in both the public and private schools in Boston. The public schools, Franklin, Bowdoin, and Hancock, were set aside for girls in 1831.[55] In 1825, through the influence of the Rev. Mr. John Pierpont, a high school for girls was established and two hundred girls, mostly Irish, applied for admission. About forty of the best prepared were selected and a single room in the boys' school was set aside for their use, but after eighteen months trial the school was abolished. Mayor Quincy explained that the school was drawing so many students that it would be too great an expense to maintain. In lieu of the high school for girls an additional year was given to the grammar school training.[56] When the high school was closed, the principal, Mr. Ebenezer Bailey, opened a school for young ladies and kept it going for ten years.[57] George Barrell Emerson started a similar school. Other schools were Mrs. Rowland's, Mr. Cummings, and Mr. Fowle's. Mr. Fowle's school was unique in that its curriculum included gymnastics, dancing, vocal music, and scientific studies, while Mr. Cummings ventured to hold classes in Latin for the young ladies of his school. It was not until much later, however, that a course of study in any school for women approximated that offered in colleges for men.[58]

Dorothea Dix's new school was to be a combined day and boarding school. Her reputation as a teacher and an author had become rather well known, especially among Unitarians, and they were glad to be able to entrust the care and education of their daughters to such an exceptional and "pious" woman. Pupils came from as far as New Hampshire. Madam Dix's home was so large that only a few changes were necessary in order to accommodate the school. Upstairs rooms were converted into a dormitory for girls who came from a distance and lived at the school. Classes were held in the large dining room and the long table served for study purposes when it was not in use for meals. Years afterward a former pupil complained how very hard it was to write at this table with so many crowded about it. "The merit of the school," she went on to say, "was not in its elaborate appointments but in the supervision of its accomplished mistress."[59]

In Miss Dix's school natural history or "general science," as such courses are now designated in elementary schools, was taught in addition to the regular studies. A special teacher gave lessons in French and perhaps beginning Latin, since it was being offered in other schools. It was character formation, religion, and morals that Miss Dix valued most highly and on these she desired the reputation of her school to rest.

The girls from Miss Dix's school, as one of her pupils said, were always "remarked for their propriety and decorum." They were never allowed to be boisterous or rude; they were taught to be modest and "lady-like"; they never ran in the street or laughed out loud in public. The eleven year old who was so indiscreet as to laugh after being solemnly warned was punished by being compelled to spend several hours in the cloakroom each day for a week. In the late afternoon one might see the boarding pupils from Miss Dix's school taking their daily walk. Two by two, they walked, their neat braids hanging down their backs, with Miss Dix always heading the procession and leading the youngest by the hand.[60]

Dorothea Dix was barely thirty. She was animated and inspired. She had come triumphant through the fire of disappointment. Restored to almost normal health by the long rest in the tropics, she threw herself prodigally into the new enterprise. She had bright visions of the work she was to accomplish, the young minds she would direct, the tender hearts she would reach. For her young pupils she had a most affectionate solicitude, though not without the stern and rigid discipline which she fancied would alone inure them to hardship and temptation, and inculcate that sense of duty which she believed was the noblest attribute of man. Too, she desired to teach her pupils piety which she declared "the wise have taught is an ornament of peculiar beauty to those who have not seen many years."[61]

Rigid in the discipline of her pupils, she relaxed none with herself. When tired, weary, or sick, she reproached herself, "I have no right to stay my efforts." She called to mind the goal she had set for ministering to the mind and soul of youth, and threw herself passionately into her work again. To her pupils she was a marvel of industry, consecration, and determination. Sickness paled her cheek and sadness mellowed her heart, but it never dimmed her clear, discerning eyes, and with the years her face took on a sort of spiritual beauty. Mrs. Margaret Merrill, of Portland, Maine, who was a resident pupil in Miss Dix's school, wrote many years afterwards:

I was in my sixteenth year, . . . when my father placed me at her school. She fascinated me from the first, as she had done many of my class before me. Next to my mother, I thought her the most beautiful woman I had ever seen. She was in the prime of her years, tall and of dignified carriage, head firmly shaped and set, with an abundance of soft, wavy brown hair.[62]

Dorothea Dix attributed the joyous progression, this self-mastery that she was beginning to experience, to prayer and introspection. Her critical cousins, however, never realized the relentless torture of self-examination to which she daily subjected herself or the constant effort she was making toward moral and spiritual improvement. She felt an exhilaration as she conquered faults of selfishness, pride, and vanity. Introspection she believed, was a virtue that every human being should cultivate if he were to master error. She made a constant effort to bring her pupils to the point of daily probing their inmost souls, developing a conscience, recognizing and "casting out tares," and nurturing only the good, the true, the beautiful. On the mantel shelf, Tiffany tells us, was kept a certain large shell, a sort of ear of God, in which the pupils dropped letters recording the results of their self-examination. To these confessions, the teacher sat up many times after midnight writing replies, suggesting ways of overcoming childish faults, encouraging and sympathizing with her beloved pupils.[63]

On Saturday evening they were free to come down to Miss Dix's quiet sitting room and talk over with her their individual shortcomings and seek her private counsel and admonition. Among Miss Dix's effects were found many bundles of these childish notes. Some were pathetic, some amusing, but in themselves, all were intently serious. Tiffany quotes the following:

You wished me to be very frank with you and tell you my feelings. I feel the need of some one to whom I can pour forth my feelings, they have been pent up so long. You may, perhaps, laugh when I tell you I have a *disease*, not of body but of mind. This is *unhappiness*. Can you tell me anything to cure it? If you can, I shall indeed be very glad. I am in constant fear of my lesson, I am so afraid I shall miss them. And I think that if I do, I shall lose my place in the school, and you will be displeased with me.[64]

What a sympathetic reply this disturbed little girl must have received from the teacher who had herself once been the victim of the same unfortunate mental condition. Sometimes the notes were sentimental and effusive but they serve to indicate the affectionate regard which the young pupils had for their teacher.

One child who had been struggling with the terrors of composition derived new hope from a quotation in Mr. Gannett's sermon that "an iron will can accomplish everything," and hurried to tell her teacher, "I will have this iron will and I *will do* and *be* all that you expect from your child." Another child pleads for a note from Miss Dix and even encloses the paper on which it is to be written. "The casket is ready, please fill it with jewels. Your Mary."

That such a régime of introspection and self-examination would be too much of a strain on tender sensibilities and emotions, there is no doubt, but it was one to which the teacher had long accustomed herself and she did not suspect that her young pupils were not of the same material as martyrs are made. That it might have a tendency to make them nervous, high-strung, and neurotic like herself, Miss Dix never dreamed, and for five years she went guilelessly on, teaching, counseling, and laboring until her own strength was gone. When Mr. Tiffany prepared his life of Miss Dix, many of her former pupils were still living and he endeavored to secure their reactions to this method of reaching young people. He found that while some acknowledged they were over-stimulated at the time, they were nevertheless "spiritually revolutionized" by these seasons of close personal contact and felt that they owed to Dorothea Dix the best in life. "Others," he said, "retain none but painful and bitter memories of their early relation with one the stress of whose immense demand was further accentuated by the inevitable bodily penalties of exhaustion, sleeplessness, and pain entailed on her by overstrain."[65]

It was no small task to be matron in a girls' boarding school and attend to the needs of a dozen or more girls who were away from home for the first time in their lives. To watch over them and see that they were neat and orderly, well, and free from homesickness was difficult work. To be matron, teacher, dietitian, purchasing agent, mother confessor, moral and religious counselor all in one, was a superhuman undertaking. Much of the planning and routine of housekeeping and management about the school had to be done after the candles were out upstairs, and her young charges had said their prayers and were asleep in their beds. Nor did she neglect her interest in the poor; as long as she taught she kept a charity school for children from poor and humble homes. She often remarked that it was to these poor children that her Christian duty came first. For five years the success of the school and sheer force of will carried Dorothea Dix through each day's work and on to the next, but the beautiful voice that was one of her most outstanding personal charms, grew husky again, hemorrhages from the lungs came almost daily, and the pain in her side was incessant. As she had written Ann ten years before, again the wheel revolved heavily at the cistern.

CHAPTER III

RESTIVE YEARS

IN THE spring of 1836 the school in Orange Court was closed. Dorothea Dix had suffered a complete nervous and physical collapse. At first Dr. Hayward solemnly shook his head, he did not know whether she would ever recover; if she did, she must never teach again. Grandmother Dix now in her nineties sat beside her. "Poor, dear Dolly, why had she worked so hard," the old woman murmured over and over again as she looked at her granddaughter lying there so pale and wasted except for the two hectic spots upon her cheeks. As she looked backward it seemed as though she were always giving up some one that she loved. First there had been her baby, Joseph, for whom she had named Dorothea's father, then her own parents, next William, her eldest son, her son Alexander and her husband in the same year; Clarendon, then Dorothea's father, and Henry Elijah had been the next to go. How much Dolly reminded her of Henry, her youngest son! As a physician and lieutenant in the marines, he had been her pride and comfort; then came the epidemic of fever at Norfolk in the winter of 1821-1822, and he had fallen a victim of the disease and a martyr to duty. John, her last son, had died six years later and now there was only her daughter, Mary, left. Sorrow and tragedy had often been the lot of Madam Dix, but she bore her troubles with fortitude, and the young woman lying there so still little suspected that the proud bearing might be a mask for deeper feelings.

Dorothea knew that she was very ill. She watched Dr. Hayward as he counted her pulse, and then looked at Aunt Mary Harris' anxious face as she stood in the doorway. Before when ill, she had been comforted by repeating the words of her favorite hymn, *"Come," said Jesus' Sacred Voice,* now she wanted to live.[1] Dorothea Dix believed in heaven, but she knew earth and here she wished to tarry. She composed hymns and repeated them as if to stay the hand of death. The following published in the *Christian Register* under the initials, "F. C." is illustrative of her struggle against disease.

A Communion Hymn

(Matthew XXVI, 38, 42
Luke XXI, 41, 42, 44)

My soul the scene revive
Within yon garden's bound
Behold the Lord of all below
Prostrate upon the ground
Baptized in midnight's cold and palsying dews
In agony of prayer to heaven for help he sues.

This cup, this cup of bitterness
Oh, Father, let it pass
This agony, this agony
My spirit sinks, alas
Abba, Eternal Father. Pity thou thine own
Send thy spirit down to help thy fainting son.

. . . .

Thou who art in heaven, we wander
Oft lose the narrow way
Thy counsels, precious, gracious, kind
Too oft we disobey
Suppliant, returning, now we come to thy safe fold
Good Shepherd, nourish, guide, and guard us as of old.

F. C.[2]

Miss Dix did not forget the welfare of her school. She could not bear the thought of seeing wholly abandoned the projects into which she had thrown her energies so unreservedly. As soon as she was able she made an appeal to George Barrell Emerson, principal of a prominent girls' school in Boston. Mr. Emerson was not an intimate friend, but she appreciated his ability and depth of purpose. Upon his graduation from Harvard in 1817 he had become principal of a private school in Lancaster, Massachusetts, and later returned to Harvard as a tutor in mathematics. In 1821 he became principal of the English Classical School, and in 1823 opened a school for young ladies. He was interested in natural history and shared Miss Dix's views on the place of science in the curriculum. He was instrumental in 1830 in organizing the American Institute of Instruction, a precursor of the state board of education and of normal training for teachers. He made a memorable address before the institute in 1831 on "Female Education." Dorothea Dix had been greatly impressed.[3]

In a long letter written early in the spring of 1836 she entreated him to take over the work of her charity school, "The Hope." She imagined that she had not long to live. "With me," she wrote, "the axle of human life turns more heavily and the silver cord winds more tenuous." She was unwilling to depart this world until the future of her school was assured. As a special mark of favor she enclosed, as she said, without apology some articles she had written when it was not easy to give attention to study or teaching. "These beguiled me of pain," she wrote along the margin.

This letter intended as a sort of valedictory, a "last will and testament" in which she bequeathed her beloved charity school to a man whom she admired but did not know, was the beginning of a long and valued friendship. George Emerson and his wife were a generous and public-spirited couple and identified themselves with numerous humanitarian and social reforms. He was a man of practical vision, and to him Dorothea Dix went for many years for advice and direction. The Emerson home had a welcome for the frail, enthusiastic and lonely woman and she soon idealized the friendship it offered.

Dr. Hayward realized that Dorothea Dix would give no rest to either her mind or her body as long as she remained in Boston. Her life was bound up in her schools and what she needed was a complete change in thought, scenery, and climate. He advised an ocean voyage, summer in England, autumn in France, and winter in Italy. Her grandfather Dix had left her certain property holdings, a small annuity[4] which she had allowed to accumulate, and she had also gained a pecuniary independence from teaching. She no longer needed, moreover, to feel any responsibility for her family. Charles Wesley had finished the Latin school in 1832 and had gone to sea, while Joseph, the elder brother, had entered business. The proposed journey was a long one for a woman who had never traveled farther than Alexandria, Virginia, but in the late spring she seemed strong enough to undertake the journey and there was no reason why she should not follow Dr. Hayward's prescription.

Miss Dix went about arranging her affairs as though she never expected to return. A couple of weeks before sailing she wrote Mr. Emerson:

Tomorrow evening perhaps you will give me half an hour but it is not necessary; it is merely to please myself that I ask you. I am getting a little nervous. My resolves falter a little but I trust will not fail. . . . Pray for me that at the last, rest may be found; and that the most High may bring me out of darkness into the light of health. Yet His will be, He who hath smitten can heal. I will trust. I will believe that he will restore.[5]

In another letter of that same period to Emerson she expressed the hope that they might meet "where all trials are unknown and where infirmity is exchanged for perfection."[6]

In company with Mr. and Mrs. Frank Schroder, and Mr. and Mrs. Ferrer, she set sail from New York on April 22, 1836. Miss Dix was not a good sailor and when she arrived in Liverpool she was greatly weakened instead of improved. It was her plan to spend several months in England and later to join the Ferrers in France or Italy. She was too weak for sight-seeing and was taken at once to a hotel in Liverpool. On a similar quest for health Dr. Channing had visited England in 1822 and had met William Rathbone, a prominent merchant and Unitarian near Liverpool. They had become fast friends and when Dorothea Dix set out for Europe Dr. Channing had given her a letter of introduction to his English friends. As soon as they heard that a friend of Dr. Channing lay sick in a Liverpool hotel, they called and insisted that she be removed to "Greenbank," their country home.

Miss Dix went to Greenbank expecting to stay only a few weeks and then resume her travels on the continent as soon as she had recuperated sufficiently. Greenbank was a delightful country place about three miles from Liverpool and the family into which she was received was one of the happiest and most genuine that she had ever seen. For nearly half a century there was scarcely a charitable or philanthropic enterprise in the city with which William Rathbone or his family was not associated. Liverpool was beginning to be industrialized and the coming of the great mills and factories had brought all of the ills attendant upon the concentration of population—poverty, bad housing, and disease.

William Rathbone had concurred with the Rev. Mr. Thom in his memorable Christmas sermon, "What we as Christians are, may be judged from what we suffer the poor around us to be,"[7] and now together with a group of Quaker and Unitarian friends he was giving serious thought to the matter of alleviating distress and poverty in the slums of the rapidly growing city. Miss Dix told of similar conditions in the mill towns of New England and the social work that was being done about Boston and Lowell, the Sunday schools, the missions, and her own charity school in the barn loft in Orange Court.

In this cultured and cheerful atmosphere, Dorothea Dix seemed free of the orphan and martyr complexes which had so long dominated her life. Surrounded by these generous friends even imaginary troubles were deprived of their realism. The sad, unhappy experiences of her childhood slipped out of her consciousness until one day a letter came from Mrs. Hayward in Boston. It told of the death of Dorothea's mother in Fitzwilliam, New Hampshire. How vividly it brought back the memory of those tract-stitching days, the miserable poverty-stricken home, the irresponsible father, and the neglected little brothers. Mary Bigelow Dix had died at the age of seventy-six. For thirty-five years she had been more or less of an invalid, dependent on her daughter and her husband's people for support. Mrs. Hayward no doubt surmised the flood of memories that would rush to the mind of the sick young woman, and she tried to console her.

The remembrance of duties so faithfully performed, and the consciousness that you could have done nothing more had you been at home, will be a comfort to you. Your mother's departure was so unexpected that even those in the room were totally unprepared; no sickness nor suffering, but a sudden summons to go to her rest after a life of suffering from a lingering disease.[8]

After a time Miss Dix began to gain slowly. In November, she suffered a slight relapse, and in January 1837, she wrote Ann that for the first time since September she was allowed to walk about the room.[9] With the coming of spring she was able to take occasional excursions from Greenbank to visit other friends of Dr. Channing or people with whom she had become acquainted while an invalid in the Rathbone home.

The young woman reveled in the social contacts at Greenbank. In Boston she had delighted in the scientific and philosophical lectures at the Pantheon and Concert Hall. She knew by sight most of the "intellectuals," Theodore Parker, the great preacher, Edward Everett who edited the *North American Review* for which she

aspired to write, Daniel Webster, George Bancroft who had published the first volume of his history in 1834, George Ticknor who
taught literature at Harvard, John Quincy Adams, and Ralph
Waldo Emerson. With some of them she had a speaking acquaintance, and one or two she knew quite intimately. Among the friends
of the Rathbones were many persons of distinction, men of letters,
lawyers, physicians, ministers, and statesmen. Many of them were
Quakers or Unitarians who, like William Rathbone, had felt a
humanitarian impulse, and were bent on reforming and alleviating
distress among the poor. Dorothea Dix while respected in Boston
as a successful and capable teacher of young ladies, was never regarded as being one of the brilliant coterie that made the city
famous for its culture; there is no record that she was ever invited
to a meeting of Hedge's club or the Concord Symposium where
Margaret Fuller, Elizabeth Peabody, and Sophia Ripley were always
welcomed among the company of Emerson, Orestes Brownson,
Henry Hedges, Bronson Alcott, William E. Channing, and Theodore Parker.[10] At Greenbank, Dorothea Dix did not have to sit
far back, a timid but interested spectator; she actually entered into
conversations with the "good and great." She never forgot these
rare minds, this year of intellectual and spiritual jubilee.

It is probable that on this visit to England, she met Dr. Samuel
Tuke, long a friend of the Rathbones, and learned from him of the
work that was being done at York Retreat in the care and treatment
of the mentally ill. York Retreat had been founded in 1792 as an
asylum for Friends, by his father, William Tuke, a well-to-do
Quaker, who had become incensed at the treatment accorded inmates at the York County Asylum. Here he did for England what
Pinel had done for France.[11] It may have been at Greenbank that
Miss Dix's interest in the scientific care and treatment of psychosis
was first aroused.

Due to her illness, Dorothea Dix's sojourn in England was extended over a period of eighteen months. From childhood she had
had a habit of making protracted, often self-invited visits to the
homes of relatives where she was not always welcome, and now
her aunt and grandmother were worried for fear she might become
a burden to the kind and benevolent strangers. Would not the
English household tire of this perennial guest? Why did not Dorothea come home if she were not able to continue her travels into

Italy? Nearly a year had elapsed and Madam Dix was shocked to learn that her granddaughter had made no plans to return to Boston. That relations between the young woman and her ninety-year old grandmother were becoming quite strained is evident in a letter to Ann Heath written from Greenbank on November 12, 1836. Dorothea wrote in detail of her illness, her pleasure in the English home, how she hoped to regain her health and resume her teaching, and ended her letter with the request, "Visit my grandmother if you can summon the moral and physical courage to face the Medusa. The flint heart may yet be softened."[12]

"Medusa" and "flint heart" were rather harsh epithets to apply to one who had always been so generous as Madam Dix, but Dorothea was very ill at the time, her nerves were taut, and her sense of justice was distorted. No doubt, she afterward regretted writing such a letter but the deed was done and unfortunately the letter was not destroyed; fifty years later a biographer ignorant of the circumstances seized upon the letter and delineated Dorothea's grandmother as a Puritan devoid of sympathy, tolerance, and charm, and for two generations this apocryphal description quite obscured the true Madam Dix who was depicted by her son-in-law as "affectionate, gracious, and charitable."[13]

At ninety-one Madam Dix's health began to fail. When she realized that she did not have long to live, she longed to see "Dolly" again, and asked that she come home. Dorothea was still very weak, and as the trip home was a very long and uncertain one, she was advised to remain in England. On April 29, 1837, Madam Dorothy Dix passed away. When the word reached Dorothea a month later, she resolved to stay in England until fully recuperated.

"I feel the event," she wrote, "as having divided the only link save the yet closer one of fraternal bonds which binds me to kindred."[14] There was no need to hurry home now; the only place she could call home was broken up. Her brothers, Joseph and Charles, were grown and could take care of themselves; she no longer felt a responsibility for them, and her invalid mother was no longer there. It was autumn of 1837 before she returned to New England and claimed the part of the estate which had been bequeathed her by her grandmother.

The amount of this legacy was estimated by Roe, Tiffany, and members of the family to have been enough "with the earnings of her school teaching days to provide for the moderate wants of a single woman."[15] Alfred S. Roe, in a paper before the Worcester Society of Antiquity, November 20, 1889, estimated her income at $3000 a year.[16] According to Madam Dix's will, she left certain furniture, bedding, linen, and other property to her granddaughter, "Dorothy" Dix. When the real estate and personal property were sold, one-half of the proceeds was to go to her daughter, Mary Harris, and certain provision was also made for the latter's two daughters, Sarah and Dorothy Harris.[17] Although the exact amount of Dorothea Dix's holdings and income can not be computed for any one time, there is sufficient evidence to indicate that there was no necessity for her to take up teaching again; nor would her health permit it.[18]

The situation which confronted her upon her return to America was not an easy one. Dorothea's cousins never regarded her illness as serious and suspected her of subscribing to the "cult of frailty,"[19] which was not uncommon among the refined women of her day, and too, they censured her for not returning at her grandmother's request. Madam Dix had taken Dorothea and her two brothers into her home, clothed, educated, and cared for them for more than twenty years. It seemed to them that Dorothea owed something in return. It was known that she would inherit the bulk of the Dix fortune; it appeared that she might have at least been in Boston to minister to the old grandmother in her last hours and to have been with her when she died. "Ingratitude," they termed her conduct, and when Dorothea returned to Boston she found a chill welcome. There was no need to make explanations, Dorothea told herself. Boston had never understood or appreciated her. Ann Heath, Mrs. Hayward, Mrs. Torrey, and Dr. Channing might understand; as for the others it did not matter.

But the problem could not be idly dismissed; daily it haunted her. Where could she go? What could she do to occupy her mind? She faced an uncertain future. For the first time in her busy life she became keenly aware that she was on the awkward side of thirty, unmarried, unoccupied, and unsettled. In the eighteen months that she had been away she saw many changes in Boston and in her friends. Lydia Francis was married to Mr. Child and had moved away, and many of her other friends were gone. She missed her grandmother and the old home in Orange Court. Ann

Heath was still in Brookline but she was busy with her household cares and looking after her brother's children. Surrounded by married sisters and affectionate nieces and nephews, Ann would never feel this same barrenness of life. There was no place Dorothea could go now and call it "home." The rest of her days she would have to spend in boarding houses or in occasional visits to the homes of friends which more often augmented than assuaged her loneliness.

Now that her health would not permit teaching, Boston seemed to have so little to offer. Massachusetts seemed so chill and harsh after England. She went to Washington, D. C., and to Alexandria, Virginia, for the winter but she was not contented there. She was thirty-six; it was hard to realize the years that had passed. It seemed as if the best years of her life were gone. She fell back into her old habit of introspection. What had she accomplished? To what could she look forward? Youth and romance lay in the past. She smiled sadly for she had not forgotten that first love and she had not dared to love again. She treasured it too dearly; no other would ever take its place. When word came to her of the death of Edward Bangs that spring, it brought a flood of memories to her mind. It was now fourteen years since he had married Mary Grosvenor. Time had gone more swiftly than she realized. When he became secretary of state in 1824, he had brought Mary as a bride to Boston.[20] Dorothea had almost forgotten the date; it was that spring Dr. Hayward had first warned her that she was working too hard in her school. Dear, wise, old Dr. Hayward, there were some things he did not know.

She knew it was not a wholesome thing for one no older than she to be living in the past. She was restless, and she worried about her unsettled frame of mind. She knew she must rise above it; she must find peace and security. She had not realized so great a trial was to confront her upon her return from England. She was lonelier now than she had ever been; she craved the association of other minds as she had never craved before. At the Rathbones' friendship was no unreal thing; it was not an image created of vivid fancy and wild imaginings, there "hearts met hearts, minds joined with minds." Yet she knew she must not brood over the past. "Life is not to be expended in vain regrets," she wrote Ann.[21]

No day, no hour comes but brings in its train work to be performed for some useful end, the suffering to be comforted, the wandering led home, the sinner reclaimed. Oh, how can any fold the hands to rest and say to the spirit, "Take thine ease for all is well"?

Slowly a vision of social service was evolving, but the form it should take was not yet clear. She determined to find activity for body as well as for mind. During the winter in Washington, she had visited the Orphans' Asylum. She loved children after a strange and tender fashion, but she no longer knew how to approach them, and the older she grew, the more difficult she found it to make the responsive friendships among children that she desired. She delighted in giving them useful inexpensive presents, but all too often she gave thimbles to little girls who would have preferred jumping ropes, and religious picture cards to boys who would have liked marbles or tops instead. Her own childhood had been bereft of loving attention and caresses much as these poor orphans and she longed to find some way of bringing to them happiness and pleasure that she herself had never known.

While in the vicinity of Washington she visited not only the Capitol but Mt. Vernon, Christ's Church in Alexandria, and other places sacred in American history. She delighted in souvenirs from historic shrines, a sprig of rosemary, three chestnuts from Mt. Vernon, and a bit of ivy from an old English Abbey. Three hairs, said to have come from the head of George Washington, were sent as a rare treasure to Ann Heath who shared her friend's enthusiasm for curios and things both patriotic and romantic.

To Ann she wrote long descriptions of the places that she visited, and the emotions that she experienced. The days in Washington were long and she often went to the Library of Congress or the Congressional Library as it was then called, to read. She wrote Ann that it was a very good place to read but that it "would be much nicer or more inviting if so many members did not come there. . . ." It was, she thought, "too public for ladies to desire to spend too much time there."[22] She loved to watch the flag floating over the Capitol. The flash of colors never failed to thrill her and when the nation presented her with a standard some thirty years later in token of her meritorious service during the Civil War, she felt her cup was filled to overflowing.

During 1838 she journeyed through Virginia, Pennsylvania, and New York and on to New Hampshire on business, no doubt, to look after the few possessions that her mother left. There were only a few railroads at that time so she was compelled to make most of the journey by stage and by canal boat; and as it was some distance she did not return to Boston until rather late in the season. She then visited relatives and friends in Weston and Dorchester and stayed for a while in Jamaica Plain. She called on Dr. Channing who was growing more and more feeble, and she often visited with Ann Heath and her sisters, Abby and Susan. They too were still unmarried, and knew something of Dorothea's restiveness in an age which had not yet come to place its stamp of approval upon women entering into an independent life or going into business or the professions in competition with men. The Heath sisters were fortunate, thought Dorothea; they still had each other and a growing flock of nieces and nephews to give variety to otherwise drab and prosaic lives. Ann and Dorothea still exchanged notes. These missives were tender, pious, and affectionate, but they had lost some of the sweet, romantic trappings of youth. Dorothea, instead of signing her letters with the effusive and sentimental "Thea," now substituted the more dignified and formal "D. L. Dix" or simply the initials, "D. L. D." There was less of the neighborhood news, the Fragment Society, various calls and callers, and more of the struggle for self-improvement, frequent outbursts of loneliness, and her futile attempts at social adjustment. "Perhaps it is within myself, the fault lies," she told Ann. She searched her Bible daily thinking that there she might find an answer to her problem.

By the late thirties Boston was full of searchers and seekers. The renaissance of which the first murmurings had been heard in the late twenties and early thirties had now come into full vigor. From a theological principle had evolved an ethical program, a social ideal. Out of the reverence for man had come a desire to improve the conditions of his daily life. This humanitarian impulse did not burst forth like a bugle in the night. New Englanders were not startled into the consciousness that they were their brother's keepers and that the heavenly command meant more than seeing that their morals were fashioned after the models of orthodox dogma; nor had the new ideal been evolved without protest and misgivings. When Harvard succumbed to the liberal theology, Andover was promptly founded to defend the law of Moses and the prophets, and the tenets of John Calvin.

By the forties the leaven had done its work; pew rent had begun to decline in the orthodox churches, and by the very nature of things their straight-laced pastors were beginning to look less askance at those who denounced predestination and reprobation; however it is not in doctrine so much as in the fine character of the men and women who subscribed to its precepts that the noblest evidences of the new spirit are found. Among the hopeful coterie were such men as Longfellow, Holmes, John Quincy Adams, Channing, Emerson, Ezra Stiles Gannett, and James Freeman Clarke. They preached and lived a dynamic faith; in a wider sense they perceived New England in transition, a commonwealth that was being rapidly changed, industrialized. Their hopes ran high. By the time Dorothea Dix returned from England the Symposium was holding regular meetings at the Ripleys', the Channings', or the Cyrus Bristols'. There the members discussed the philosophies of Kant and Rousseau, ancient and modern scriptures, and current literature. George Ripley and his wife discussed their plans for Brook Farm, and Bronson Alcott recited some of his "Orphic Sayings." In Boston Margaret Fuller was holding private conversations in her home as Elizabeth Peabody had done some six years earlier, and was discussing literature, art, and philosophy, now and then touching upon some such novel and yet pertinent topics as "Woman" and her place in society.

These staunch souls were throwing aside the narrow confines of New England and partaking of a world culture, but Dorothea Dix who had drunk deep at the fountain while in England, still remained outside the charmed circle of intellectuals in Boston. It is possible that had she been admitted she would have found their society too visionary, too philosophical, and impractical for a woman of energy and humanitarian impulse. Had she been admitted to the Symposium, she would, no doubt, have been drawn over to the "Humanity and Reform" wing as Emerson styled the "left" or "direct-actionist" group.[23] She would have taken her stand with men like Orestes Brownson, William E. Channing, and James Freeman Clarke, who were soon talking temperance and abolition. Acceptance by Boston's intelligentsia would have been pleasing to Dorothea Dix but she would have mingled better in the company of William Lloyd Garrison, Harriet Keziah Hunt, Samuel Gridley Howe, and R. C. Waterson, men and women who offered society a program as well as a philosophy. She was not a utopian philosopher; she had no desire to bring about a heaven on earth and she would have been too modest to attempt it. She was willing to meet the world on its own terms so long as it offered her work for idle hands and a friendly niche in which to live.

Such was her frame of mind in 1841 when she heard that some one was needed to teach a Sunday School class in the East Cambridge jail. She had often passed the jail but she had never gone inside. Her opportunity came when John T. G. Nichols, then a student in the Harvard Divinity School, was one of a body of students to whom the East Cambridge jail was assigned for Sunday School instruction.[24] To young Nichols was given a class of women convicts. There were at this time about twenty women in the jail; some were innocent, some were first offenders, while others were habitual drunkards and hardened criminals. Some were incarcerated for theft, some for immorality, others for vagrancy, and one or two were there simply because they had no other place to go. Some were bold, uncouth and vile in their speech, others were retiring and ashamed. It was a motley lot of sinners, and after young Nichols had tried to hold services with them a few times, he became convinced that it was a task for a mature and sympathetic woman rather than a youthful theological student. Only a strong, noble-minded woman could reach them, secure their confidence, and uplift their minds.

Nichols talked over with his mother the possibility of finding a woman who would be willing to go down to the filthy jail and carry a message of hope to those degraded and unhappy women. She suggested that Miss Dix might be able to help him find some one. "On hearing my account," Dr. Nichols wrote many years afterward, "Miss Dix said after some deliberation, 'I will take them myself.' I protested her physical incapacity as she was in feeble health. 'I shall be there next Sunday,' was her answer."[25]

It opened up a possibility for Christian service and Miss Dix looked forward to teaching those poor unfortunate women. She visualized them in their dingy quarters, repentant many of them, some of them more sinned against than sinning. She thought of how she would talk and pray with them, and bring them the gospel of love and piety and of how she would read beautiful promises of the scriptures to them. Some of these poor souls might yet be redeemed to useful Christian lives. Early the next Sunday morning with her hymn book and her Bible under her arm and a prayer upon her lips she set out for the East Cambridge jail.

After the services Miss Dix walked through the jail and talked with the prisoners. Among them she found a number of insane persons. She was shocked to see them among hardened criminals, and entirely devoid of medical and moral treatment. Upon inquiry she learned that their only crime against society was their affliction. She inspected their quarters and to her horror found them bare, cold, and unheated. She asked the jailer why there was no stove or other heat in the part of the jail reserved for the insane, and why nothing was done to make their living as comfortable as that furnished for persons who had committed actual crimes against society. The jailer tried to dismiss the matter by saying that "lunatics" did not feel the cold as others, and that a fire would be very unsafe.

It was a raw March day, and the wind whipped sharply around the corners and rattled the window panes; the mentally ill huddled closer together in their cold, damp quarters, their teeth chattering at times, and they drew their thin garments tightly about them. They looked appealingly at the sad-faced woman in the dark cashmere, and she was moved with compassion. During later visits she asked the jailer repeatedly to make provision for warming their quarters, but to no avail. She determined not to drop the matter. Court was then in session in East Cambridge and she had the case brought before it. She was deeply affected by the inhumanity of it all, and in vivid language she depicted the wretchedness of those poor demented creatures, their suffering, their neglect, their wild frenzy; the guilty, the innocent, the diseased and the unfit, all herded together in unsanitary, inadequate, and in some instances freezing quarters.

She enlisted the support of other philanthropic persons among them R. C. Waterson, George Emerson, Charles Sumner, and Samuel Gridley Howe who was doing so much to help blind and afflicted children, and asked that they corroborate her statements. They investigated conditions in the Cambridge jail. Dr. Howe wrote an article for the *Daily Advertiser* in which he reported conditions as he had seen them. "Untrue, lies, slander," was the public reaction. But it was true, and Sumner who accompanied Howe replied in a public letter.

My dear Howe:

I am sorry to say that your article does *present a true picture* of the condition in which we found those unfortunates. They were cramped together in rooms *poorly ventilated and noisome with filth.* . . . You cannot forget the small room in which were confined the raving maniac, from whom long since reason had fled, never to return, and that interesting young woman, whose mind was so slightly obscured that it seemed as if, in a moment, even while we were looking on, the cloud would pass away. In two cages or pens constructed of plank, within the four stone walls of the same room, these two persons had spent several months. The whole prison echoes with the blasphemies of the poor old woman, while her young and gentle fellow in suffering, doomed to spend her days and nights in such close connection with her, seemed to shrink from her words as from blows. And well she might; for they were words not to be heard by any woman in whom reason had left any vestige of its former presence. It was a punishment by a cruel man in heathen days to tie the living to the dead; hardly less horrid was this scene in the prison at Cambridge.

Ever faithfully yours,

Charles Sumner.[26]

Dorothea Dix was incensed by man's inhumanity to man. This had, no doubt, been going on for generations. Cambridge was perhaps not the only place in Massachusetts where the indigent mentally ill were housed with criminals, and neglected as outcasts when they deserved only mercy and kindness. Why had no one ever raised a hand in their defense, or spoken a word in their behalf?

She was haunted by the scene until at last there came the blessed thought: Here was a work that she might do. As Esther before Mordecai, perhaps she too "had come into the kingdom for such an hour as this."

CHAPTER **IV**

PSYCHOSIS: SUPERSTITION AND SCIENCE*

CONDITIONS such as Dorothea Dix found in the Cambridge jail were not unusual; wretched though the facilities there appeared, they were superior to those in most parts of the country. In the early years of the nineteenth century it was very common to find the indigent psychotic housed with criminals, vagrants and paupers. There were no great psychopathic hospitals maintained at public expense where the mentally ill might be given scientific treatment and where pleasant surroundings, carefully regulated diet, exercise, and occupational therapy might contribute toward the restoration of mind and usefulness. Poor farms and jails were the only places available for lodging unfortunate persons bereft of reason and funds; seldom then was there an almshouse or a prison that did not number among its inmates two or three, or even a dozen "insane" persons.† As soon as these poor souls were incarcerated and no longer menaced society, they were forgotten.

The sixth census, taken in 1840, which was the first to take cognizance of the problem, reported the number of "insane" in the United States as 17,434 out of a total population of 23,191,876. The ratio was 1 to 977. Of the mentally diseased, 5,172 were supported as public charges, and the remainder were cared for privately. Because of the difficulties in securing authentic information in such cases, it is probable that these figures are considerably lower than the actual number of persons mentally ill.[1] In 1840 there were fourteen hospitals for mental disease in the United States, but their total capacity was less than 2,500 beds.[2]

The general neglect of the mentally ill in America and the common failure to discriminate between idiocy and psychosis, the criminal and the abnormal, were due in a large measure to ignorance,

* This chapter deals primarily with the history of the care and treatment of the mentally ill prior to 1840. It may be omitted by readers interested solely in the biography of Miss Dix, without impairing the narrative.

† In this study the terms, "mentally ill," "psychosis," and "psychotic," are used to describe persons of diseased mind. Only by a process of law may the term "insane" be rightfully applied to an individual. "Insanity" is a legal not a medical term.

certain widespread misconceptions of the nature of the disease, and
the lack of an aroused social consciousness. Psychosis is as old as
humanity, and throughout the ages, superstition, theology, and
science, in turn, have been invoked to explain the bleak phenom-
enon. Modes of treatment have run the gamut from social ostra-
cism, chains and dungeons, charms and magic to public asylums and
the present-day psychopathic hospitals with their fine equipment,
skilled physicians, trained nurses, and dietitians. As the cultural
level of a people has changed so have the popular notions regarding
the nature and treatment of mental diseases. Here and there
prophets have appeared who preached a rational theory of the disease and advocated treatment far in advance of their time, but unfortunately few of these were in a position to put their ideas into
practice and their lessons were lost to humanity.

For purposes of classification and historical comparison the evolution of methods of caring for the mentally ill has been conveniently
divided into four periods. In the first the victims were regarded
as being possessed of evil spirits; hence society held aloof and feared
contamination. Queer behavior or abnormal mental states were
associated with the devil or divine powers. Based on the same general outlines were the beliefs of the ancient Jews, which have been
perpetuated through the literature of the Old Testament.[3] In the
second stage society was indifferent and its chief concern was public
safety rather than the well-being of the afflicted. It had often been
called the "chain and dungeon" period because of the frequency with
which these defenses were employed in caring for mentally ill. The
third era is marked by the "asylum," which bore witness to a new
humanitarian spirit but it was intended to harbor rather than cure
the sick. It manifested itself in its earlier years as an ecclesiastical
and not as a civil institution. Except for private charities and an
occasional royal or municipal house of refuge such as Bethlehem
Hospital in London and the House of Grace in Bagdad, monasteries
and nunneries took over the great burden of ministering for the
mentally diseased when they were not allowed to run at large. The
treatment in this era was empirical rather than rational. In the
fourth, or present-day, mental derangement is regarded as a disease
to be cured, and not as a scourge of God to be patiently accepted.
Hospitals are organized to meet the needs of various types of
psychosis and to make possible a treatment whose aim is the restora-

tion of the individual. Historically this era may be said to begin with Pinel's work in the closing decade of the eighteenth century, when he made a practical demonstration of the new theories regarding the nature and care of mental disease.[4] Non-restraint, occupational therapy, and scientific medical treatment were to be characteristics of this new régime, while the state was to assume responsibility for the care of the indigent mentally ill.

At the close of the eighteenth century the theoretical side of the care and treatment of psychosis was in the main "nebulous philosophic speculation." Mental diseases were still generally attributed in terms of the Galenic tradition to black and yellow bile or to dog-days; symptoms of the disease, such as exaggerated self-esteem, jealousy, envy, sloth, and self-abuse, were mistaken for causes. Drugs were constantly used in treating the disease regardless of cause or type. Opium pills were prescribed for melancholia diaphoresis and pruritis, while to belladonna and tartarus tartarisatus were ascribed mysterious powers for quieting and curing the mentally diseased. Other resources were mustard plasters on the head and feet, clysters and plasters of Spanish fly, venesection at the forehead and thumbs, the nerve-racking cold douche, and the costly *aqua benedicta Rolandi* which it usually took three stout men to administer. The case that did not respond to drugs was considered beyond human help or hope.[5] Incarceration under the most adverse conditions, cold, damp walls, rags, and a simple diet of hard bread and water was the lot of the "insane" pauper until at last fatigued by hunger, disease, and cold, he lay down to die. In the remote rural sections where the causes of mental diseases were still attributed to the moon and strange bewitchings of the human soul, recourse was made to charms, mysterious rites such as the nude bathing of the afflicted at Lochamanur in the north of Scotland, and pilgrimages to shrines such as Saint Dymphna at Gheel or the well of St. Winifred.[6] Queer portions of lupin, bishop wort, henbane, ale, and cathartic grains, and holy water were drunk out of church bells or sacred shells as the priest repeated over the patient the *domine sancti pater omnipotens.*[7]

At the turn of the century there was no more of a social consciousness in Europe than in America and except for a few of the great cities and medical centers, the mentally ill were grossly neglected. For generations the Church and various orders of nuns and monks had performed a commendable service in conducting houses of refuge and asylums for deranged persons, but even in these institutions the humanitarian spirit of the modern age was not present. Benevolence and compassion moved the hearts of those in charge, but knowledge of the true nature of disease was sadly lacking; within walls surmounted by a crucifix, treatment was accorded the mentally ill which would be considered criminal today. Straight jackets, cribs, muffs, wristlets, iron collars, balls and chains were used to restrain the violent. At Strasbourg, the mentally ill were housed in dens, 4 x 4 x 6; at Mareville, cages containing patients were put in cellars;[8] at Lille, they slept in holes underground, while at Samur they were given troughs to serve as beds.[9] For nearly two centuries Bethlehem Hospital in London, and the Narrenthurm or Lunatics Tower in Vienna were showplaces where for a penny or two the public might view the patients.[10]

By 1837 Bethlehem, or Bedlam as the name was pronounced, had over four hundred patients.[11] This institution, a "royal foundation for lunatics" was incorporated by Henry VIII in 1553. In the beginning everyone connected with the hospital—patients, abbots, brothers, and nuns wore black robes with a single white star upon the breast. The hospital built at a cost of £100,000 had an annual income of £18,000, but this was not sufficient to maintain the institution and for many years in the spring a large number of simple-minded and harmless inmates were turned out to beg for bread. Ragged and poor, with their white stars upon their breasts, people recognized these "Toms o' Bedlam" and set out food for them.

There was no effort made in these hospitals to treat patients as individuals; all were treated *en masse*. About the last of May or the first of June, depending on the weather, they were all bled. Following this, they were given weekly vomits, and after that they were purged.[12] The violent were confined in chains, or caged, or encased in muffs, leggins, or straight-jackets. They snapped and snarled, and tore and tugged at their chains like wild beasts. In the seventeenth century a man might take his entire family on a holiday outing through this chamber of horrors for a sixpence, a sum considerably less than the cost of seeing the lions in the Tower. For half a shilling they might behold reincarnations of Oliver Cromwell, Mary Magdalene, Julius Caesar, the Virgin Mary, and even

Instruments of restraint used in the early treatment of the mentally ill. Included in the photograph are muffs, anklets, wristlets, chains, a camisole, a straight jacket, a restraining sheet, and a Utica crib. A woman was confined in this crib in an Illinois institution for fourteen years. From the museum of Dr. George Zellers, at old Jubilee College, Jubilee, Illinois.

the Messiah. Blackguards about the town and even women jeered and mimicked the demented inmates to greater fury.

By 1840 some progress had been made in the hospitals of Europe. The influence of the three great medical centers of Edinburgh, Vienna, and Paris was beginning to be felt in other parts of the continent, and there was a more lively interest in the treatment of mental diseases. Physicians were inquiring into the nature of psychosis and advocating more judicious modes of treatment. Between 1800 and 1840 a number of valuable works on mental diseases were published in England and France and several in Germany. Their acceptance, however, was not spontaneous.

The first evidences of reform may be said to begin with Pinel in France, although recent investigations tend to show that similar reform was going on in England and in Belgium, quite unnoticed by the world. Philippe Pinel (1745-1826), published his treatise on diseases of the mind in 1791. The following year he became physician to Bicetre, the men's hospital for the mentally ill in Paris.[13] By striking chains from the limbs of madmen and substituting a gentle and humane system of therapeutics for a barbarous one, he earned for himself the title of "liberator of the insane."

The French Revolution was at its height. Three years before the Bastille had fallen; the gospel of freedom was being proclaimed far and wide. Liberating the "insane" from the thralls of chains and medieval practices was in keeping with the spirit of the French Revolution and the dramatic incident at Bicetre, reënacted at Salpetiere, the woman's hospital in Paris, in 1793, was given much publicity.

Philippe Pinel, trained in the medical schools of Paris, had been greatly influenced by his observations of the methods employed in caring for the insane at the Gheel colony in Belgium. Here several thousand mentally ill persons were managed without resort to violence and restraint; less than one hundred were quartered in a central hospital, while the others lived about the village, leading as natural a life as possible, adhering to a careful diet and exercise and helping with the farm and household tasks, such as gardening and weaving, which would not interfere with their health. No patient in Gheel was ever deceived, threatened, or disciplined by force.[14] Pinel saw no reason why the principles of kindness, non-restraint, and occupational therapy might not be successfully applied in a great city hospital; nor was Pinel the first to advocate reorganization of the French hospital system, if indeed, it could be called a system.[15] Tenon had made a survey of Paris hospitals in 1736 and reported the urgent need of better accommodations. In 1785 J. Colombier and F. Doublet prepared a manual of "Instruction on the Management of the Insane and the Asylums in which They are Confined."[16] It was 1790 before the Legislative Assembly took action and gave Pinel his opportunity.[17]

Unfortunately for the cause of reform, the continental wars absorbed the resources and interests of the French people and until the restoration of the Bourbons in 1815 very little was done outside of Paris toward ameliorating the condition of the mentally ill.[18] Esquirol, who was to write the first great work on psychosis in French, complained in 1818 that asylums and hospitals of other cities did not approach at all the high standards set in Bicetre and Salpetiere.[19] In 1838 the French legislature passed an act requiring each department to care for its mentally ill; most of them preferred to pay a franc a day to one of the religious orders for the care of each insane person.[20]

In England the Quakers early became interested in social reform. Few things moved them quite so much as the pathetic state of demented Friends who had been committed to public asylums, or incarcerated in British workhouses. In 1792 William Tuke, in the city of York, had become indignant over the treatment of the mentally ill in the York County Asylum and had established York Retreat.[21] A man of means and influence, Tuke went to wealthy Quakers and solicited funds to erect a hospital or asylum where mentally sick Friends could obtain decent quarters, good food, humane treatment, and the proper medical attention. He had followed closely Pinel's experiment in France and resolved that the Retreat at York should be conducted along the same lines.[22]

The fame of York Retreat and Pinel's experiments spread throughout England. The Friends were joined by others and an appeal was made in the House of Commons for legislation regarding the mentally ill.[23] Anthony Ashley Cooper, Seventh Earl of Shaftesbury, became interested and throughout his long life was devoted to the cause of reform in behalf of the indigent insane.[24] In 1807, 1815-1816, 1827, and at other times the Lunacy Select Committees investigated and made recommendations to the House of

Commons.[25] Appropriations were made from time to time that alleviated conditions somewhat by providing additional quarters and removing many mentally ill persons from workhouses and gaols, but it was in hospitals that the most phenomenal changes were made.

Elimination of restraint was the most outstanding reform made in hospital care in England in the generation before Miss Dix began her work in America. In 1821 Dr. Charlesworth became physician to Lincolnshire Asylum and soon began to do away with instruments of restraint. At the Lincoln Asylum in 1835, Dr. Gardiner Green inaugurated a similar policy.[26] In 1839 Dr. John Conolly was appointed physician to the Middlesex Lunatic Asylum at Hanwell, and within four months had discarded all implements of restraint, including forty-nine restraining chairs and six hundred leg and hand cuffs.[27] Meanwhile Dr. John Reeve, long an observer of Pinel's methods, was called to Bethlehem Hospital where he instituted the system of non-restraint.[28]

When Dr. Pliny Earle made his tour of European hospitals in 1857, he commented that the principle of non-restraint was universally accepted in the hospitals which he visited in England. No definite system of royal or municipal control had been evolved; thousands of persons of deranged mind were still incarcerated in gaols and workhouses under the most wretched conditions. In the remote sections of the country hundreds of mentally ill were confined in cellars, damp and musty cells, or left to roam the streets.

In America

The United States by 1840 was still in transition from the second to the third stage. A few states and some cities had taken measures for the indigent mentally ill but they had provided "asylums" rather than true hospitals. These so-called "lunatic asylums" were little better than specialized almshouses where the inmates were victims in varying stages of the disease; the superintendents of these institutions served as wardens and keepers. James Galt, the first of the illustrious family so long connected with the Eastern State Hospital, in Williamsburg, Virginia, entered upon his duties as "keeper" of the "Public Hospital for Persons of Insane and Disordered Minds," upon its opening October 12, 1773, without any medical knowledge or experience in institutional management; nor had his wife, Mary, who became the first matron, any special training.[29] They brought good insight and common sense to their task, however, and had a talent for discipline and wise administration.[30] Few hospitals were so fortunate, and the lack of qualified medical supervision was one of the chief weaknesses of the early state asylums. As late as 1850, Dr. J. M. Higgins, Superintendent of the State Lunatic Asylum, Jacksonville, Illinois, read a paper before the Association of Medical Superintendents of American Institutions for the Insane, in which he plead "The Necessity of a Resident Medical Superintendent in an Institution for the Insane."[31]

There were no special psychiatric nurses nor trained attendants in those days, and help in these early institutions had to be recruited from among the ne'er-do-wells of the community who were not able to find more desirable employment. Attendants were frequently afraid of patients and their fear led to an unnecessary use of instruments of restraint, cuffs, anklets, straight jackets, iron collars, and other gross inhumanities. In Charity Hospital, New Orleans, where a special wing was set aside for mental patients in 1820, there were no regular nurses and convalescents were given a small compensation for looking after patients; the nuns acted largely as directors and purchasing agents. In 1832, Savannah, Georgia, hard pressed for nurses in the city hospital, hit upon a plan as unique as it was inefficient. Free persons of color were required to labor twenty days each year on public works, but women were allowed to commute this to service in the hospital. Thus there was a succession of time-servers and untrained help passing in and out of the Savannah hospital.[32] In such northern cities as Boston, Philadelphia, and New York, where Irish and native white labor could be secured for reasonable wages, hospitals were much better regulated; even here the personnel shifted from time to time and there were loud complaints about wages. There was a general strike in the Philadelphia Almshouse and Blockley Hospital in 1833 when the servants demanded higher wages.[33] In the north a few Catholic hospitals had followed in the wake of Irish and Portuguese immigration; there gentle nuns devoted themselves to the relief of suffering among the sick and poverty-stricken foreigners with such tenderness and efficiency that evntually their hospitals were to become models for public institutions.

The early nineteenth century looked askance at hospitals of any kind and perhaps not unwisely, for in those days of poor sanitation and lack of antisepsis, a hospital might spread disease while attempting to cure it.   Yet hospitals had to be provided; epidemics were common and segregation at times was necessary; and provision had to be made for sick travelers, homeless seamen, derelicts and improvident persons who had no other place to go.   Weird stories were told of the awful experimentation that went on in hospitals, the low morals of attendants, the frequent neglect of patients, and the vast numbers of deaths that occurred.[34]

The attitude of the general public toward idiocy and psychosis in the immediate family was another deterrent to progress in the methods of caring for the mentally ill.   The disease was regarded as a disgrace and something to be concealed, a skeleton in the closet. The unfortunate member was locked up if violent, and always kept out of sight when callers came.   Once the disease was discovered, invariably the victim began to lead an unnatural life.   "Queer," "a little off," he was no longer taken seriously; he was obviously humored or ignored, either of which modes of procedure tended to accentuate abnormalities.   The pious saw in the dire phenomena "the hand of God," "the sins of the father visited upon the children"; insanity was a cross to be borne.[35]   It followed that their attitude toward the homeless and indigent mentally ill was one of indifference, and for generations the sufferers were allowed to be sent indiscriminately to county jails and poorhouses, or farmed out to the lowest bidder.

There was also the puzzling problem of the legal status of the psychotic.   Were they criminals, potential criminals, disorderly persons, or public enemies?   Public sentiment had never been crystallized, and there was a great diversity in the statutes of the respective states as to the treatment that should be accorded the insane.   It was 1838 before Dr. Isaac Ray published his treatise on the *Medical Jurisprudence of Insanity,* the first work in America which attempted to synthesize the laws governing the mentally ill and to lay down principles which legislation should follow.   In 1798 the Commonwealth of Massachusetts passed a law which provided "that lunatics who were furiously mad, so as to render it dangerous to the safety or the peace of the good people to be at large" might be placed in the House of Correction.[36]

Under the act of February 2, 1793, Delaware vested the care of idiots and "insane" over the age of twenty-one in the courts of chancery.[37] In 1799 the question arose in New York of whether the state had the authority to execute an insane person or a person who committed a crime while mentally ill. John Pastano, convicted of murder and sentenced to be executed, was found to be mentally ill. Under the laws of New York, 1788, the mentally deranged were classed as disorderly persons. An appeal was made to the legislature and a special act was passed pardoning Pastano on the condition that he be kept in prison until he could be sent to his place of legal residence.[38] An act passed in New York in 1827 specified that no insane person should be confined in any prison, jail, or house of correction, or in the same room with any person charged with or convicted of any criminal offense; such persons were to be sent to the asylum in New York City, or to the county poorhouse, or other places as provided by county superintendents for the reception of the insane.[39]

The attitude of medical men toward the care and treatment of psychosis was slightly in advance of that of the laity. Despite the low standards of training and practice still common in American medicine prior to 1850, numbers of physicians in the United States had been well trained in Edinburgh, London, or Paris, or had availed themselves of such superior instruction as that offered at the medical colleges of Columbia, Harvard, and the University of Pennsylvania. A few of these men began to take an interest in psychosis and in the possibilities of a scientific treatment for the mentally ill. Most notable of these was Benjamin Rush (1745-1813). He was in many ways the first outstanding American physician and the first American to make a serious contribution to the study of psychosis.[40]

Rush attended Princeton, learned the rudiments of medicine from Dr. John Redman, and then went to Edinburgh for his degree. He "walked" the London hospitals, and assisted by Benjamin Franklin, spent several months studying in Paris. When he returned to America in 1769, he became professor of chemistry in the Medical College of Philadelphia. In turn he was physician-general of the continental army of the middle department, and "Professor of the Institute of Medicine and of Clinical Practice" in the new University of Pennsylvania.[41]

In his earliest work, *The Influence of Physical Causes upon the*

Moral Faculty, he showed the moral sense to be subject to physical influences and indicated how scientific treatment might be applied. Between 1789 and 1798, he published five volumes on *Medical Inquiries and Observations,* and in 1812, *Diseases of the Mind.* The latter is considered his most significant contribution to medical science.

Dr. Rush rejected the current beliefs that the primary causes of mental derangement were either a diseased condition of the abdominal viscera, of the peritonital covering of the intestines, or of the brain-cells. He advanced the theory that "madness is seated primarily in the blood vessels of the brain, and it depends upon the same kind of morbid and irregular actions that constitute other arterial diseases."[42] This was in accordance with his general theory of disease as a condition of the blood and blood vessels. He based his theory upon the premise that certain treatments used in fevers and blood diseases were beneficial in the treatment of mental disease and that mental disease is nearly always accompanied by some arterial or skin disorder. He classified the causes of "intellectual derangement" as being of two kinds, (1) those which act directly upon the body as malconformations and lesions of the brain, and (2) those which act indirectly upon the body through the medium of the mind. He classified contributing causes as "physical" and "corporeal"; under the "physical" were listed contusions, abscesses, apoplexy, headache, use of spirits, sex-indulgence, extreme exercise, and sudden change of temperature; under the "corporeal" were those things which acted sympathetically upon the brain such as narcotics, consumption, hysteria, cutaneous eruptions, and intense shock.[43]

Rush's contribution to psychology was considerably impaired because he coupled with it a sort of realistic phrenology in which imaginary faculties were confined in so many arbitrary compartments. His cerebral localization was erroneous and he never recognized the true function of the brain in the higher thought processes. He shared the ancient belief that the moon had a strange influence upon the mentally ill. He believed that mentally ill were possessed of a sort of sixth sense which well persons lacked, and that the full moon rarified the air so that the mentally ill, with their increased sensibilities, responded to those atmospheric changes and became more agitated.[44]

Around Benjamin Rush and his theories developed the Philadelphia school which emphasized the reciprocal or coördinate influences of the physical and psychic. Dr. Rush was the first prominent physician in America who tried to popularize institutional treatment for the affluent as well as for the indigent mentally ill. He believed that the food and surroundings should be in keeping with the patient's former social status. He recommended the substitution of women for male nurses, and called attention to the importance of labor in restoring the mind.[45]

Not all of Rush's methods of treating the mentally ill were so progressive,[46] particularly where patients were violent and where discipline seemed to be involved. To meet these conditions he recommended the tranquilar or straight chair, depriving the patient of his customary food, pouring ice cold water into the coat sleeve of the patient, a shower bath for fifteen or twenty minutes, the fear of death, great pain, prolonged abstinence, and the use of the gyrator,[47] a cheap rotary machine which Rush had himself invented. Last, but not least, he advocated bleeding. Rush often took from twenty to forty ounces of blood from a patient. He was convinced that this early and copious practice was "wonderful in calming mad people." Rush never laughed or talked with his patients. He believed it necessary to maintain a frozen dignity and an attitude of great power, believing that those in charge of mental patients should control them through fear or other dubious means. Rush's interest in the mentally ill was mainly one of therapeutics. In his writings there is no evidence that he was deeply struck by the inadequate provision made for the insane, although he used the Blockley almshouse as a laboratory for his classes, and as a leader in the prison reform movement, he must have at various times visited Philadelphia's miserable jails as well as the basement cells of the Pennsylvania Hospital where so many mentally ill were confined.

The University of Pennsylvania was for many years the leading medical school in America, and the influence of its most eminent professor was far-reaching. As late as 1842 Dr. Stribling, of the Western State Hospital, complained to the Virginia Legislature that seldom did he have a patient come in that had not been well-bled, blistered, and purged.[48]

In 1840 there were three types of provision for the insane—namely, municipal, county, and state administrative agencies; nowhere was there any very definite policy. The county system was most prevalent, except in counties where there were large cities, the number of mentally ill dependents was not sufficient to warrant separate institutions and by force of necessity the insane had to be placed in jails and almshouses. Miss Dix was soon to find in hundreds of places throughout the land, conditions not only as bad as those in the Cambridge jail, but even more appalling. In some parts of the country, as in Rhode Island, local boards farmed out paupers and mentally ill dependents to the lowest bidder. These practices led to much cruelty and gross neglect, for it was a mean nature that would undertake to make a profit out of lodging insane for $1.25 or $2.00 a week. County boards were by law administrative rather than legislative in function, and were powerless to levy additional taxes to meet the ever increasing cost of providing for the indigent. This may explain although it does not justify the devices to which county boards frequently resorted. At best it was a drear and inefficient system.

Outstanding examples of municipal provision were in Philadelphia, Boston, and New York City. The first hospital for mental patients in the United States was founded in Philadelphia. As early as 1709, members of the Friends Society in Philadelphia began efforts to secure an asylum for deranged Quakers. In 1751 with the help of Dr. Thomas Bond, who made appeals for contributions, they interested Benjamin Franklin, and on January 25, 1751, a petition signed by thirty-three citizens was presented to the provincial assembly.[49] Not long afterward an act was passed chartering "a small provincial hospital to care for the insane and others." Originally only one wing was set aside for the insane, but in 1796 a separate building was erected. In a few years it was overcrowded and Blockley almshouse was again used to house the mentally ill. In 1840 the almshouse in Philadelphia was overflowing with a heterogeneous lot of paupers, mentally diseased persons, and criminals.

The Boston Lunatic Asylum was opened in 1839 to care for the insane from the city of Boston. Before this the public charges were housed in the almshouse on Leverett Street, in the jails, and in the House of Industry in South Boston, or in the state hospital at Worcester. A report to the legislature in 1833 says, "Instead of a House of Industry, the place is a general infirmary, an asylum for the insane, a refuge for the deserted and most destitute children of the city. It contains the aged, the infirm, the sick, the insane, idiots, and helpless children."[50] Suffolk County provided for one hundred patients in the South Boston Hospital. The state made provision for 229 patients in the Insane Hospital at Worcester, but the poor did not have easy access to it. The Boston Lunatic Asylum had a capacity of about a hundred, and this slightly relieved the congestion in the jails and poorhouses.

Provision for the indigent mentally ill in the City of New York was much the same as in Boston and Philadelphia. Originally they were housed in the basement of the New York General Hospital, but in 1806 a separate building was set aside for mental patients.[51] Beginning with the year 1806 the state legislature made small appropriations to the governors of the New York City Hospital in caring for the indigent. In 1822, as an outgrowth of this combined and enlarged program, Bloomingdale Hospital was constructed near the city; it provided for about a hundred patients."[52] It soon proved inadequate and in 1836 the New York City Hospital for the Insane was established on Blackwell's Island. The new hospital with its capacity of 350 patients offered temporary relief, but in a short time jails and poorhouses were again numbering "lunatics" among their inmates.

In the south, conditions were similar. New Orleans until 1847, cared for its mentally ill through the agency of the famous Charity Hospital whose history dates far back into the French and Spanish régimes. Under the management of the Sisters of Charity, the institution was supported by popular subscriptions, bequests, appropriations by the town council, a municipal tax on gambling houses, a tax on travelers to New Orleans, and a twenty-five cent fee charged all visitors to the hospital.[53] In 1813 state aid was first granted to the hospital and after that date a council appointed by the governor participated in the management. Charity was primarily a general hospital whose chief function was caring for the vast number of travelers who became ill in the city during the frequent epidemics of malaria and yellow fever. When the new hospital was built in 1820, a special wing was set aside with twenty-four apartments for the mentally ill, but during emergencies these were converted into wards for fever patients. Iu 1840 an appropriation of $25,000 provided a separate building to which all "lunatics" sent from any part of the state should be admitted.

In Charleston there is record as early as 1762 of a charitable organization for the purpose of providing an infirmary for the "reception of lunatics or other diseased persons." The Revolution interrupted its plans and the "madhouse" in Charleston, in the Colonial Records of 1776, no doubt refers to the combined poorhouse and asylum that was started about the year 1712. Upon the establishment of a state hospital in 1828, Charleston abandoned its program of municipal care for this class of unfortunates.[53a]

Of the private institutions maintained exclusively for the treatment of psychosis, there were few. People have ever been sensitive about mental diseases, and those who could afford to employ special attendants preferred to keep distressed members of their family at home rather than entrust them to the care of strangers. This was not always possible, and now and then a physician would take a few mentally ill persons into his home for closer observation and treatment. As his success became known he was asked to take more patients; thus a number of private institutions had their beginnings. Seldom did these households include more than five or ten patients at one time; usually these sanatoriums bore no names. There was no stigma attached to residence in the home of a physician, and where good work was accomplished these private hospitals served to break down prejudices against institutional treatment for the better classes of society.[54]

One of the most notable private institutions was Hartford Retreat, founded in 1824. In 1812 Dr. Nathan Dwight of Colchester read a paper before the Connecticut State Medical Society in which he urged hospital care for the mentally ill. The society moved to have a survey made of the number of "insane" persons in the state. Nothing was accomplished by the committee and in 1814 the Medical Society enlisted the help of the General Association of Congregational Clergy, an organization which extended into every town in the state, as church and state had not yet been separated in Connecticut. The clergy reported 146 persons as "deprived of reason" but this figure was thought to be too low. Nothing was done about the matter, and in 1821 Dr. Eli Todd reported to the Hartford County Medical Society that there were five hundred cases of mental disease in seventy towns in Connecticut and as he had yet to hear from fifty-four towns, he roughly estimated the number at 1000.[55]

A committee raised $12,000 through private subscriptions ranging from twelve and one-half cents to three hundred dollars for the purpose of establishing an asylum. The state contributed $5,000 and the state medical society $600. A total of $20,000 was secured and in January 1824, the Hartford Retreat under the management of Dr. Todd and Dr. Samuel Woodward was opened. The hospital had a capacity of fifty beds. The state granted a lottery which brought in $40,000; ten thousand dollars of which was applied on the building fund and the remainder set aside as a perpetual fund to defray maintenance.

Dr. Todd did not approve of depletion, especially bleeding, in cases of mental illness; neither did he advocate violent purges or blisters. He recommended a generous diet and frequent resort to tonics and narcotics. This course of treatment had been prescribed by the best European writers on mental diseases but as it was contrary to the Rush school of thought it was not followed in American hospitals prior to the time of Dr. Todd.

The McLean Psychiatric Hospital, one of the leading institutions of its kind in the world today, dates from 1813.[56] Originally it was a department of the Massachusetts General Hospital, but it received little help from the state. Trustees were selected in 1813 and a few years later they began a subscription for funds to be used in the construction of a hospital for the sick and special accommodations for the mentally ill. Fifty thousand dollars was secured for the department for mental diseases, a building was constructed and in 1818 it was opened for patients. In 1821 John McLean left $100,000 to the hospital corporation and in accordance with the terms of the gift, the name was changed to McLean Hospital. In 1835 Mary Belknap left a legacy of $90,000 for the construction of separate quarters for women.[57]

Edward Sturit Abdy, an English traveler in America, from 1834 to 1836, wrote enthusiastically of a hospital for mental diseases near Boston, unmistakably McLean Hospital, whose methods, he said, were "astonishingly modern."

The principle on which the establishment is conducted differs very considerably, and from what I saw and heard, very successfully from the methods usually pursued in the treatment of lunatics. No kind of deception, and if possible no restraint, is exercised upon the patients who are allowed every indulgence and gratification that are not incompatible with the object for which they are sent hither . . . with the aid of soothing language, occupation suited to their inclinations, proper exercise and appropriate medicines, an alleviation, if not a cure of the malady is effected. . . . No one is confined, however violent and intractable, in irons or in solitude. No breach of promise, no attempt to mislead, is ever permitted. . . . Riding on horseback for both sexes is found very serviceable, or any other occupation that may interest or amuse, is employed with good effect; and as the house is open to visitors at all times, and the same courtesies are observed toward the inmates as are practiced in common life, a constant succession of objects presents itself, to give gentle exercise to the tastes and affections and dispel the morbid illusions of the imaginations. To gain his confidence and imperceptibly lead him to the exercise of his disused energies and faculties . . . is all that the physician studies in the management of his patient.

McLean was then as now a very exclusive and costly hospital, and while providing for many charity cases, so numerous were requests for care that only a comparative few could avail themselves of its superior facilities. There was a striking contrast between the treatment given the mentally ill in McLean Hospital and in the Boston jails and almshouses. It is no wonder that Dorothea Dix, who knew of the splendid things that were being done for patients at McLean, was shocked and horrified to see mentally ill persons, idiots, and little children huddled together with prostitutes, vagrants, drunkards, and even murderers in the Cambridge jail. Were not these wrecks of humanity entitled to something better?

State hospitals, however, made slow progress. By 1840 eleven of the twenty-six states had provided in some way for institutional care of the indigent mentally ill within their borders. South Carolina appropriated funds for a state hospital in 1822. In 1837 Georgia made appropriations for a "hospital for the insane" but it was 1841 before the buildings were ready for occupancy. Some of the states such as Virginia, Massachusetts, and Kentucky, owned and operated hospitals or subscribed to private institutions after the manner of Louisiana and the Charity Hospital in New Orleans. Virginia, as already noted, was the first state to build a hospital devoted exclusively to the mentally ill. In 1828 a second institution, the Western Lunatic Asylum, was opened at Staunton, Virginia. After

1830 idiots were not admitted to Virginia state hospitals, but were sent back to the counties from which they came to be looked after by the county overseer of the poor.[58] The Maryland State Hospital was opened in 1816; it was financed by the state and operated by the Sisters of Charity. For a time it was leased to private physicians, but in 1834 the state assumed control and management of the institution.[59]

Beyond the Alleghanies state provision for the mentally ill was made little by little. In 1821 Ohio passed an "Act Establishing a Commercial Hospital and Lunatic Asylum for the State of Ohio," but it was 1830 before the hospital at Columbus was ready to receive patients. On May 1, 1824 the Kentucky State Hospital at Lexington was opened.

In 1836 as a result of a memorial from the New York Medical Society, the New York legislature provided for a state hospital to be located at Utica. Pennsylvania provided for her mentally ill through the hospital in Philadelphia. The Vermont Asylum for the Insane at Brattleboro, was opened December 12, 1836; it was founded as the result of a bequest of $10,000 from Mrs. Ann Marsh, the widow of Dr. Perley Marsh, of Hinsdale, New Hampshire. In 1840 Maine opened its hospital at Augusta. In the same year the Tennessee State Hospital, near Nashville, for which appropriations were made in 1832, was also opened.

On the whole the need for hospitals was still appalling. No provision whatever had yet been made in Alabama, Mississippi, Illinois, Arkansas, Indiana, and Michigan, and the territories of Florida, Wisconsin, and Iowa, to take care of mentally ill paupers in either state or privately owned institutions. Hartford Retreat was utterly inadequate for the needs of Connecticut. Indiana had no asylums of any kind whatever and had the greatest number of mentally ill of any of the states that had not yet made accommodation for this class of defectives. In Michigan, the indigent insane were sent to prisons. In 1842 a "crazy house" was built at the Wayne County almshouse. In 1843 there were only fourteen hospitals in the United States, either private or public, that were devoted solely to the care of mental diseases. The total bed capacity of these hospitals was only 2,547.

By 1840 France, England, and America all possessed a few hospitals which were doing notable work in treating mental diseases but the great mass of the mentally ill were without the benefits of this superior equipment, or of any medical treatment which would today be termed scientific and humane. The rich were able to avail themselves of the services of costly physicians but the indigent in all countries suffered. The world had yet to be shown the relationship between social responsibility and taxation.

That was to be the work of Dorothea Dix.

CHAPTER V

THE MASSACHUSETTS MEMORIAL

DOROTHEA DIX was by no means the first person before 1843 to take cognizance of the evils in the Massachusetts system of providing for the indigent mentally ill. She had no sooner asked herself why no one had ever raised a hand in their defense than she began to recall previous surveys and agitations. They were thought-provoking, indeed: Thirteen years before, Horace Mann, of Dedham, soon to become her friend and close associate in the cause of reform, called attention to the miserable status of the mentally ill and to the law of 1816 which made it the duty of the supreme court to commit to prison any person whom a grand jury refused to indict or a jury to convict by reason of his mental condition, and to keep him confined there until his health came to be compatible with his release and the public safety, or until a friend would assume responsibility.[1] Mann declared that "had the human mind been tasked to devise a mode of exaggerating to the utmost the calamities of the insane, a more apt expedient could scarcely have been suggested, or had the earth been searched, places more inauspicious to their recovery could scarcely have been found."[2] It was 1827 before the law was changed so that "persons furiously mad" were committed to the hospital "lunatic asylum" instead of the jails.[3]

For two years Mann worked upon a survey of Massachusetts prisons, almshouses, and houses of correction. Response to the legislative committee's questionnaire was slow and the final report represented only half the population of the state; however, the 114 towns which replied reported 289 "lunatics" or "persons furiously mad." Of these 78 were in poorhouses and houses of industry, 37 in private houses, 19 in jails and houses of correction, 10 in insane hospitals and the remaining 17 were in other places of confinement. At least sixty were confined in the hospital in Charleston.[4] In 1830, as a result of the efforts of Mann and his committee, the legislature voted an appropriation of $30,000 for a state hospital for the insane to be established at Worcester.

It was the desire of the Massachusetts board of welfare commissioners that all mentally ill persons then lodged in prisons and jails should be removed to the hospital. Governor Lincoln made a proclamation to that effect in 1835, and on January 17 the first patients were received.[5] The hospital at Worcester, Miss Dix reflected, was an exemplary institution. Under the management of Dr. Samuel Woodward it ranked high as a hospital for mental diseases. In eight years it had received over a thousand patients, of whom nearly one-half had been restored to health and usefulness. Except for the occasional use of mittens and wrist-bands, there was no resort to instruments of restraint. Amusements such as riding, walking, dancing, and blind man's buff, were enjoyed by the patients. There was a library for reading, and when the capacity of the hospital was increased from 120 to 230 in 1837, a chapel was added.[6]

Miss Dix remembered that this increase in appropriation made at the suggestion of Mr. Mann, was granted as he said "without a single murmur of opposition, nay with the greatest apparent cordiality toward the hospital." It even surprised Mr. Mann and he wrote in prophetic vein to his friend, Charles Sumner:

Ah, I never thought of this, when in 1830, we stormed the dungeons of inhumanity. The outer gates were broken down and some of the captives are coming forth every day to enjoy the light and the beauty of the physical and the holier light and beauty of the moral universe; yet here in this midnight silence, as I write, I hear more from their interior cells, as audibly as if it were the voice of the thunder cloud, the voices of many victims awaiting in unconsciousness the day of their deliverance.[7]

Despite its enlarged quarters the Worcester Hospital was in no way attempting to care for all the mental defectives in Massachusetts. In his inaugural speech as Mayor of Boston in 1837, Samuel Eliot called attention to the many unfortunate idiots and "insane" persons in the House of Industry and Correction.[8] He asked if it would not be more becoming in a community of large resources and liberality, to provide for the comfort and safety of those who were inmates of the House of Industry. "A hospital fitted for the application of suitable treatment of these patients," he said, "would not only be honorable to the philanthropy of the city, but it might result in such diminution of their number as materially to lessen the expense of their support."[9] Through Mayor Eliot's efforts and those of the

Boston Prison Discipline Society[10] the Boston Lunatic Asylum[11] was established and opened for patients on December 11, 1839.

So there was progress toward the solution of the problem of the mentally ill though it was only natural that Miss Dix was shocked two years later when she found such terrible conditions in the Cambridge jail, scarcely an hour's walk from the new Boston asylum. It seemed incredible. In terse impassioned words she laid the case of the poor shivering demented inmates of the Cambridge jail before the judge. Was not the court champion of the innocent, the defenseless? Was justice blind to the distress of men and women simply because they were devoid of reason? Why in the name of decency must innocent persons be housed with criminals, murderers, and prostitutes, and if they were imprisoned on the same basis as criminals, were they not entitled to the same treatment? Why should they be denied warm clothing and comfortable quarters? Should their poor bodies be denied warmth because their minds were broken? The court listened. Heat was provided in the apartments for the "insane." Miss Dix was encouraged. She visited the inmates in their renovated quarters. They seemed calmer and less afraid.

March passed and then April. The ground thawed and the trees began to leaf. The more Miss Dix visited the prisoners in the Cambridge jail, the more she began to wonder about conditions in other prisons and almshouses. Trips to nearby towns convinced her that a survey of the state would reveal far worse abuses. If the facts were laid before the Massachusetts legislature, certainly some action would be taken. The law permitting the incarceration of insane and idiotic persons along with criminals would surely be changed, and the practice of farming out insane paupers such as she had heard was employed in some townships would be abolished and adequate appropriations made so that every mentally ill person in the commonwealth could have proper medical and moral treatment.

The mass of people, Miss Dix reflected, had no contact with hospitals, almshouses, and prisons. Literature on mental diseases was at that time directed toward only a small audience of doctors and practitioners. The idea of more and larger state hospitals would have to be popularized and the public convinced that it was the function of the state to protect its defectives. Current practices had to be stopped. New England in the forties was becoming cultured on the one hand and industrialized on the other. Miss Dix smiled dryly. The Brahmins might have to be shocked.

She talked over her plans again with Dr. Howe and Charles Sumner, both prominent members of the Boston Prison Discipline Society. It was an excellent idea, they agreed, but had she thought of the expense involved. The questionnaire method such as Mr. Mann had used was unsatisfactory. To make the right kind of an investigation every jail, house of industry and correction in the state of Massachusetts, even farmhouses where mentally ill persons were kept, should be visited. It would take months, and such an intensive survey was beyond the resources of any organization then in existence. Did Miss Dix realize that?

Miss Dix did realize it. For a long time she had been considering ways and means. There was the money she had saved from teaching, the royalties on her books, the annuity left her by her grandfather Dix, and the income from her grandmother's estate. She had more than enough to keep her as long as she lived, and to what better use could the surplus be put than in doing good for mankind.

Both Sumner and Howe were confident that the legislature would do something if the facts were put before them. Such a move would certainly command the support of all philanthropic persons. Boston was seething with projects. Some of the fine energy expended in conversational groups in discussing the *summum bonum,* the efficacy of water cures and vegetarianism, or woman's rights, might be profitably diverted to a movement to alleviate distress among the "insane." Moreover the time was propitious. "The fruits of experimental and practical ventures of divers sorts were ripening for the harvest."[12] Half a dozen idealists never met together without some one advancing a plan for reform, some scheme for world betterment. Ripley and Alcott were delving into Fourierism and trying to prove through the Brook Farm and Fruitlands experiments that the hope of the world lay in the organization of communistic societies. Garrison was throwing all his resources into *The Liberator* and appealing for the abolition of racial privilege, and Margaret Fuller was gleaning ideas for a book on the changing status of women. Orestes Brownson, Henry Hedges, and Emerson were all preaching a gospel of world brotherhood. The *North American Review,* prophet of the new age, was giving ear and space to all manner of innovations ranging from animal magnetism, clairvoyance, and spiritualism to philosophy and political economy. If both the pulpit and press could be enlisted in the interest of the mentally ill, Dr. Howe believed that invaluable service might be rendered to the cause.

The medical profession could also be relied upon to give support. A few years before Dr. Amariah Brigham had published in the *North American Review* an article on "The Insane and Insane Asylums," in which he tried to popularize institutional care and to point out the need of better scientific treatment for the insane. Dr. Willard and Dr. Chandler of the Worcester Hospital, Dr. Luther Bell of the McLean Hospital, and Dr. Butler of the Boston Hospital would readily testify as to the inadequacy of their institutions to care for the increasing number of mental cases. Physicians in small towns and villages were beginning to look more favorably toward institutional treatment. It remained to get statistics and to inform the public of the critical state of the mentally ill and to appeal to their humanitarian instincts.

Miss Dix thought the matter over carefully. It was a stupendous undertaking to inspect the living conditions of every insane person in the state of Massachusetts. Dr. Howe warned her of her own delicate health and the fatigue and exposure to which she must subject herself if she carried out the project; but the cause loomed large and she forgot self. She resolved to depend on no agency for direction or support; she would make it a personal survey. It might take six months, or eight, or even longer; she would not be content until she had covered every step of the ground and taken notes on every jail, farmhouse, or poorhouse where pauper insane were quartered.

She talked over her plans with Dr. Channing, now very weak and rapidly failing in health. Long her spiritual adviser, he encouraged her in the ambitious undertaking. In this new venture he foresaw the full flowering of a beautiful and unselfish character. In ministering to the wretched and neglected of humanity, he believed she would find the peace and happiness for which she had so long been searching. The frail body had withstood the rack of pain and disease for many years; it was the spirit of the woman that concerned him now. The gray blue eyes revealed new depths as she described conditions in the Cambridge jail and the House of Industry in South Boston, and pictured the joyous relief which decent moral and medical treatment might bring to the mentally ill. When she had finished, Dr. Channing was gravely silent, strangely moved. Here was one of his flock about to go out into the world and make a practical demonstration of what he had been preaching all these years. He wondered if he would live to see the fruition of her work. He held out a trembling hand. "Even as ye have done it unto the least of these. . . ."

And so from Dr. Channing's home, 85 Mt. Vernon Street, Dorothea Dix started on her survey. Cambridge jail and the South Boston workhouse had been bad enough but now each day's visitations brought forth new horrors. Deeper and deeper she descended into the inferno of neglect and cruelty. Through the warm beautiful days of spring, the torrid heat of summer, on into the autumn and the bitter cold of winter, she went about her work. Eight months passed and less than half of the poorhouses, jails and workhouses had been visited, but what a story her notebooks were beginning to tell! It was a journey such as Howard had taken through the prisons of England years before, although there is no evidence that the one inspired the other.

Across the pages she wrote, often with nervous hand, the painful and shocking details of what she had seen; the poor helpless, forgotten mentally ill and idiotic sunk into a degraded condition. Day by day she recorded the revolting story of the unfortunate human beings that she saw "confined in cages, closets, cellars, stalls, pens . . . chained, naked, beaten with rods, and lashed into obedience."[13] Before she had gone a dozen miles from Boston she witnessed scenes of terrible filth, cruelty, and barbarism. At Medford she found one idiot in chains and another that had been kept in a stall for seventeen years.[14] At Dedham there were insane in both the jail and the almshouse. At the almshouse two insane women were lying on bunks of straw in tightly closed stalls; one of the women was thought to be curable but the overseers of the poor refused to give her a trial at the state hospital because of the expense. At Granville an insane man was so closely confined that he was losing the use of his limbs. There was one violently deranged person at Pepperell, several peaceable, and one chained hand and foot. At Plympton one "insane" and three idiots were in a miserable condition. In the almshouse at Concord an insane woman was kept in a cage and in the Concord jail were housed several violent, noisy, and unmanageable persons.[15]

Occasionally Miss Dix saw mentally ill persons who were humanely treated and who were responding to this care by gradually regaining their health and reason. These happy exceptions spurred her on and pointed to the worth of the cause to which she was devoting her time and energies.

It was November when Miss Dix first visited Danvers. The almshouse was a large building greatly in need of repair. It had between fifty and sixty inmates of whom one was idiotic and three were mentally ill. Before Miss Dix reached the house she heard wild shouts, snatches of rude songs, oaths and obscene language proceeding from a shed at a distance from the main building. She immediately suspected that an "insane" person was incarcerated there and asked the mistress to let her see the "maniac." This forlorn young person, wrote Miss Dix, exhibited "a condition of neglect and misery blotting out the faintest idea of comfort and outraging every sentiment of decency." She had been a respectable person, industrious and worthy, but disappointments and trials had shaken her mind:

There she stood, clinging to, or beating upon, the bars of her caged apartment, the contracted size of which afforded space only for increasing accumulation of filth,—a *foul* spectacle; there she stood, with naked arms and dishevelled hair; the unwashed frame invested with fragments of unclean garments; the air so extremely offensive, though ventilation was afforded on all sides save one, that it was not possible to remain beyond a few moments without retreating for recovery to the outward air. Irritation of body, produced by utter filth and exposure, incited her to the horrid process of tearing off her skin by inches; her face, neck, and person were thus disfigured to hideousness. She held up a fragment just rent off. To my exclamation of horror, the mistress replied, "Oh, we can't help it. Half the skin is off sometimes. We can do nothing with her; and it makes no difference what she eats, for she consumes her own filth as readily as the food which is brought to her."[16]

As winter came on, traveling became more difficult. It was necessary to depend largely on stage and private means of transportation as there were only a few railroads in Massachusetts in 1841. The Boston and Lowell, Boston and Providence, and the Boston and Worcester railroads, which were opened in 1835, touched only a few of the points that Miss Dix found it necessary to visit. Even railroad travel had its disadvantages; seldom did trains make more than fifteen miles an hour. The early trains had no springs on the coaches, and braking and stopping were so difficult that Miss Dix, like other travelers of the day, frequently complained of headache after riding only a short distance. Snow and rain added to the discomfort of traveling, but she allowed nothing to stay her efforts; every day that she could possibly be about, she was on her way. If ice and sleet detained her for a few days at some country tavern, she rested, caught up on the sleep she had lost in catching early morning stages, organized her notes, and wrote letters informing friends of the progress she was making and enlisting support for her project.

Back in Boston between journeys up-state, down-state, and back-state, she consulted with Dr. Bell and Dr. Chandler as to the best methods of treating mental diseases; in Worcester she talked with Dr. Woodward. She became thoroughly familiar with the treatment given in the McLean, Boston, and Worcester hospitals. The contrast in the care given in hospitals and that in the poorhouses and prisons of Massachusetts weighed heavily upon her, and she resolved to write a memorial describing so vividly the things that she had seen that even the hardest heart would be touched.

Some of the scenes that she witnessed haunted her for days. In the poorhouse at Westford there were twenty-six paupers, one idiot, and an insane person. Miss Dix was told that the latter was not fit to be seen. She insisted and was finally conducted upstairs to a rather large apartment. A young woman whose body was covered with portions of an old blanket, was sitting upon the floor. Her hair was uncombed and her naked arms lay languidly over her breast, "a distracted, unsteady eye and low murmuring voice betrayed both mental and physical disquiet." Around her waist was a heavy chain, the end of which was attached to the wall. As Miss Dix entered, the young woman blushed and tried to draw about her the insufficient fragments of the blanket. Miss Dix knelt beside the girl and asked if she did not want to be dressed. "Yes, I want some clothes." "But you will tear 'em all up, you know you will," interposed the caretaker. "No, I won't, I won't tear them off," screamed the girl as she started to rise. The chain pulled her down again, and pointing to it, she burst forth in a wild shrill laugh, "See there, nice clothes." Despite her appeals for clothes, the attendant only sneered and ignored the piteous request.[17]

Not long afterward Miss Dix found a pathetic old man chained to a bunk in the woodshed of the Newton almshouse. Half buried in the dirty straw that made his bed, and his features concealed by long tangled hair and unshorn beard, for all appearances he might have been taken for a wild animal sleeping there. "Filth, neglect, and misery reigned." Miss Dix begged that he might not be aroused. "If sleep could visit a wretch so forlorn, how merciless to break the slumber." Protruding from one end of the box on which he lay were stumps which had once been feet. From his maimed legs, chains were fastened to either side of the building. It was a terrible sight but Miss Dix said nothing.

Although mercy and prompt action had been the guiding principles of her schoolteaching days, she realized that this was not a fit occasion for reproof, and she concealed her indignation. Lifting her skirts slightly, she tiptoed out of the stench-laden room. Out in the open air she asked for the history of the case. The old man had been mentally ill for twenty years. Until the town had established the poor farm a few years before, this man, along with other paupers, sick and infirm, had been annually auctioned off to the lowest bidder. Each year this poor wretch had had a new master. For the major part of twenty years he had been chained in sheds and outhouses about the community. One winter when he was being kept in an outhouse, his keepers being warmed and clothed, did not "reckon how cold he was" and his feet froze. Since then he had not been able to walk. Miss Dix asked why he was kept in chains. The reply was, "Oh, he can crawl, and when he gets mad he might do some damage."[18]

Day after day Dorothea Dix noted in her journal heart-rending and appalling scenes of misery, degradation, and cruelty. In graphic phrase she reproduced the piteous wail, the frenzied scream, the raucous laughter of the demented, the clank of iron chains on frosted pavement, the fetid odor of unwashed bodies, soiled clothing, and putrid food. Here and there among her observations she scrawled quotations from the Bible. "My kinsfolk have failed and my own familiar friend hath forgotten me." Sometimes there were entries that reveal her own good work among prisoners and insane— a box of clothing to one almshouse, a bundle of magazines to

THE MASSACHUSETTS MEMORIAL 91

another, and hours spent in conversation with the inmates of the homes in which she was making investigation. Letters from inmates as early as 1842, found among her papers, bear eloquent testimony to her quieting and comforting presence. One thanks her for books and magazines, and another refers to her call as a "heavenly visit."

Eighteen months passed and Miss Dix had visited at least once every almshouse, workhouse and prison within the state of Massachusetts. Some of them she had visited innumerable times. As she became acquainted with the keepers, she talked over the possibilities of improving the condition of the inmates. Some expressed a willingness to coöperate but deplored the lack of funds; others were indifferent, protesting that it was no use, that "crazy" people were insensible to cold, and that no one could teach a lunatic to be clean. To many keepers chains and bars were as essential as food. Miss Dix called on the overseers of the poor in almost every community that she visited and solicited their coöperation; she stressed particularly the dangers of a system of poor relief that permitted the insane, the old and decrepit, and helpless children to be auctioned off after the manner of cattle at a fair. There was scarcely a mentally ill person in the commonwealth with whom she had not had some acquaintance.

Back in Mrs. Channing's home on Mt. Vernon Street, she began arranging her materials, preparatory to writing the memorial to the legislature that was to awaken Massachusetts from its moral apathy, and to arouse humanitarian sentiment not only in that state but throughout the nation. Miss Dix greatly missed the wise and friendly counsel of Dr. Channing who had died in October 1842. She now discussed the outline of her memorial with her friends, George Emerson and his wife, with Horace Mann, Dr. Howe, Dr. Bell, and Dr. Woodward. Carefully she weighed and sifted the evidence she had been collecting. She could not enumerate and describe every place that she had visited. So complete a report as that would fill a substantial volume. She could only give the total number visited and describe in detail but few of them. She discriminated carefully as to types of places and location. The people of Massachusetts must know that she wrote of a condition common not to one locality but to the entire state. The material which she had gathered had dramatic possibilities. Her technique was graphic, convincing. She stated conditions as they were in jail after jail, poorhouse after poorhouse. She emulated the chaste diction of her friend, Charles Sumner, and the fine spiritual touches of Theodore Parker. In intensity and conviction, the memorial had something of the power of Jonathan Edwards' *Sinners in the Hands of an Angry God*. Sentence after sentence, paragraph after paragraph, was rewritten until the whole acquired unity, power and eloquence. At last it was finished and turned over to Dr. Howe for his approval.

He was amazed at its strength, its clarity, and force. It was as though the woman were speaking directly into the heart of every citizen of Massachusetts; as though she were taking each one into her confidence, and laying bare before him the sordid panorama of Massachusetts prisons and almshouses. To an outsider it might seem incredible, but to Dr. Howe, who had visited many of these same places, it was all very real. Such a memorial could not but touch New England sensibilities. He read on. Miss Dix had begun as though she were speaking in low, well modulated tones, but as she went on, the appeal took on a forcefulness, a personal animation, and conviction that Massachusetts was to find irresistible.

I come to present the strong claim of suffering humanity. I come to place before the Legislature of Massachusetts the condition of the miserable, the desolate, the outcast. I come as the advocate of the helpless, forgotten, insane and idiotic, men and women; of beings sunk to a condition from which the most unconcerned would start with real horror; of beings wretched in prisons, and more wretched in our almshouses.

And I cannot suppose it needful to employ earnest persuasion, or stubborn argument in order to arrest and bring attention upon a subject, only the more strongly pressing because it is revolting and disgusting in its details. . . .

If my pictures are displeasing, coarse, and severe, my subjects, it must be recollected, offer no tranquil, refined, or composing features. The condition of human beings, reduced to the extremest states of degradation and misery, cannot be exhibited in softened language or adorn a polished page.[19]

She cited cold, severe facts. She felt obliged to refer to persons and to indicate definite localities. Legislators from the neighborhoods of Danvers, Ipswich, Newton, and Berkshire might blush and squirm in their chairs, but it was upon the miserable condition of the insane, not upon localities or upon individuals that she wished to fix attention. Of wardens, keepers, and responsible officers, Miss

Dix spoke briefly, believing that most of them erred not so much "through hardness of heart and willful cruelty as want of skill and knowledge and want of consideration." "Familiarity with suffering," she alleged, "blunts the sensibilities, and where neglect once finds a footing other injuries are multiplied."

As soon as the legislature assembled in January 1843, Dr. Howe made plans for presenting Miss Dix's memorial. He knew that the facts about to be presented were startling, gruesome, almost inconceivable, and that a storm of protest would follow. He was glad that the January number of the *North American Review* had contained an article by Dr. Edward Jarvis on "Insanity in Massachusetts," which would substantiate and corroborate Miss Dix's contentions. The night after Dr. Howe presented Miss Dix's memorial to the legislature, he wrote her briefly:

I presented your Memorial this morning, indorsing it both as a memorial and as a petition. Your work is nobly done, but not yet ended. I want you to select some newspaper as your cannon, from which you will discharge often red-hot shot into the very hearts of the people; so that, kindling, they shall warm up the clams and oysters of the house to deeds of charity. When I look back upon the time when you stood hesitating and doubting upon the brink of the enterprise you have so bravely and nobly accomplished, I cannot but be impressed with the lesson of courage and hope which you have taught even to the strongest men. . . . You are pleased to overrate the importance of my efforts. I can reply that if I *touch off* the piece, it will be you who *furnish the ammunition.*[20]

Miss Dix waited with anxious heart for news of the reception of her memorial and of the action which the legislature and the press would take. Daily she prayed that they might exercise that "wisdom which is the breath of the power of God."[21] The debates were postponed from day to day. She became worried lest the "conscript fathers" entrenched in their political fortress would forget that they had anything to do except fight the battles of party.[22] She was soon to learn that society regards as an effrontery any unpleasant truth which casts reflection upon its self-righteousness and which at the same time demands reform which will increase taxes.[23]

"Sensational, slanderous," blustered the angry selectmen and almshouse keepers. "Impossible in such a neighborhood as ours," declared the loyal townspeople as they lingered on the meeting-house steps on Sunday or gossiped over the counters or across the clothes-lines on Monday. "Whoever heard such awful things?" And a woman had made all those terrible discoveries! What manner of person could she be to go about prying into places and reporting such horrible things as she said she had seen. It really should not be discussed above a whisper. Had she no sense of the propriety of one of her sex?

In a counter-memorial the overseers of the poor at Danvers denounced Miss Dix's report. An official of the town of Shelbourne published such a contradictory statement in the *Greenfield Gazette* regarding the description which she had given of the wretched homes in which paupers were boarded out, that the *Boston Courier* long so favorable to Miss Dix and the cause of reform, began to retract the approval that it had once placed upon her memorial.[24] Although Dr. Howe and Mr. Waterson made a prompt refutation as soon as they heard of these attempts to impeach Miss Dix's testimony, the *Courier* remained skeptical. Such details as were embodied in the Danvers counter-memorial and in the *Greenfield Gazette* led the editor to express the opinion that suspicion was cast upon the whole memorial, and that on the whole the public would be quite liberal if they received her facts at a discount of 50 per cent.[25]

Dorothea Dix was deeply pained. Dr. Howe was indignant. He sensed the reluctance of the citizens of Massachusetts to acknowledge their neglect, or to admit the veracity of her report; on February 22, he moved that the resolves relating to the State Lunatic Asylum be taken up and that nine o'clock on Saturday, February 25, be set aside for their consideration. Gray, of Boston, opposed the motion on the general ground that the orders of the day ought not to be disturbed. Dr. Howe pointed out once more the large number of insane poor who were suffering in almshouses. Two hundred applications to the State Hospital at Worcester had been rejected for lack of room.[26]

When the memorial was finally taken up in the senate on Saturday, Dr. Howe defended Miss Dix in her charge that the keepers were inhumane and neglectful of duty.[27] He sought to explain that it was a system and not individuals that she arraigned and that when the pauper insane were placed under untrained authority of ignorant willful persons there was no hope for afflicted minds and broken bodies. The lot of such inmates was little better than a living hell. But hard-fisted legislators complained of the increase in taxes and Dr. Howe was compelled to tell Miss Dix of the unfavorable outlook for the measure:

I do not like to indulge in feelings of distrust, but have been irritated by the cold, pecuniary policy of these men. A friend overheard one of those very men who talked so sympathetically to you say, "We must find some way to kill this devil of a hospital bill!" Speaking about these traitors, another friend, and one versed in the wiles of politicians, said to me, "Doctor, never mind: there is a hell; these fellows will find it."[28]

Not only Dr. Howe, but Charles Sumner, the orator, statesman and idol of Massachusetts, replied to the editorial in the *Boston Courier*. The attempt to discredit Miss Dix's memorial, he said, made it the duty of all who knew anything about the condition of the pauper insane in the state to rise up in refutation and support of her testimony. Sumner had visited the almshouses at Sudbury, Wayland, Westford, and Groton; he had seen the naked maniac caged in the filthy woodshed at Wayland, and the poor old man chained to his cell at the poorhouse in Groton, and he replied through the columns of the *Courier*.

I have read over very carefully the account of the visit to the four almshouses . . . and for the sake of humanity, I am obliged to add that it accords most literally with the condition of things at the time of my visit. It seems superfluous to describe those scenes anew. But even the vivid picture of Miss Dix does not convey an adequate idea of the unfortunate sufferers in the almshouse at Wayland. The correctness with which Miss Dix has described the four almshouses which I have seen leads me to place entire confidence in her description.[29]

Dr. Luther V. Bell, of the McLean Hospital, Horace Mann, the beloved educator, and others likewise respected, came to her support. Dr. Bell quoted extensively from his own notebook, citing instances similar or identical to those in the memorial. He described the scenes he had witnessed at Groton and elsewhere. His plea for institutional treatment was an eloquent one. Like Pinel, he would strike the chains from the insane. Mann wrote, "I have felt in reading your Memorial, as I used to feel when formerly I endeavored to do something for the welfare of the same class—as though all personal enjoyments were criminal until they were relieved."[30]

With the publication of these letters, the first waves of indignation and shock began to subside. Perhaps Miss Dix was not a sentimentalist. Sumner had said these things were true, and Massachusetts trusted Sumner. Perhaps Miss Dix was after all only a sensitive and compassionate woman bent on bringing home to the citizens their obligation to their defective brothers. "Massachusetts," said Dr. Jarvis, "is not too poor to do anything that can be shown to be her duty."

The committee to whom the memorial was referred at once endorsed Miss Dix's petition and appealed for immediate action. The report verified Miss Dix's assertion that the entire provision then existing in the state, namely, in three "insane asylums" and the hospital at Worcester, could accommodate less than 500 patients, while there were in Massachusetts 958 indigent idiots and mentally ill maintained as public charges and around 800 at private expense. The committee recommended that additional buildings be erected at the hospital at Worcester near the existing buildings to provide accommodations for two hundred more patients.[31]

As soon as the report of the committee became known, the public came to its senses, investigated local conditions, acknowledged facts, and Miss Dix's labors were then the object of praise. Politicians withdrew mercenary objections, and the bill for immediate relief as well as additional accommodations for the mentally ill at the State Hospital in Worcester passed by a good majority.

In the silent library where she had spent so many hours with Dr. Channing, Dorothea Dix waited to hear the result of the vote. The passage of the bill meant so much. A copy of the memorial lay in her hands as she waited for Dr. Howe's carriage. "Men of Massachusetts, I beg, I implore, I demand, pity and protection for these of my suffering, outraged sex. Fathers, husbands, brothers, I would supplicate you for this boon." Wearily she turned the pages. "Gentlemen, I commit to you this sacred cause."

There was a gentle knock at the door. Her heart seemed to stop. "Miss Dix, your bill has passed." The blue-grey eyes sparkled at the triumph, the thin lips parted into a radiant smile, and the rich low voice trembled with emotion as she greeted the friends who had come to congratulate her.

In the quiet of the night she wrote a long letter to Ann Heath. Dear Annie, how happy she would be to know that the hospital bill had passed, and that the citizens of Massachusetts were at last aroused to their obligation to the indigent insane. If only her journeyings had not brought the sad knowledge that there were other states where the mentally ill fared no better. Her work was not done; there lay ahead other surveys, other memorials. As she wrote, her days of teaching and her years of quest for health and happiness fell from her as a mantle. Suddenly she was conscious that for her a new life had begun. Ann would understand.

She held the letter before the light for an instant, then sprinkled powder over it, carefully folded and sealed it.

"Father, I thank thee!"

CHAPTER VI

DECADE OF VICTORY

WHILE making the survey of Massachusetts jails, almshouses, and prisons, Miss Dix often crossed the borders and observed conditions in adjoining states. In New York, Rhode Island, and Connecticut she witnessed distressing scenes in overcrowded almshouses and prisons, mentally ill paupers auctioned off to the lowest bidder, and then housed in cellars, pens, and outbuildings. In neglecting her indigent sick, Massachusetts had not sinned alone.

Two years of patient observation had taught Dorothea Dix that reform could not be accomplished overnight and that her natural sensibilities had to be constrained. Indignant though she might be at the sight of cruelty, avarice, and heartlessness, she could ill afford to give expression to personal feelings. The calm manner and the well modulated voice so greatly admired by Miss Dix's friends suggested a hidden power and an indomitable will. Jailers, wardens, and keepers might resent her coming but they did not resist her entrance. She visited and inspected every crack and cranny from the cellar to the garret, climbing rickety stairs and stepping cautiously into cold damp dungeons amidst vermin and scattering rodents. Now and then she paused to ask a searching question or warm the hands of some shivering inmate. She developed a technique for inspection, a method of going quickly to the bottom of things.

Already she was spending her spare time in reading books on mental disease. She wanted to learn all that was known of its nature and causes, and the treatment that the best medical authorities of the world were recommending. Into her neatly packed portmanteau alongside her Bible she placed a volume on mental diseases. Inured by years of habit and privation, she required but little sleep; long after the tavern-keeper had banked the coals and retired for the night, Miss Dix might be found still reading by the light of a candle or a sperm oil lamp, a shawl about her shoulders and a blanket over her knees. She converted hours of waiting in lonely junctions and wayside inns between stages and trains into hours of study. Now and then she made pencil notes along the margin of her texts or jotted down questions that she wanted to ask her medical friends.

The Massachusetts Hospital bill was no sooner passed than Miss Dix was off on another mission of mercy. In January 1844, she presented a memorial to the New York state legislature depicting the condition of the mentally ill in the county poorhouses. She recommended four or six additional hospitals to care for the rapidly increasing number of insane, but she succeeded only in obtaining a larger appropriation for the Utica Hospital.[1] During the next two years she was to travel over ten thousand miles and to visit eighteen state penitentiaries, three hundred jails and houses of correction, and over five hundred almshouses and other institutions, in addition to hospitals and houses of refuge.[2] She was to secure during this time the establishment of five hospitals for the insane, several county poorhouses, and a number of jails on a reformed plan. Her travels were to take her from the Canadian boundary to the Gulf, and from the Atlantic coast to the Mississippi River;[3] from June 1843 to August 1847 she traveled thirty thousand miles.

Miss Dix did not always remain in one state until she had secured reforms there before beginning her work in another state. She was concerned for the mentally ill of all America. By having a number of surveys and memorials under way at the same time she was able to keep the general problem of the insane before the public. Stage and train connections sometimes made it more convenient to travel longer distances, cross into other states and double back. One week might find her in Philadelphia, another in Baltimore or Trenton, and a third in Kentucky or on a steamboat on the Ohio.

In the spring and summer of 1843 Miss Dix had also turned her attention to Rhode Island where as yet no adequate provision had been made for the mentally ill. Dexter Hospital in Providence, opened in 1828 through the generosity of Ebenezer Dwight Dexter who bequeathed $60,000 to establish an institution for the benefit of the poor of his native town, could hardly begin to take care of all the indigent sick who knocked at its doors. In the state at large the justices of the peace continued to commit, according to law, "furiously mad persons dangerous to the peace and safety of the good people . . ." to the county jail while the less violent were confined at home, boarded out, or provided for in the local almshouse.

As early as 1725 a law had been enacted by the General Assembly of Rhode Island empowering the towns of the mainland to construct houses of correction for vagrants and "mad persons." The state in 1742 turned over to the town councils the care of the insane and imbecile together with the authority to appoint guardians for the estates of the mentally incompetent.[4] Miss Dix's investigations a hundred years later revealed this law to be practically unchanged.

Thomas G. Hazard who accompanied Miss Dix on many of her inspections in Rhode Island, wrote a friend that she had ferreted out some cases of human suffering almost beyond conception or belief.[5] Abraham Simmons, a man whose name Hazard said should go on the rolls of martyrdom, was discovered in the town of Little Compton.[6] He was confined in a stone roofed, stone floored cell seven feet square. It was double doored and double locked, and without light or ventilation. The day that Miss Dix visited poor Simmons the walls of his cell were coated with an inch of frost. The two comforts which made his bed were wet and the outer one was frozen stiff. The man himself, chattering and shivering, was tethered to the stone floor by an ox chain.

"Sometimes he screams dreadfully and that is the reason we had the double walls and the two doors," explained the woman who had conducted Miss Dix to Simmons' cell. "His cries disturb us in the house."

"How long has he been here?" inquired Miss Dix.

"Oh, above three years," was the answer.

Despite the attendant's protests that the man would kill her, Miss Dix walked into the cell, spoke gently to Simmons, took his hands and began to warm them in her own. She talked to him of release and care and kindness. The dim light of the lantern revealed a tear stealing down his hollow cheek. As Miss Dix turned to leave, she stumbled over the iron chain linked to the iron ring about Simmons' leg.

"My husband," remarked the woman, "sometimes of a morning rakes out half a bushel of frost, and yet he never freezes."

"And yet he never freezes!" Those words rang in Miss Dix's ears. She called public attention to the case in an article in the *Providence Journal*, April 10, 1844.

It is said that grains of wheat taken from within the envelope of Egyptian mummies some thousands of years old had been found to germinate and grow in a number of instances. Even toads and other reptiles have been found alive in situations where it is evident that they must have been encased for many hundreds, if not thousands, of years.

It may, however, be doubted whether any instance has ever occurred in the history of the race where the vital principle has adhered so tenaciously to the human body under such a load and complication of suffering and tortures as in the case of Abraham Simmons, an insane man. . . .

Then follows the story of poor Simmons. As Miss Dix preferred to remain in the background and concentrate attention upon the cause rather than upon the dramatic figure which she as an ardent reformer made as she went from almshouse to prison, she described the scene through the eyes of the local townsman who had accompanied her. Briefly she sketched Simmons and his icy tomb-like dwelling. She concluded almost bitterly:

Should any persons in this philanthropic age be disposed from motives of curiosity to visit the place they may rest assured that traveling is considered quite safe in that part of the country, however improbable it may seem. The people of the region profess the Christian religion, and it is said that they have adopted those forms and ceremonies which they call worship. It is not probable, however, that they address themselves to poor Simmons' God. Their worship mingling with the prayers of agony which he shrieks from his dreary abode, would make a strange discord in the ear of the Almighty Being in whose keeping sleeps the vengeance due to all his wrongs.[7]

Miss Dix collected data on conditions in Rhode Island and would have appealed to the state legislature through a memorial as she had done in Massachusetts had not a circumstance arisen by which private philanthropy promised speedier relief. Not all of Rhode Island had slumbered while the mentally ill suffered. Many of her citizens were not impervious to the universal quickening of conscience and the need for reform; among them was Nicholas Brown, distinguished merchant and founder of Brown University. He had long been impressed that an insane or lunatic hospital or retreat for the insane should be established under an act of the legislature.[8] In order that an institution might be established more quickly, he bequeathed $30,000 to be used toward the erection or endowment of such a retreat. Brown died in 1843 and when the General Assembly met in January 1844, a charter was issued and the Rhode Island Asylum for the Insane was incorporated. A unique provision in the act of incorporation gave legal sanction to alter or change the name of the institution by inserting or substituting that of any distinguished patron. The incorporators realized that the $30,000 left by Nicholas Brown was inadequate to build and endow a hospital, but that there were a number of other wealthy merchants who might be induced to make additional gifts.

Miss Dix inquired the names of persons whom she might interest in the project. Cyrus Butler, a penurious old bachelor who ultimately left an estate of $4,000,000 was the one to whom she decided to make the first appeal. The Rev. Mr. Edward Hall, in whose home she was staying in Providence, gave her little encouragement as Butler was not noted for his generosity but offered to accompany her to Butler's office. At the door she told him good-bye and went in without an introduction. She inquired for Mr. Butler. A clerk pointed to his desk. Butler, who heard her speak, whirled around in his chair and looked in her direction. Butler was seventy-eight, gruff and brusque.

"What do you want?" he asked. She stepped over to his desk.

"If not intruding, I wish to make a statement that will hurt no one but will give the opportunity of a monument to your name as a benefactor of the poor which will never be forgotten." She had come immediately to the point instead of letting the shrewd old merchant divert her attention to some trivial matter as was his habit with solicitors.

"Are you Miss Dix?" he inquired. "If so, sit down."

She seated herself and told him of what she had seen at Little Compton. She talked as though Cyrus Butler might be called to judgment by Simmons' God.

"What do you want me to do?" Butler asked abruptly.

"Sir," replied Miss Dix, "I want you to give $50,000 toward the enlargement of the insane hospital in this city, to be called henceforth Butler Asylum."

"I will give $40,000 provided $40,000 more shall be obtained from other sources or shall be subscribed by responsible persons within six months from April first."

Miss Dix nodded her approval.

"Furthermore," he went on to say, "there should remain a sum not less than $50,000 as a permanent fund whose income should be applied solely on the support of the institution."[9]

The proposition sounded fair, sound, and business-like. Cyrus Butler turned to his checkbook and wrote a draft for the designated amount. Miss Dix rose, thanked him, and as Pliny Earle said years later, "walked forth the marvel of Rhode Island which had always been hearing how Moses smote the rock but had never yet witnessed such a miracle."[10]

There remained the other $40,000 to be raised as well as certain legislation to be passed pursuant to the matter of reform in the matter of poor relief. She prepared the article previously referred to, for the *Providence Journal*. Miss Dix then went to Newport where the legislature was sitting.

She was determined to bring relief to Simmons at Little Compton. When members of the legislature called to talk with her about the proposed hospital, she pressed his case and told them how the town had promised ten months before to move him to a hospital but had taken no further action. She had come to Newport, she said, to secure his removal; she could not take him away without the consent of the town but the legislature might intervene.[11]

Mr. Updike, one of the legislators, was greatly moved and declared that the assembly should interpose at once. He went to the house of representatives and made a speech that roused everyone. A member from Little Compton then arose and announced the death of Simmons. There was an awkward pause—mercy had come too late. Finally another member arose. There were other insane paupers in Rhode Island; he moved that a committee be appointed to investigate their condition. The motion carried.

In their desire of shift responsibility from their own shoulders, the members of the Assembly became quite communicative and told Miss Dix of other instances of maltreated paupers.

Another case in Little Compton was very touching. A young girl, the daughter of poor but hard-working parents, was violent, most of the time suicidal. Miss Dix investigated and found the situation much worse than she had expected. The girl had at one time tried to cut her throat, another time to set fire to her clothes, and had jumped into a well, but each time her attempts at self-destruction had been thwarted. Simmons, old, helpless, and beyond the restoration of mind was gone. Here was a young girl who might yet be redeemed to health and reason. Miss Dix decided to pour coals of fire upon the heads of Rhode Island's complacent, self-

centered legislators. She wrote authorities at the hospital in Charlestown for reservations. Meanwhile she made clothes for the girl to
wear and took up a subscription to defray the expense of the eighty
mile journey. Four days later George Emerson met them at the
train in Boston.[12]

Miss Dix's next visit to Rhode Island saw the hospital fund over-
subscribed.

By this time Miss Dix's reputation as a reformer was beginning
to be widely known. *Niles' Register* repeatedly spoke of her as "the
American Mrs. Fry," and her friend, Lydia Maria Child had written of her in *The Present* as the "God-appointed missionary to the
insane." Each day's post now brought her letters from ministers,
physicians, and reform-minded persons in distant parts, inviting and
urging her to assist them in securing better conditions in prisons,
almshouses, and insane asylums. Macedonian calls these were to
Dorothea Dix. Prisons had to be visited, interviews made, memorials written. "I must be on my way," she wrote Ann Heath.

As soon as the hospital for Rhode Island was secured and brief
trips made into Vermont and New Hampshire where the mentally
ill were very well cared for, Miss Dix concentrated her attention on
New Jersey and Pennsylvania. In New Jersey no provision had
been made for the insane. After the State Medical Society appealed
to the legislature in 1839, $500 was appropriated to defray the ex-
pense of a survey of the idiotic, epileptic, and insane of the state. A
report was submitted in 1841; the governor in his inaugural address
called the attention of the legislators to the philanthropic efforts of
sister states in providing for their mentally ill and urged similar
action in New Jersey. Nothing was done, however, and when
Dorothea Dix arrived in 1844, she had to make a survey from the
ground up. As in Massachusetts, New York, and Rhode Island, she
visited every county, jail, and almshouse.[13] She demonstrated that
as early as 1839 there were 305 "insane" persons and 200 idiots in
the state of New Jersey. In numbers these unprovided-for mental
defectives exceeded the total population of the state prison.[14]

Miss Dix incorporated into the memorial to the legislature not
only her own observations but the tabular statement made by the
commissioners of 1839. She told how many of the mentally ill of
New Jersey were housed in the institutions of other states and
briefly stated conditions of local prisons and almshouses. There

were no beds in the Salem County Jail while at the Shark River poorhouse only sixty cents a week was allowed for the upkeep of each inmate. At the county poor farm near Sharpstown there were 100 paupers, eight of whom were mentally ill and a number epileptic. She continued:

I do not come to quicken your generous impulses and move you to emotion by showing the existence of terrible abuses, revealing scenes of almost incredible suffering. I come to ask justice of the legislature of New Jersey, for those who, in the providence of God, are incapable of pleading their own cause, and of claiming redress for their grievances.[15]

She told of Pinel's work and quoted extensively from the memoirs which his son had written for the French Royal Academy of Arts and Sciences. She discussed the new and more humane methods of treating mental diseases, and gave a résumé of recent cases and cures in an attempt to show that the sooner a deranged mind was treated the more probable its complete restoration and the longer treatment was delayed the more unlikely recovery. An institution for the mentally ill, she said, should be a hospital whose object was to cure diseased minds and not a mere madhouse in which to incarcerate maniacs and persons dangerous to society. Swiftly and unsparingly she pictured the responsibility of the state toward its defectives. As if to give her appeal added strength, she quoted, "As ye mete to others, so shall ye receive." "I will have mercy and not sacrifice," saith Jehovah. "Blessed are the merciful, for they shall obtain mercy." She dwelt upon the danger of delay.

On January 23, 1845, Joseph S. Dodd, a senator who was an ardent supporter of Miss Dix and a staunch advocate of the plan, presented the memorial and moved that measures be taken during that session of the legislature to effect the reforms which had been recommended. It was moved that the motion be laid on the table. Mr. Dodd brought up the resolution the next day and modified it by calling for a joint committee of both houses for the consideration of the subject. This resolution passed.

A month later, on February 25, the joint committee reported favorably upon Miss Dix's memorial and made a fervent appeal for action. Three weeks before the Salem County poorhouse in West Jersey had burned to the ground. The hundred inmates had been rescued in safety although several of the insane paupers had been chained in their cells.

In order to secure the hospital program, it was necessary not only to convince the public of the need of a hospital and the responsibility of society as a whole for the mentally ill, but to meet objections to increased taxation. Regardless of the compassion and desire for reform which her memorials always precipitated, Miss Dix found that a certain reaction invariably followed. A few legislators always grew wary and remembered forgotten pledges to constituents that taxes would be reduced. Her most difficult work began after the memorial was presented; early and late she was busy making interviews, overcoming objections, and winning over reluctant and timid legislators, and shaming cold and niggardly ones. Some of them faced her openly with their objections, while others preferred to make them on the floors of the legislature.

In the debate on the measure, one member lauded the state for having kept clear of debt. Indignant that New Jersey should consider the construction of a building 487 feet long by eighty feet wide for a "few lunatics" he boldly asserted that the state would have been better off "if Miss Dix had been paid $500 or $600, and escorted over the Delaware or to Philadelphia, or even $1000, and . . . enshrined in the White House."[16]

It was annoying to have such remarks made publicly but Dorothea Dix ignored them. She cultivated a mien of reserve, poise, calm. She learned to rationalize quickly and quietly. She could not afford to have the press brand any action as "brazen" or "vulgar." She was well aware that many questioned the propriety of her traveling about alone, and she was careful to see that she did nothing which might cast reflection upon her sex.

As soon as the memorial was out of the way, Miss Dix began her study of the personnel of the legislature. By skillful questioning here and there she learned which members could be counted upon to support the measure, and which were doubtful, those that were humanitarian in principle, and those that were self-seeking. She found out who could be depended upon to convert others to the program, and who would shape public opinion, and who would be followers. Sometimes she met legislators singly and privately, sometimes in groups. It was a grilling performance night after night. After such an evening, she wrote her friend, Mrs. Hare in Philadelphia:

I must write to you, I must have your sympathy. How I long for your heart-charming smile! Just now I need calmness; I am exhausted under this perpetual effort and exercise of fortitude. At Trenton, thus far, all is prosperous, but you cannot imagine the labor of conversing and convincing. Some evenings I had at once twenty gentlemen for three hours' steady conversation.

The last evening, a rough country member who had announced in the House that the "wants of the insane in New Jersey were all humbug," and who came to overwhelm me with his arguments, after listening an hour and a half with wonderful patience to my details and to principles of treatment, suddenly moved into the middle of the parlor, and thus delivered himself, "Ma'am, I bid you good-night! I do not want, for my part, to hear anything more; the others can stay if they want to. *I am convinced;* you've conquered me out and out; I shall vote for the hospital. If you'll come to the House, and talk there as you've done here, no man that isn't a brute can stand you; and so when a man's convinced, that's enough. The Lord bless you."[17]

Miss Dix won over obstinate and unwieldy members one by one. "I encounter nothing," she had once written George Emerson, "which a determined will created by the necessities of the cause, does not enable me to vanquish."[18] On March 25, she received a hastily written note from Senator Dodd, "I am happy to announce to you the passage of the bill for the New Jersey Lunatic Asylum."

Not a brick had been laid, not a clod had been turned, yet for this New Jersey hospital she was already developing a peculiar affection. She wished she might stay and watch it grow. She visualized it some day half overgrown with trailing ivy like York Retreat in England. The founding of this hospital had been different from her work in Massachusetts and Rhode Island; there foundations had already been laid, while in New Jersey, if one gives credit to the *Newark Daily Advertiser,* the institution was almost exclusively her own creation. She delighted in poring over the architect's drawings and picturing in her mind a beautiful long red sandstone building with a Tuscan portico and tall white columns and a dome above. She liked to think of it as situated on the top of a hill in the center of a grove of trees, commanding a view of quiet Jersey farms and perhaps the Delaware in the distance. In such a happy setting she thought that sick and turbulent minds could not but find peace. She had worked so hard to secure this institution that it seemed an infinite part of her being, and it would always be so. Years later, tired and worn out with age and disease, she would come back to rest in the apartments so gratefully set aside by the trustees for her use. One morning years later, Dr. John Ward, the superintendent and long her friend and physician, would come to her room to announce the birth of his first-born child, and she would smile and reply, "Yes, and under the roof of my first-born child."[19]

Miss Dix completed her survey of Pennsylvania while waiting for the New Jersey legislature to take up its hospital bill. On February 3, 1845, her memorial soliciting a hospital for the insane was presented to the legislature at Harrisburg. Conditions of the mentally ill in Pennsylvania were not unlike those in other states that she had visited. Friends Hospital for the Insane at Frankford, the Blockley Division of the Philadelphia Almshouse, and the Pine Street Unit of the Pennsylvania Hospital were taxed to the limit of their capacity. Most of the insane of the state were found in private families and poorhouses, and as usual in jails and penitentiaries. Miss Dix in her memorial described the Allegheny County jail in Pittsburgh as combining "all the faults and abuses of the worst county prisons in his state, or in the United States."[20] She found here transgressors of all ages, colors, sexes and degrees, promiscuously associated. "The sick were unattended, the ignorant untaught, the repentant if any, unencouraged, and the insane forgotten." She declared that "If it had been the deliberate purpose of the citizens of Allegheny County to establish a school for the inculcation of vice, and obliteration of virtue, I cannot conceive that any means they could have devised, would have more certainly secured these results, than those I found in full operation in the jail last August."[21] It was a relief for her to be able to turn to well-conducted institutions such as the Pittsburgh Orphans Asylum, the Pittsburgh Poorhouse, and the Western Penitentiary.

Pittsburgh citizens were shocked at Miss Dix's recital of conditions in Allegheny County; an editorial comment in the *Pittsburgh Daily Gazette and Advertiser* urged an investigation.[22] Mayor William J. Howard called a public meeting on February 26, 1845, and appointed committees to investigate and to outline a program for ameliorating conditions of the insane. This second committee was instructed to report in favor of establishing a hospital, and to present a plan for the prevention of crime, to be sent to the

New Jersey State Hospital, Trenton, New Jersey, 1848. This hospital, the first to be established outright through Miss Dix's efforts, was affectionately called by her "my first born child."

legislature for immediate action.[23] Miss Dix's memorial also won the prompt approval of the Philadelphia Society for Alleviating the Miseries of Public Prisons, an organization long interested in securing better treatment for the mentally ill. On April 14, 1845, the legislature voted to establish a hospital to be located at Harrisburg and to be known as the Pennsylvania State Lunatic Hospital. So far as local prison reform was concerned only a little was done. On October 27, 1845, Miss Dix addressed a public letter to the *Gazette* depicting the "want of cleanliness," the lack of system, and absence of suitable officers in the Allegheny County jail. The Pittsburgh jail was now labeled as a "public nuisance." She soon advocated a separate hospital to care for the mentally ill of western Pennsylvania.[24]

As Miss Dix had gone about from penitentiary to penitentiary and from prison to prison, she had been struck with the divergence of theory underlying their operation. It seemed to her that certain broad principles should govern the conduct of all penal institutions and that reformation of the individual and not social revenge, should be the motivating thought in prison discipline. It pained her to see the gross inhumanities that were perpetrated *en masse* in the larger institutions. She was incensed at the wretched health conditions in some of the larger prisons. Strong men were compelled to work all day at hard manual labor and then were denied the privilege of a bath at night. At Sing Sing when the water supply was low the men were on rare occasions allowed to bathe in the river. Not until 1844 did Rhode Island prison inspectors decide that convicts in good health might be permitted to take a warm bath once in three months. Everywhere poor food, dark cells, and solitary confinement spread a foul discontent that undermined all hope for regenerating the criminal.

Miss Dix resolved to put these convictions also and the facts she gathered, as well as her conception of the function of penal institutions, before the public. For the present, however, the needs of the insane claimed her efforts. Despite urgent requests to come into Indiana, Ohio, and Kentucky during the summer of 1845, she remained in Pennsylvania compiling data on the insane. But late in September she returned to Boston for a brief visit with Ann and a conference with George Emerson and Horace Mann before publishing a manual on prisons.

A Sunday afternoon call at the Heath home, a cup of tea with the Emersons, and Miss Dix was ready to begin the serious business of organizing her material. In the bright October sunshine in Mann's library she discussed the philosophy of prison reform, the relative merits of the Pennsylvania and Auburn systems, the evils prevalent in most penal institutions, and the dangers of the conglomerate assignment of hardened criminals and first offenders to county jails and houses of correction. Miss Dix, who preferred the Pennsylvania system, insisted that there should be separate houses of refuge for juvenile offenders. Mann talked of John Howard and his efforts to reform the English prisons, and the need of similar leadership in America. He spoke reminiscently of Robert Vaux and the organization of the Boston Prison Discipline Society, and of Edward Livingston. Perhaps it would be well to reorganize the society. Miss Dix thought that an aroused social conscience would be more effective. She was willing to make use of societies which already existed, such as the Philadelphia society,[25] but she felt it was often wasted energy to create organizations to achieve ends which might be obtained quite as easily through agitation in the press and through personal appeals to legislators.

They agreed that the first requisite of a prison was doubtless such physical arrangements as would secure health and comfort, and next such instruction as a parent would give to an erring child. Prison reform, Mann declared, was one that involved the whole theory of morals and religion.[26] Regeneration, not degradation, should be the result of prison discipline. He thought that there was in the instructor's hands no instrument so powerful as a rational, earnest and benign inculcation of the vital truths of religion. This was Miss Dix's belief, too; every penitentiary should have its chaplain to conduct weekly and daily worship, to walk among the prisoners, to talk with them, and to act as a father confessor and spiritual guide. Prison management should be raised above the level of low politics. Wardens should be selected with a view to character and human understanding; they should not be mere keepers but molders of men. They talked on and on. Pardons, criminal justice, prison schools. Morals and religious instruction. Crimes and punishment. It was quite late when Dorothea rose to leave.

Returning home she spread out her manuscript and began the

task of revision, changing sentences, altering whole paragraphs, inserting new evidence, crossing out a word here and a phrase there. Rapidly, untiringly as of old, she wrote. Except for an occasional trip to the Boston Public Library to consult some authority or to verify statistics, she seldom left her study. Few people knew that she was in the city; she had no time for callers.

Three main considerations she would put before her readers: (1) the philosophy and objectives which should underlie prison discipline, (2) the need of moral, religious, and general instruction in prison, and (3) houses of refuge for juvenile offenders. Illustration after illustration from her own abundant experience was set forth. She made no sentimental appeal for the relaxation of prison regulations. In correcting prisoners who were refractory she preferred the cold bath to the lash; all she asked was a demonstration of humanitarian principles. She believed that the restraining influence of penal justice was destroyed by the frequency of pardons. Moral and spiritual regeneration should be the function of prison discipline: hasty pardons and capital punishment curtailed the whole performance of this function. "Steady, firm, and kind government of prisoners," wrote Miss Dix, "is the truest humanity and the best exercise of duty."[27]

Another week's hard work and the sheaf of closely written foolscap was in the hands of the printer, and Dorothea Dix was leaving for Trenton in the interest of the new hospital and the penitentiary.

Late in October 1845, Miss Dix set out for Kentucky and began the first of the long trips that she took periodically into the west during the next twenty-five years. It was on one of these western trips that she yielded to the entreaties of her friends and engaged space in a sleeping car. She had always protested that the sight of sleeping cars was quite enough for her and after one trial was entirely convinced. "They are quite detestable," she wrote Ann. "I did make one night's experiment between Pittsburgh and Cincinnati and that will suffice for the rest of my life. I can not suppose that any person of decent habits, especially ladies, will occupy them unless some essential changes are made in the arrangements and regulations."[28]

Miss Dix had heard much of the difficulty of western travel, the scarcity of railroads, and the necessity of long journeys on stages, or in lumber wagons over muddy roads and across swollen streams.

She had read of long delays that were caused by broken axles and harness, and when she left Frankfort to make a journey into the back country of Kentucky, she prepared for all contingencies by carrying along a small kit containing carpenter tools, nails, rope, leather for patching, and a can of axle grease, to be used in case of accident in that uninhabited country.

Back and forth across the state of Kentucky, by train, stage, carriage, and lumber wagon, Miss Dix visited jails and prisons. Here and there she crossed the boundaries to inspect the prison at Jeffersonville, Indiana, or Cairo, Illinois, or for a week in Tennessee where she had promised to spend six months the following year. Very soon Miss Dix began to show the strain of her labors and from time to time she was threatened with serious illness. "How old may you be?" asked a back country woman one day. Upon being told she replied, "Well, now I should not think you was that old but it looks like age is breaking upon you powerful fast and you had a mighty heap of trouble."[29]

Miss Dix expected to spend the spring and summer of 1846 examining the jails and poorhouses of Illinois and Indiana, but learning that travel would be difficult there if not impossible on account of rains and mud, turned her course southward from Louisville and took passage on a steamer for New Orleans. Whenever the boat stopped for half a day to unload or take on merchandise, as at New Albany, Brandenburg, Owensboro, Henderson, Paducah and Memphis, she availed herself of the time to investigate local conditions.

After four days inspection of the schools, Charity Hospital, and other public institutions in New Orleans, Miss Dix declared that she had seen "incomparably more to approve than censure" and departed for Mobile.[30] She took the outer passage up the Alabama 260 miles to Montgomery, thence to Tuskegee, Columbus, Knoxville, Macon, and Milledgeville, Georgia, where she found the state penitentiary "excellently ordered" but the hospital "very bad." Miss Dix interested the governor, secured an appropriation for a library for the convicts in the state penitentiary, and promised to return the following year. From Augusta she went to Savannah and from there by boat to Charleston, where she arrived April first. After a rather cursory survey of the hospitals in Charleston and a brief visit to the state hospital in Columbia, she began the laborious return trip through Georgia and Alabama, and back to New Orleans and up the Mississippi again as far as the Arkansas River and into the interior of Arkansas as far as Little Rock. On this trip Miss Dix lost no opportunity to visit county jails while other passengers were taking their meals or while horses were being changed. She was delighted to find most of the southern jails well built, well ventilated, and clean; this was especially true in Mobile. Miss Dix spent the remainder of the summer of 1846 plying up and down the Mississippi from Vicksburg north to Dubuque and back to St. Louis, and then up the Ohio. She traversed the malaria-stricken areas of the South and southern Illinois, and visited prisons throughout Indiana, Illinois, Ohio, and going up as far as the western part of Ontario, back to the Jeffersonville prison where conditions were especially obstinate, and then across the Ohio again into Kentucky and over to Tennessee.[31]

Taken as a section, the south showed no great contrast to other sections which Miss Dix had visited. It yielded its scores of cases of cruelty and neglect as had New England. There were the same mistaken ideas regarding the causes and the modes of treating mental diseases. The statute books of the south were lacking in laws governing the jurisprudence of insanity. Very early South Carolina and Georgia as well as Virginia, had become conscious of the state's responsibility for its indigent mental defectives and had established state hospitals, but antiquated and impractical laws still regulated commitments, and all of the hospitals were overcrowded and poorly supported. The rural, isolated, self-sufficing communities adhered to old folk remedies and shook their heads at the idea of a "state lunatic asylum" as they persisted in calling hospitals for mental diseases; they continued to confine their deranged relatives at home and farmed out the pauper insane at public auction. In the large commercial centers a well-informed coterie of medical men occasionally forsook their researches into malaria and yellow fever, and took a few private cases of mental diseases into their homes and thereby disseminated some of the more modern theories of the nature and treatment of the disease. It was claimed in 1844 that the rate of insanity was considerably lower in the south than in New England and the north central states and that the ratio of colored insane to white insane was much lower in the slaveholding states than in the non-slaveholding states.[32]

For nine months Dorothea Dix struggled against odds to obtain data on prisons and the insane in the south, the middle west, and the northwest. She traveled through the bitter cold of winter and the blistering heat of summer, through dense forests and fever-infested swamps. Floods and storms interrupted her progress. She crossed the Yadkin once when it was three-quarters of a mile wide. The bottom of the stream was rough and in places there were torrents; the water was always up to the carriage bed and sometimes flowing in. Twice the horses were forced to rest on sand bars while the turbulent waters surged about them. A few miles beyond, Miss Dix had just crossed a branch two hundred yards wide when the axle tree broke and off rolled one of the back wheels.

Trips up and down the Mississippi were never peaceful or free from nerve-racking incidents. There were always dangers from over-stoked boilers, a broken paddle wheel, or a loose propeller. The passengers might awaken in the morning and find themselves stranded on a sandbar in mid-stream where they would be compelled to wait for a freshet, or until a passing steamer might tow the vessel into the current again. Sickness was invariably breaking out among the passengers or crew. The almost steady diet of salt pork, hominy, sorghum, rice, beans, and black coffee was far from being conducive to health. Mosquitoes, flies, and rats infested the boats, and added to the spread of infection. Except for purges, quinine, laudanum, hard liquor, turpentine, and salves for sprains and bruises, the medical equipment of the average Ohio or Mississippi steamer was extremely limited. After the first two or three trips, Miss Dix knew what to expect and she never went aboard without an ample supply of home remedies, bandages, and a basket of lemons and fresh fruit. Long sleepless nights she kept vigil at the sickbeds of fellow passengers, strangers far from friends. She took little heed that her own frail constitution was being saturated with malaria.

In September 1846, while making a parting call at the hospital in Columbus, Ohio, after completing a day's survey of prisons and poorhouses in the city, Miss Dix collapsed. Her illness was a most unwelcome interruption to her plans. She had under way memorials to the legislatures of Illinois and Tennessee, as well as plans for a memorial to the federal government in behalf of insane soldiers and sailors. She was also anxious to secure reforms of the prison administration in Ohio; following that she planned to go south again and make intensive surveys in the states of Alabama, Mississippi, and North Carolina. In trembling hand she wrote Ann Heath, on November 16, 1846:

> My robe of life is travel-worn
> And dusty with the dusty way;
> It bears the mark of many a storm
> And marks of many a toilsome day
> The morning shower, the damp night dews
> Have lent their dark discoloring hues.

I do not regret having come, [she said]. On the contrary am thankful for having attempted all that I have done. Heaven has greatly blessed my labors and I feel truly more and more that a leading Providence defines my path in the dark valleys of the world.[33]

An increasing conviction that hers was a God-given mission attended Dorothea Dix's recovery. "I am the Hope of the poor crazed beings who pine in cells, and stalls, and cages, and waste-rooms," she told the General Assembly of North Carolina a year later. "I am the Revelation of hundreds of wailing, suffering creatures hidden in your private dwellings, and in pens, and cabins,— shut out, cut off from all healing influence, from all mind restoring cares."[34]

Miss Dix resumed her travels in December, 1846. Her memorial in behalf of the mentally ill of Illinois was presented to the legislature in Springfield on January 16, 1847, and in March a bill was passed creating a state hospital for the insane, to be located at Jacksonville.

In the summer of 1847 Miss Dix made a hurried trip to Boston fired with new zeal. She had been delighted with the letters which she had received from Laura Bridgeman, the fifteen-year-old deaf mute, and she decided to study at close range the methods which Dr. Howe was finding so successful in Perkins Institute. On her travels Miss Dix had come across many deaf, mute, and blind children. Public schools were provided for boys and girls with normal sight, speech, and hearing, but nothing had been done for defective children. She had already talked over the possibility of such an institution with leaders in the Illinois legislature.

While in Boston she also wanted to talk over with George Emerson and Charles Sumner a plan for federal appropriation of public lands as an aid to the states in caring for their indigent insane. In the west she had heard much of Henry Clay's and Thomas Benton's schemes for the transfer of public lands to the states for public improvements. Why could not the same principle be invoked in the interest of the indigent and the defective? It was a stupendous program, but it would provide a perpetual endowment for the care of the needy, and the longer Miss Dix thought about the matter the more attractive the plan became.

Provision for the insane was still her major interest and true to her promise, she returned to Tennessee in November 1847, and worked into final shape the memorial to the legislature then in session. Again success crowned her efforts. On February 5, 1848, her recommendations were approved, and $40,000 was appropriated for the purchase of one hundred acres of land and the construction of a building large enough to care for two hundred and fifty patients. The appropriations were subsequently increased to $75,000.[35] Following the work in Tennessee Miss Dix undertook to make an appeal to the federal government and early in 1848 she prepared her first memorial to Congress.[36] In the fall she again turned her attention to state legislation in behalf of the insane, this time making a three months' investigation of the jails and poorhouses of North Carolina.

There the ground was not entirely unbroken. As early as 1817 Archibald Murphy had included in his plan for a comprehensive school system, provision for mental and physical defectives. Governor Morehead in his first message to the legislature in 1842 had recommended the establishment of asylums for the deaf, dumb, and blind, and for the "protection of unfortunate lunatic persons."[37] In a special message on December 31, 1844, he again urged that these three institutions be established.[38] No action was taken, however. Of the thirteen original colonies only North Carolina and Delaware now remained without state hospitals.

This situation was the more deplorable because it was estimated that there were more than 1000 insane, epileptic, and idiotic persons in North Carolina in 1848. A few of these were sent to the hospitals established in sister states, some were in cells and dungeons, county jails, or the comfortless rooms and cages of county poorhouses, but most of them were kept in the dwellings of private families.[39] Miss Dix solicited an appropriation of $100,000 for the erection of a state hospital. ‑It was uncertain whether the appropriation would be granted. The Democrats, long out of power, were in again; jealous of their position, they had at once become conservative. A project for a railroad into the western counties overshadowed all other issues. Miss Dix wrote her friend, Mrs. Hare, in Philadelphia:

They say nothing can be done here. I reply, "I know no such word in the vocabulary I adopted." It is declared that no word will be uttered in opposition to my claims, but that the Democrats having banded together as a party to vote for nothing that involves expense, will unite and silently vote down the bill.[40]

One morning, several gentlemen, all Whigs, called to see Miss Dix and reported the most discouraging things. She immediately requested the leading Democrats to come to the Mansion House where she was stopping. She laid before them the memorial which she had written "under the exhaustion of three weeks most fatiguing journeys and labors." "Gentlemen," she said, "here is the document I have prepared for your assembly. I desire you, sir, to present it," handing the manuscript to John W. Ellis of Rowan, the champion of the Charlotte and Danville railroad, and popular leader of the Democratic party. "You gentlemen," she said, facing the astonished delegation, "you, I expect, will sustain the motion this gentleman will make."[41]

Ellis introduced the memorial as Miss Dix had requested. It was presented in both houses and referred to a joint committee of seven from the Senate and seven from the Commons.[42] On December 8 Ellis, as chairman of the House committee, reported a bill for $100,000 for a hospital for the insane, which was to be a special order for December 21. A fight was made over section 5, which provided the amount of $100,000 and the method by which the funds were to be raised. At this time the annual revenue of the state exclusive of the Literary Fund was less than $200,000. It looked as though the measure would be defeated, and had it not been for James C. Dobbin the measure would, no doubt, have been lost.

From this point, the story of the North Carolina memorial illustrates well the human and personal elements that so often entered into the passage of Miss Dix's hospital bills. In the spring of 1848, James Dobbin had returned from Congress, and declining to run again, had been elected a member of the General Assembly. He had been a member of the joint committee which had gone over the hospital bill. Since he and his wife also had rooms at the Mansion House, circumstances brought about a close acquaintance with Miss Dix. Shortly after the session opened, Mrs. Dobbin who had been in poor health for some time, became very ill. Miss Dix became her devoted nurse. Every hour away from official duties was spent at Louisa Dobbin's bedside. Deeply grateful, Mrs. Dobbin expressed a wish that she might do something to show how much she appreciated her kindness.

"You can do something," replied Miss Dix. "Ask your husband to speak in favor of the hospital bill." Louisa Dobbin died on December 18. As a last request, she asked her husband to support Miss Dix's project. James Dobbin promised. Miss Dix accompanied him to Fayetteville with his wife's body. While they were absent from Raleigh the section of the bill relating to the appropriation was struck out. Thereupon Mr. Raynor, a Whig, on December 21, offered an amendment to levy a special tax of 2½ cents on every $100 worth of land and 7½ cents on the poll, but this too was defeated.

Dobbin did not observe the customary period of mourning but on December 23, resumed his customary place in the assembly. He asked for a reconsideration of the hospital bill. His request was granted and he rose to speak in its favor. He offered an amendment to the objectionable section 5; he asked for a tax of one cent on every $100 worth of land and 2½ cents on every poll for four years. Earnestly and eloquently James Dobbin pleaded the case of the mentally ill in North Carolina. He was scarcely aware that he was effecting anything until he noted the stillness of the hall and the tears in the speaker's eyes. When the bill came to a vote, it passed 91 to 10.[43]

Miss Dix now bent all her energies on getting to Washington where a bill soliciting 5,000,000 acres of the public lands for the benefit of the insane was about to be brought before Congress. Her North Carolina friends stayed her. "Not yet. The site must be selected. You must not leave us until that is decided upon." Miss Dix smiled. Wherever she had helped to secure a hospital that request followed. She always preferred a hill commanding an expansive view, where good spring water was available, a place not too far removed from the city, and at enough distance that noise and smoke might not be encountered. South and west of the town of Raleigh was such a place. A grove of oaks surmounted a great knoll and overlooked a wide and peaceful valley. Through this valley the new railroad wound its way. From the summit of the hill one could see the narrow rails sparkling in the sunshine and the thin wavy ribbons of smoke that accompanied the little locomotive laboriously puffing to bring its load of freight into Raleigh. "You will let us call it, Dix Hill?" the commissioners asked. Miss Dix hesitated.

"You accept no money, no gifts from legislatures. Can we not express our gratitude in this way? If not in your honor, is there not some one dear to you, whose memory you like to perpetuate in this fashion?" Yes, she thought a hospital named in his honor would be a fitting tribute to her dear grandfather, Dr. Elijah Dix. She recalled how her grandfather had once dreamed of establishing a medical school in Boston and how he had brought back from England a large supply of surgical instruments, much new chemical apparatus, and many books. But for one reason or another he was not able to carry out his project. It is in his honor that the North Carolina Hospital is known as "Dix Hill."

Dorothea Dix's generous expenditure of time and money in making the survey, and her tender care for Louisa Dobbin endeared her to the people throughout the state. Her greatest tribute from North Carolina, however, was to come during the Civil War. In 1863 while traveling in Pennsylvania her train was stopped by Confederate troops. The officers, one of whom was a surgeon from North Carolina, boarded the train. He recognized Miss Dix immediately, introduced himself and presented the other officers. Miss Dix inquired after the hospital in Raleigh and certain North Carolina friends. The surgeon whispered a word to his superior officer who in turn bowed and said that inasmuch as Miss Dix was a passenger the train would be released. She expressed her appreciation of this signal courtesy and assured the officers that when the war was over she would again visit North Carolina.[44]

After Congress adjourned in 1849, Miss Dix visited Philadelphia and then turned her attention to the southern states again. Her real objective for the winter months was a memorial to the legislature of Alabama, where as yet no provision had been made for the mentally ill.

In the memorial which was presented to the legislature on December 14, 1849, she attacked the practice of confining the mentally ill in jails. "Society," she said, "must pay the tax levied by its false modes of life, its defective organization, its self-indulgence, and its self-will in the frequent results of these,—poverty and insanity."[45] The population of the United States at that time was about 22,000,-000, of whom at least 22,000 were insane or idiotic, and of this latter group only about 5,000 had the advantage of hospitals. In 1849 the United States had only twenty state hospitals located in nineteen states.

As a result of the memorial, considerable interest was manifested in Alabama, and it looked as though a substantial appropriation might be secured until the burning of the capitol at Montgomery gave rise to a program of retrenchment against which the supporters of the hospital bill were powerless.[46]

While waiting for the Alabama legislature to take action on the hospital bill, Miss Dix prepared a memorial to be presented to the legislative assembly of the Province of Nova Scotia. In 1843 and 1844, and again in 1848, she had visited Canada and inspected hospitals, jails, and poorhouses. Miss Dix observed there the same general neglect and abuse of the insane as she had witnessed in the United States. Hospital physicians pursued in the main the same old systems of cupping, bleeding, blistering, and purging. In the jails and hospitals only the smallest quantity of food was served, and that of the poorest quality. This memorial followed much the same lines as those which she had presented in the United States except that in Canada her research had not been so intensive. She emphasized more than ever before the vital need of institutional treatment for recent cases. She cited the opinions of leading European and American psychiatrists and medical administrators. The memorial was presented on January 21, 1850. No immediate action was taken but later an appropriation was made and in 1858 the Nova Scotia Hospital for the Insane was opened for the reception of patients.[47]

There being no further prospect of action in Alabama, Miss Dix next appealed to the Mississippi legislature. Despite her fears to the contrary, the Mississippi bill passed the legislature by a majority of twenty-four in the senate, and eighty-one in the house. She confided to Ann:

Here was something of a conquest over prejudice and determination not to give a dime. Therefore to give $50,000 and 3,000,000 brick besides the farm and foundations of the structure is no small matter. Great was my surprise at the really beautiful vote of thanks, first by the legislature, then by the commissioners, and finally by the citizens.[48]

Before Miss Dix left Jackson, not only had an appropriation been made for the hospital for the mentally ill, but an act was also passed to rebuild and reorganize the state penitentiary.

The legislature, commissioners, citizens, all insisted that the hospital be named for her. This honor she refused. A sort of legend by this time had grown up around Dorothea Dix. There were tales of her great beauty, her brilliance, her modesty, her magnetic personality and her ability to influence legislators, as well as the peculiar soothing effect which her conversation or reading had over mentally deranged persons.

Mary Mann said that as Dorothea Dix extended the cause of reform from her native state to the borders of the civilized world, her husband's "worship of her divine prowess waxed and became a part of his consciousness, and that he counted it happiness, as he sometimes said, to be the lackey to do her bidding." He told his wife that "he loved to picture her entering alone realms of darkness where man did not dare to set his foot and reading words of cheer . . . or with a hymn upon her lips quieting the fiercest raging of madness.[49]

Miss Dix abhorred notoriety and display, and cultivated the virtues of modesty and refinement. She gave no public lectures and except in prisons and reform schools, rarely spoke in the presence of more than six or a dozen persons. In talking before small groups of legislators that she frequently invited to her hotel, she never made what might be called a formal address.

A woman who had traveled as widely and beheld so vast a pageant of injustice as Dorothea Dix could not help being alert to the rights and wrongs of her sex; yet she denied that she was a feminist. She had little patience with the extremes to which some of the leaders of the so-called feminist movement carried their theories. Fanny Wright was an abomination to one of Miss Dix's principles. Miss Dix felt that Amelia Bloomer and Lucy Stone sacrificed something fine in their natures and hurt their cause when they advocated such radical reform in women's dress. Why a few more inches of exposed pantalette should symbolize the emancipation of woman was something Miss Dix never understood. In an age that looked askance at women who took to the platform, pulpit, or stage, or went off traveling by themselves, Dorothea Dix never suffered opprobrium. In the south, where the most inflexible standards for women have always been enforced, editors vied with each other in praising her as "the gracious lady," "the chosen daughter of the Republic," "the angel of mercy," and "the apostle of humanity."[50]

Civil strife was pending in 1850 and as Dorothea Dix journeyed through the southern states she felt the tension more and more. The issues of territorial expansion, tariff, and abolition were beginning to place tremendous strain on federal relations. The proposed Nashville Convention threatened to precipitate disunion. Miss Dix found herself unwittingly dragged into discussions. Did she know Mr. Garrison and what did she think of his *Liberator?* Had she ever met Mr. Toombs? Did she read Webster's seventh of March speech? Did she think there was a possibility of civil war or would the compromise go through? She did not want to commit herself on sectional controversies. "I do not feel sure that I shall not become quite willing to expatriate myself," she wrote Ann, "if a summer sky does not displace the dark clouds which now threaten our peace. I have no patience, and no sympathy either with the northern abolitionists or southern agitators."[51] She analyzed the situation keenly: "I am quite sure that neither the one nor the other party would willingly see the question of slavery determined; in that case they would lose the whole political power which they possess or are likely to command."[52]

Miss Dix turned north from Jackson, Mississippi on another itinerary of prisons, poorhouses, and hospitals. She planned to visit Nashville, St. Louis, Pittsburgh, Philadelphia, Washington, D. C., Baltimore, Halifax and the Carolinas before the summer was over. Ann Heath was pleading with her to come to Brookline. "Few accidents of my life," she wrote Dorothea, "are so pleasant to meditate upon as our early friendship." "My dear friend, our affection must, will live when Time is no more."[53] It was calming and comforting just to look at Annie's fine neat, round script; each character was as unmistakably plain and evenly proportioned as the tiny stitches which she took in fashioning Thea's dresses. It was always hard to refuse Ann, so she promised to stay at least a couple of days with her when she came east again. Meanwhile, perhaps Susan would knit her a light blue scarf similar to the "lovely rose-colored one which had been admired away (from her) as a specimen of New England industry."

While Miss Dix's memorials were before Congress she confined her activities to investigations in the nearby states. During the Christmas holidays she made trips to southern hospitals and prisons and in the summer between sessions made hurried trips into Canada. On February 25, 1852, she submitted a memorial to the legislature of Maryland petitioning a state hospital for the insane. The memorial had the support of the *Baltimore Sun* and humanitarian-minded persons such as Moses Sheppard, and before the session was over an appropriation was made for enlarging the facilities of the Maryland Hospital and for the purchase of a new site.[54]

As Miss Dix traveled back and forth between state capitols and from city to city she became endeared not only to the lowly and afflicted, but to many of the powerful and distinguished. The growing richness of her life in human relationships in a large measure offset and relieved the strain placed upon her by the more tedious and painful side of her work. She was the close friend of three presidents, Polk, Fillmore, and Lincoln. She had known the Polks in Tennessee, and when they came to Washington, she was invited to the White House. Dorothea's letters to Ann Heath as frequently bear the imprint of the Executive Mansion, Albany, Raleigh, or Montgomery, as of the Eastern Penitentiary, or the Bloomingdale Hospital for the Insane. Her benevolence and self-sacrifice was a constant example and inspiration to others. She was frequently asked how she might be aided in her philanthropic ventures. Presidents of railroads, steamship and packet lines presented her with annual passes. After the first few years she seldom purchased a ticket out of her own funds. Express companies for years forwarded free of charge the books, magazines, tools, toys, clothing, and miscellaneous materials that she was always gathering for hospitals, prisons, and orphans' homes.

As she visited in the homes of friends she always impressed upon children how thankful they should be for health, and happy, comfortable homes. To the amazement of these children she sometimes told how grown men, sick of mind, would amuse themselves for hours with the simplest games or with building blocks, or rolling hoops down a hillside; she told of insane women who delighted in dressing and rocking dolls. As boys and girls of eight and ten and twelve listened to Miss Dix as she talked of that strange melancholy world she so often visited, they were moved to part with their choicest possessions. Later many of them regretted their spontaneous outbursts of charity and grieved for the loss of their dolls, tin soldiers, and picture collections.

While Miss Dix was working on projects for legislative appropriations for the insane in two or three states, she might also be championing prison reform, collecting books for prison libraries in the respective states, gathering up tools for workshops in schools for feeble-minded children or insane hospitals, soliciting clothing for almshouses or orphanages, or flower seeds and shrubs to beautify the grounds of some hospital or penitentiary. She always found some use for what others discarded. Dr. Godding's son said that while Miss Dix lived at the Government Hospital in Washington he never knew her to throw away a single thing that might ever be of use to herself or any one else. In the days before the sewing machine and the ready-to-wear factory, one of her favorite charities was to supply layettes for indigent mothers. Miss Dix had no time to sew herself but she knew a great many women who she thought could find a few spare hours in which to sew up the tiny garments which she had so fondly cut out. Dorothea's sister-in-law in Dorchester, the Heath sisters, and other friends seldom saw her arrive without the inevitable bundle of muslin and flannel under her arm. She was deeply moved by all who suffered, the poor, sick and afflicted, orphans, the aged, and storm-tossed sailors. Miss Dix's activities in behalf of the latter first brought her philanthropies to the attention of the English crown.

In June 1853, she visited St. Johns, Newfoundland again, at the behest of Dr. Stabb and others interested in the hospital movement. Meanwhile there was a terrible storm at sea. Miss Dix was awakened by the booming minute guns. There was a ship in distress. The wind and rain continued all night and the next morning guns, heavily charged, from the battery sent a warning up and down the coast. More than a thousand fishing vessels had been off the coast the day before. Miss Dix listened anxiously for news of the night's disaster. Sable Island, a hundred miles to the east was known as the graveyard of ships. Since Sir Humphrey Gilbert, the gallant courtier of Queen Elizabeth, had been shipwrecked there in 1583, Sable Island had taken high toll of ships and seamen. The whole region around was a trap and a snare. The island itself was desolate, covered with sand dunes, and without a harbor or shelter.[55]

As soon as the storm and fog abated, reports came in of the shipwrecked and broken vessels. On inquiry Miss Dix learned that between 1830 and 1840 at least sixteen full-rigged ships, fourteen brigs, thirteen schooners, to say nothing of hundreds of fishing smacks, were victims of storm and shoal off Sable Island.[56] She had seen many storms along the New England coast and had been in a few at sea herself, but never had she experienced anything so terrible as that of the past night. She determined to devise some means of rescuing storm-tossed mariners. As soon as it was safe, she set out for Sable Island to study the life-saving apparatus and equipment used there and to consider what might be done to reduce the storm toll of the island. She rode on one of the little native ponies from one end of the island to the other, taking note of shifting dunes, the coves, and reefs. "The whole island bristled with stark timbers and débris of wrecks." Broken spars pierced the fog, bleak reminders of tragedies of the past, silent portents of storms to come. Bits of barnacle-encrusted wood crunched beneath the pony's feet as they lay there strewn like bleaching bones over the sandy waste. While Miss Dix was looking over the island, "The Guide," a fine new vessel, bound for Labrador with a cargo of flour, went aground in a fog on the south side of the island.

Miss Dix quickly hurried to the beach and arrived just as the last boat was being landed. The ship had been abandoned by all except the captain, who in fright had suddenly become mentally deranged and refused to leave. She pleaded with the sailors to return to the wreck and bring him ashore, binding him if necessary. In a little while they returned with him, tightly bound. Miss Dix talked to the man, unbound the cords and led him to the relief station, where she calmed his troubled mind and persuaded him to express his gratitude to the sailors for saving his life.

The wreck of "The Guide" strengthened Miss Dix's conviction of the need for more adequate lifesaving apparatus for Sable Island.

The few lifeboats that were there were clumsy and antiquated, and unfit for the perilous business of riding a rough sea; there were no mortars for throwing lines across wrecked vessels, no provision of cars and breeches buoys.

Dorothea Dix returned to Boston on August 20, 1853, and immediately addressed a note to Captain Robert B. Forbes, chairman of the Humane Society of Boston, requesting him to call to see her at the earliest hour convenient on the following morning. Captain Forbes, wealthy merchant and seaman, had taken command of the "Jamestown" when she had been sent out laden with corn for the relief of famine-stricken Ireland; he had also founded the Sailors' Snug Harbor at Quincy, Massachusetts, as a home for disabled sailors. Miss Dix told him of her plan to solicit funds from merchant friends in Boston, New York, and Philadelphia, for the purchase of some lifeboats and a full equipment of the latest innovations in lifesaving apparatus for Sable Island.[57]

She accompanied him to inspect life-preservers and to observe demonstrations of various kinds of apparatus. In a short time she collected enough money to warrant the construction of four lifeboats, one financed entirely by Boston merchants, one by Philadelphia merchants, and two by New York subscribers.

By November 25, 1853, the boats were completed and the three boats constructed by Francis of New York, were placed on exhibit in Wall Street where they attracted considerable comment because of their beauty, strength, and modern equipment. Miss Dix wished to send the fleet to Halifax by the very first sailing vessel and thence to Sable Island, but Captain Forbes warned against "putting all the eggs in one basket" and the "Victoria" which had the gift of Boston merchants was sent separately by Cunard steamer.[58]

The brig "Eleanora," bearing the New York boats, set out for Halifax on November 27. It carried two surf boats, one lifeboat, two boat wagons, one life car, the mortar, with firing ammunition, coils of rope, all provided through Miss Dix's efforts. The following letter accompanied the boats.

New York, November 29, 1853

His Excellency, Sir George Seymour, K.C.B. etc.,

When I was in Nova Scotia last summer, an opportunity occurred of visiting Sable Island. I found it deficient in libraries, opening a source of amusement and instruction to isolated mariners stationed there, and that there was neither a lighthouse for warning, nor life-boats for rescue in event of perilous shipwrecks. The first and last deficiencies I was confident I could by myself and my friends at home supply but the second, the lighthouse I could only hope to see established through your Excellency's influence, met and sustained by the gubernatorial authority of Sir Gaspard le Marchand. . . .

The opinions of civilians differ, but as they suffer none of the dangers of maritime life, I presume they will concede the decision to those who unite prudence with courage, and who, while they unshrinkingly meet perils do not despise aids for avoiding destruction. I shall regard elaborate argument unseasonable in presenting this subject to your Excellency for cordial support; and in the confidence which your reputation for humanity and energy inspire, leave this work in your hands for early accomplishment.

I may inform you that a library of several hundred volumes, the joint gift of some of my friends and several liberal booksellers in Boston, has already been forwarded to Halifax to constitute a Mariners' Library for Sable Island.

In view of supplying life-boats to meet a necessity, in a spirit of "neighborly good will and fraternal kindness," I asked a few of my mercantile friends in the cities of Boston, New York and Philadelphia, a sufficient subscription for four first class life-boats, a life car, with mortar cables, trucks, harness, etc. . . . I have named the Philadelphia, *The Grace Darling,* the New York boats, severally, *The Reliance,* and *The Samaritan,* the car, *The Rescue,* and the Boston boat, *The Victoria of Boston.* . . . I shall be grateful if you will do me the honor of inspecting them. I have already seen them conquer the breakers in a stormy sea. . . .

I have, your Excellency, the honor to be with sincere respect and high appreciation, your Excellency's friend,

D. L. Dix.[59]

For a long time Miss Dix heard nothing from the brig or its precious freight. In January 1854, she had a letter from her friend, Hugh Bell, telling of the fate of the lifeboats. The brig had been driven ashore in a terrible storm off Canterbury Head, nine miles from Yarmouth, and was a total wreck. Bell had telegraphed to learn the condition of the lifeboats. The reply had come back, "One totally lost (went to sea), one badly broken, other in hold, uncertain, buoys, etc., I believe saved." Miss Dix would permit the good intentions of her friends to be frustrated only for the time being. She gave instructions to have the broken boats, as well as the one that had gone to sea and been picked up later, together with all the equipment, sent back to New York for repairs. She ordered the "Victoria" to be kept in Halifax until the rest of the little fleet should be in condition to proceed to Sable Island. Because of numerous delays it was not until October 1854 that the boats reached Halifax, and were then forwarded to Sable Island.

Ten years had now elapsed since the beginning of Dorothea Dix's humanitarian enterprise. Success marked her efforts in behalf of the mentally ill as she had proceeded from state to state. Rich and poor alike had been enlisted in the cause of reform; men, women, and children had subscribed to her charities. A glorious decade it had been; eleven states had hearkened to her appeals and established hospitals. She had inspected almshouses, jails, and prisons; libraries, workshops, and hospitals rose as monuments to her labors. She had continued to go about her moral crusade in a "spirit of devout humility" as Francis George Shaw had written of her in *The Harbinger* at the outset of her career.[60]

To Mrs. Rathbone in 1850, she wrote:

Shall I not say to you, dear friend, that my uniform success and influence are evidence to my mind that I am called by Providence to the vocation to which life, talents, and fortune have been surrendered these many years. I cannot say, "Behold now, this great Babylon which I have builded," but "Lo! O, Lord, the work which Thou gavest thy servant, she does it, and God in his benignity blesses and advances the cause by the instrument He had fitted for the labor."[61]

CHAPTER VII

THE APPEAL FOR FEDERAL AID

IT WAS NOW 1848, a year of much agitation at home and abroad. Discontent animated by idealism and secret hopes ran high. Europe still reverberated with the clarion call of Karl Marx's *Communist Manifesto* of 1847. In London the Chartists presented their demands and in France republicans led by that soldier of fortune, Louis Napoleon, were to displace the old monarchy of Louis Philippe, while at Frankfort, idealistic Germans were to set forth the principles by which they hoped to effect an *anschluss,* and in Piedmont, Italians under Mazzini were to proclaim their behalf in the *risorgimento.* In America, a presidential election was at hand, and the public mind was distracted by a multipliciy of issues and movements, northern demands for abolition, southern demands for fugitive slave legislation, nativist propaganda, woman's rights, and expansionism. Over it all rumors of secession cast a menacing shadow. Miss Dix, however, was animated by a zeal which stopped for nothing. The cause of the indigent mentally ill had to be brought to the attention of Congress.

For several years Miss Dix had been trying to formulate a plan which would provide not only for the mentally ill of her own day but of the future. Statistics revealed that along with the rising tide of immigration, industrialism, and the growing complexities of modern life there was an increase in the number of people who were becoming mentally ill each year. Miss Dix acknowledged herself to be the voice of the inarticulate insane of her own time, but what of tomorrow? To what persons or agencies was their fate to be entrusted? By this time it had become the settled policy of the national government to grant tracts of lands to the new states for the purposes of establishing schools and promoting internal improvements. By 1845 when Miss Dix first conceived the idea of federal aid for hospitals for the mentally ill, 134,704,982 acres of the public domain had already been ceded to the various states; over a hundred million remained. There was much talk, said Miss Dix, of retaining the public land for the benefit of the poor and creating homesteads. Why not reserve a part of this vast domain in trust for the indigent insane? "The insane poor," she declared, "through the Providence of God, are wards of the nation."[1] A government which provides schools, homesteads, and highways for the sane of its population owes to its destitute and mentally defective at least shelter and humane treatment.

John A. Dix, a highly respected and influential senator from New York, presented Miss Dix's Memorial to Congress on June 27, 1848.[2] He spoke of her disinterested efforts in ameliorating the condition of the insane. He told of how her time, health, and means had been freely spent in this charitable service, and how through her perseverance and the impression created by the information she had gathered, institutions for the insane had been established in various parts of the country. The wealthy had contributed from their abundance, and states laboring under heavy burdens of debt had taxed themselves further for the relief of this class, which above all others had the strongest claim to the public sympathy and support.[3]

After traveling 60,000 miles and personally visiting over 9,000 insane, epileptic, and idiotic persons in different parts of the United States, Miss Dix was now appealing to the federal government for an appropriation of 5,000,000 acres of land to constitute a fund out of which this "too much neglected and most hopeless class might be provided." Among the thirty states of the union according to the ratio of their populations, the total proceeds of this grant should be distributed.[4] Such was her proposal. Never before had any government or earthly potentate been asked for so great a boon to charity; valued at one dollar an acre the land was equal to one-third the cost of the entire Louisiana territory. Five million acres seems a stupendous amount of land, but in 1848 land was the most plentiful thing in America. Statesmen and politicians spoke glibly of hundreds of thousands of acres. Railway promoters, private speculators, and projectors of highways and canals jostled each other in the mad scramble for land. Congress had been generous and in many instances lavish and indiscreet in parceling out the federal lands. Through machination and manipulation, greedy adventurers were yearly securing enormous grants. Miss Dix asked herself, "Why can I not too, go in with this selfish, struggling throng, and plead for God's poor and outcast, that they shall not be forgotten?"

Dorothea Dix was not unknown to members of Congress nor was she without legislative and lobbying experience. Most of the senators and representatives were familiar with the work she had done in their respective states. Many of them were acquainted with her personally; with their constituents her name was a household word, revered and honored as those of Clay and Webster and Calhoun. A petition from Miss Dix could not be entirely ignored.

Miss Dix had hoped to have the memorial introduced by Colonel Benton of Missouri, sponsor of a number of popular projects to dispose of western lands, but at the last minute the wary colonel pleaded illness and she turned to Senator Dix.[5] John Dix was selected not only on account of personal friendship but because he was interested in the work, came from a powerful state, and was a prominent member of the Democratic party. Although Miss Dix never wished to make a political issue of her appeals for the insane, she was always desirous of securing the approval of the leading party.

In her memorial to the federal government she synthesized her investigations of the past six years. In language as vivid and fearless as that in which she addressed state legislatures, she told Congress of the hundreds, even thousands, of insane that she had seen in jails, poorhouses, and in private dwellings, "bound with galling chains, bowed beneath fetters and heavy iron balls attached to drag chains, lacerated with ropes, scourged with rods and terrified beneath storms of profane execrations and cruel blows; now subject to jibes and scorn and torturing tricks, now abandoned to the most loathsome necessities, or subject to the vilest and most outrageous violations." Strong terms, these were, Miss Dix admitted, but not too potent to describe the things she had seen. Out of a population of 22,000,000, she estimated 22,000 insane persons. According to her investigations the existing hospitals, excluding those institutions not considered remedial, provided for less than 3700 patients. Where were the remainder and what was their condition?[6]

Commencing with the state of Maine, she quoted extracts from her journals. State after state was arraigned before Congress. Some of the incidents had already appeared in memorials to the respective state legislatures, others were related for the first time. Witness an illustration from Georgia, one of the states that had years before established an institution for the insane and then had failed to pass proper laws governing commitment, or to make further provision.

It was an intensely hot day that I visited F. He was confined in a roofed pen, which inclosed an area about eight feet by eight. The interstices between the unhewn logs admitted the scorching rays of the sun then, as they would open the way for the fierce winds and drenching rains or frosts of the later seasons. The place was wholly bare of furniture, *no bench, no bed, no clothing.* His food, which was of the coarsest kind, was pushed through spaces between the logs. "Fed like the hogs, and no better," said a passerby.

His feet had been frozen by exposure to cold in the winter past. Upon the shapeless stumps, aided by his arms, he could raise himself against the logs of his pen. In warm weather, this wretched place was cleaned once a week or a fortnight; not so (often) in the colder seasons. "We have men called," said his sister, "and they go in and tie him with ropes and throw him on the ground, and my husband cleans out the place." But the expedient to prevent his freezing in winter was the most strangely horrible. In the center of the pen was excavated a pit, six feet square, and deep; the top was closed over securely, and into this ghastly place, entered by a trap door, was cast the maniac, there to exist till the returning warm weather induced his caretaker to withdraw him; there without heat, without light, without pure air, was left the pining miserable maniac whose piteous groans and frantic cries might move to pity the hardest heart.[7]

In nearly all of the states where the cold of winter was sufficient to cause freezing of the body by exposure, Miss Dix found many mutilated insane, deprived of either the hands or the feet, and sometimes of both.

"It is a fact not less certainly substantiated than it is deplorable that insanity has increased in an advanced ratio with the fast increasing population in the United States," said Miss Dix. The ratio had changed from one insane to every 1000 persons to one for every 800. There were more insane in the cities than in small towns. The percentage varied from state to state and from section to section. In Rhode Island the rate of insanity was one to 503, and in South Carolina, one to 6158, in New England, one to 600, in the South, one to 900, and in the West one to 1300.[8] "Wherever the intellect is most exalted and health lowest," she alleged, "there is an increase in insanity." The Millerite movement was cited as contributing many persons to asylums and attention was called to the large percentage of foreigners among the patients received at the various large hospitals for the insane.

Briefly Miss Dix reviewed the history of the hospitals for the insane. She quoted extensively from the greatest European and American physicians on the causes and treatment of mental diseases, among them, Dr. Isaac Ray of the Butler Hospital, Rhode Island, Dr. Conolly of England, and Dr. Hayward of Boston. It was impossible, she concluded, to cope with the terrible evils of the insane without the establishment of scientifically conducted institutions.

Should your sense of moral responsibility seek support in precedents for guiding present action, I may be permitted to refer to the fact of liberal grants of common national property made, in the light of a wise discrimination, to various institutions of learning, also to advance in the new states common school education, and to aid two seminaries of instruction for the deaf and dumb, viz., that in Hartford, Connecticut, and the school at Danville, Kentucky.

Miss Dix was not asking benefits for one section of the United States while all others were being deprived of direct advantages. "I ask relief for the East, and for the West, and for the North, and for the South." "I ask for the people that which is already the property of the people."[9]

Following Senator Dix's introduction of the memorial, five thousand copies were ordered to be printed. Miss Dix expressed a wish for a select committee to consider the 5,000,000 acre bill. This was an unusual request but she pleaded that she "at least be suffered to propose it." She wrote out her list, the majority of whom were Democrats, and it was accepted. Colonel Benton, Mr. Dix, Mr. Harnegan, Mr. Bell and Mr. Davis of Massachusetts comprised the committee.[10] Benton was at this time one of the most important figures in the Senate and Miss Dix would not listen to his protest against serving on the committee. She realized that her proposition was not one of peculiar interest to politicians; her experience of the past six years had taught her that philanthropy and party politics did not often travel in the same company. Although adroit at the game herself, Dorothea Dix had little use for the average politician. As soon as she had recovered from the influenza which had attacked her while she was at work on the last draft of the memorial, she went to see Colonel Benton. He tried to cut her off with promises that he would do everything for her that was "feasible under the circumstances."[11]

"Sir, I have not come to ask any favor for myself, not the smallest," replied Miss Dix. "I ask for *yourself,* your *state,* your *people.* Sir, you are a Democrat, and profess above all others to support the interests of the people, the multitude, the poor." "This," she declared, "is the opportunity of showing the country how far profession and practice correspond." The blue grey flashed a warning. "Reject this measure, you trample on the poor, you crush them." "Sustain it," the rich voice was soft and mellow again, "sustain it, and their blessings shall echo round your pillow when the angel of the last hour comes to call you to the other life of action and progress."

It was more than the doughty westerner cared to resist. "My dear Miss Dix," replied Benton, "I will do what I can."

"Then, sir," said Miss Dix, "the bill and the measure are safe." In winning over Colonel Benton, she felt that the greatest difficulty in the Senate had been surmounted. The new Democratic movement in the northern states, protesting against the congressional policy of free disposition of the public domain, greatly imperiled the security of her measure. A thousand million acres of the public lands were yet unsold and the cry was raised that those vast areas must be reserved for the benefit of the poor man. To grant these lands to railroad or public improvement companies or speculators was regarded as the robbery of the poor; these great areas must be retained for the man who was willing to move out into the wilderness and create a home for himself and his family. To him these lands must be sold at a fixed price of $1.25 and $1.50 an acre. Knowing Colonel Benton's position on the land question, Miss Dix was doubly anxious as to the attitude he would have toward her proposal of reserving 5,000,000 acres for the benefit of the indigent insane. It was with something of a joyous relief that she was able to write to her friend, Mrs. Hare, on July 21, 1848.

You, who understand me, you who always sympathize with my anxieties and rejoice in my successes, will be glad to know that my whole committee, even the impracticable Colonel Benton, concurred in my 5,000,000 acre bill, and it was read this morning in the senate.

Despite these favorable beginnings, Miss Dix was not too elated. "I, you know, am never sanguine and feel confidence only when a bill passes into an act, and is sealed by the governor or president."[12]

Congress set aside a small alcove in the Capitol Library for Miss

Dix's use, and here each day she was on hand to explain to members the measures which she advocated. Her days in Washington were always busy, crowded with interviews and the inevitable correspondence, all carried out meticulously according to schedule. Much of the time she rose at four-fifteen. After the duties of the first hour, dressing and reading the Bible, she wrote until eight-thirty when she came down to breakfast. She always carried her knitting down to the dining room and after the meal she would knit while some member of the family read aloud from the morning paper. At ten o'clock she might be found at her desk in the Capitol Library. She returned home at three and read the papers or wrote letters until four-thirty, when the family had dinner. She usually sat with the family until six, then went to her room and wrote until eight, when she returned to the parlor for tea. After that she either retired or wrote for an hour or two. On Sundays she was on her way to the penitentiaries by eight, and either remained there until one or returned to the city in time for morning services. She seldom attended church in the afternoon or evening. On Saturdays she frequently went to Baltimore to visit the prisons and hospitals but she always returned by eight.

In answer to Ann's questions about social functions in Washington, Dorothea replied:

Now for the dissipations, the fashionable life you think I lead. One day from twelve to four, since I have been in Washington, dating from December 6, I have appropriated to returning calls, and left about fifty cards. Except these I am still in arrears. These visits only have I paid, namely, dined at the President's, was one of the three hundred friends at the mansion of the secretary of the navy, and one of the two hundred at a select party given . . . to the heads of the departments, leading officers and families of the army and navy, and the foreign ministers. So you see, I am not greatly dazzled by attractions of the gay life in Washington, and probably if I remain here, I shall not find myself consenting to be again in public. Society at large does not attract me, though if any person has reason to be satisfied with compensations, perhaps it is myself.[13]

Twenty years before, she had thrilled to an invitation to attend an informal reception in honor of the distinguished Lafayette, but now in the nation's capital and surrounded by notables, society had lost its lure. She was content to spend her evenings in Mrs. John-

son's quiet boarding house, knitting, writing letters, preparing talks
to be given before Sunday School classes in nearby prisons, or composing birthday verses for some friend in Boston, Philadelphia, or
St. Louis. Abby Heath was engaged to be married and a shopping
expedition had to be wedged in between interviews. Dorothea was
pleased with Abby's prospects. Women who married, she reflected,
had better chances for happiness than those who did not. She
wished that Ann were being married too. It would be lonely on
Heath Hill without Abby.

Miss Dix's mind flew back like a shuttle between the past and
present, memories of pleasant visits to the great white house in
Brookline, and conferences with conniving politicians and weary
legislators. Some days she found herself growing strangely tired
and she began making plans for the rest that she would take when
her bill was passed. Ann suggested that she go to Vermont and
take one of the water cures, so much in vogue during the forties,
but Dorothea was firm. "I should prefer a voyage to Maderia, a
trip to England, and a land journey at home for a year occupying
my mind with new and pleasant objects than the risks of that
aquatic amphibious life at Brattleboro."[14]

She found the members of Congress "in general a good deal
more occupied with party politics than devoted to the duties of
statesmanship." It was difficult to bring up any measure for their
consideration that did not bear upon their own political fortunes,
but one by one she managed to secure their promises to support her
5,000,000 acre bill. In the struggle over the disposition of the federal
lands, they pledged not to forget "the piteous claims of the helpless
ones" whose rights she pleaded. Loyal supporters she had, both
in and out of Congress. In 1844 the Association of Medical Superintendents of American Institutions for the Insane was founded, and
since that time it had gone on record at every meeting as endorsing
Miss Dix's work in behalf of the insane.[15]

A journal was published from the inception of the association,
and during its earlier years placed much emphasis on the value of
institutional care and the need of state-owned and controlled hospitals for the insane.[16] The editor, Dr. Amariah Brigham, of the
Utica Hospital, was a close friend of Miss Dix and personally did
much to bring medical men to appreciate her services.[17]

To these friends the failure of the bill seemed most improbable.

The medical superintendents were confident that the measure would pass both houses and soon receive the signature of President Polk, and premature letters of congratulation were sent to Miss Dix. Dr. Luther V. Bell of the McLean Hospital wrote as early as December 29, 1848:

Dear Madam:

Your friends cannot but trust that these terribly severe labors may be nearly at a close. And so, released by the actual accomplishment or encouraging inception of your labors, how much more remains to be done, which no one but you can do! The aggregation of misery and misfortune, of which you have sounded the depths, and have done so much to alleviate, affords yet an almost boundless field of labor with the pen, if possible of more moment than any present relief through personal devotion. In a country rushing upon the crowded population, the crimes, the miseries of the Old World with gigantic strides, cannot something be done which shall *tell* to all future time, by informing the world, at least the wise and good of the world, how these monster evils can be grappled with?

Is not our want of fixed principles owing to our want of facts? Now, it seems to me that when you have finished the specific course laid out for yourself, if you could, in the light of all your personal experience of human suffering, take a year and sit down to the composition of a volume which should meet the emergency alluded to, you might accomplish more than in any other way. A personal narrative of your last ten years' life would contain just the needed elements, if the fair conclusions could be eliminated from it, which you alone could do.

Accept, dear Madam, our heartfelt regards and sincerest prayers,

Yours truly,

Luther V. Bell.[18]

Miss Dix was grateful for the "heartfelt regards" and "sincerest prayers" but she would never find time to write anything that was in the smallest way autobiographical. There was little in her personal life which she felt worth recording for others to read, and there was so much that she wished to be forgotten or to remain unknown. There was her abnormal childhood, the difference in her parents' ages and temperaments, her own extreme sensitiveness, and her disappointment in love. She could never want the world to know that in her compassion for the neglected of mankind, she had found her own happiness and salvation, or that legislative achievements meant more than restored minds and monuments in brick and stone, that they were to her milestones in her soul's progress upward, the conquest of the spirit over the flesh. The chronicle of those years was too intimate for Dorothea Dix ever to write. She never spoke of her childhood, her family, or her thwarted plans. Ann Heath, George Emerson, Horace Mann, or perhaps Dr. Hayward may have guessed the secret of her passion for philanthropy; but there is not the slightest possibility that Luther Bell, Thomas Kirkbride, or Pliny Earle, ever realized the driving power back of her humanitarian endeavors.

As the winter of 1848-49 wore on, Dorothea Dix was less concerned over what she would do next. First the bill had to be passed; but now grave dangers loomed ahead, threatened the consummation of her labors. Legislation was a slow, uncertain process; bills sometimes went astray, were shelved, overlooked, forgotten. On January 30, 1849, she wrote her brother, Joseph:

Specially and prominently, at this particular time, I am watching and guarding the 5,000,000 [acre] bill. Through the courtesy of my friends in the Senate and House, a special committee room is assigned to my use in the Capitol. I am neither sanguine nor discouraged. I think the bill may be deferred till next session. A new difficulty is to be combated, the President having declared . . . he will *veto* all and every land bill which does not make a provisional payment to the general government. I suppose this will be gotten over by a small premium upon every acre sold. I, fortunately, am on good terms with Mrs. Polk and the President, knowing well all their family friends in Tennessee and North Carolina.

The Vice-President, Mr. Dallas, the intimate associate of many of my Philadelphia friends, is warmly in favor of the bill. I have decidedly declined the interposition of the state legislatures, preferring to rely on the "uninstructed" deliberations and acts of the two branches of Congress. The public interest is involved for *all* the States, and those who will vote negatively will do so upon constitutional grounds, imaginarily involving the federal integrity.[19]

Weeks passed by. Election was only a few months past, and retrenchment was the order of the day. Land bills suddenly became unpopular and the sponsors of Miss Dix's bill felt it best not to bring the matter to a vote until the excitement abated. "My bill has been deferred," she wrote Ann early in March. A month later she wrote, "My bill has again been deferred." Still she had not lost hope. The spring wore on and it became evident that the bill would not be brought up. Even though the bill might be deferred, the cause must not be lost sight of; daily Miss Dix continued to enlist the interest of senators and representatives. "There will be another session," she said when at last Congress adjourned and the bill was allowed to lapse.

Undaunted by defeat, Miss Dix was on hand when the new senators and representatives took their places in December 1849, and prepared to urge upon them the claims of America's defectives. Settled again in the little alcove in the Capitol Library, she held conferences and laid plans for advancing bills. This time she proposed a memorial in behalf of the indigent blind, deaf, and dumb, as well as the indigent insane. Instead of 5,000,000 acres of the public domain, she now asked for 12,500,000, of which 10,000,000 should be set aside for the benefit of the insane, and the remaining 2,500,000 for the blind, deaf, and dumb.

James Pearce, of Maryland, introduced the memorial before the Senate, and John Fremont, of California, and son-in-law of Colonel Benton, brought it forward in the House.[20]   Mr. Pearce, Mr. Benton, Mr. Davis of Massachusetts, Mr. Dickinson, and Mr. Bell were appointed by the Vice-president to constitute a committee for the consideration of Miss Dix's appeal. In a short time they reported favorably upon the memorial and it looked as though a bill would be passed. The press, the pulpit, and forum endorsed the measure. Resolutions from churches and societies, and letters from public-spirited citizens poured into Washington. The Medical Superintendents of American Institutions for the Insane, at their fifth annual meeting, in Boston, unanimously passed a resolution of their "unqualified sanction" of Miss Dix's proposal; that a portion of the public domain be devoted to the endowment of the public charities throughout the country.[21]

The summer of 1850 was unusually hot, but Miss Dix refused to leave her post. What was her personal comfort, she asked herself, compared to the well-being of thousands of mind-bereft souls? It was tiresome work, daily sitting in the stuffy alcove instructing members relative to the needs of the insane, repeating gruesome details that she longed to eradicate from her mind forever, listening to old objections, pointing out fallacies in arguments and correcting erroneous impressions. If she grew weary, impatient, discouraged, she dared not admit the fact. Patience, tact, and tolerance, she had to cultivate. Heat, delay, and political avarice had to be ignored. Not for a moment would she give way to the pressure of physical discomfort or irritation at political chicanery and perversity. Late in August she wrote Ann:

> None can tell what a mountain will be lifted from my heart if my bills pass. I shall feel almost as if I could say, "Lord, now let thy servant depart in peace, for mine eyes have seen thy salvation."

Yet in the next sentence she chides herself for this outburst of weariness and resigns herself to what she can not change.

> I recollect that my times and seasons are His and for His work. He will do as seems to Himself good. I ought to be ready to meet all changes, all events; but the troubles of this miserable world, if now no way were opened for their alleviation, make the hour of death mournful to me.[22]

Only to so close and understanding a friend as Ann Heath would she confess this feeling of exhaustion and fatigue; few others suspected the weight and weariness that was daily growing heavier. At her post of duty she managed to throw off all semblance of anxiety and lose herself in enthusiasm for the hospital measures. Horace Mann, now a member of the House of Representatives, wrote his wife on September 16, 1850, that he had just come from the Library where Miss Dix was filling all whom she called about her with a "divine magnetism."[23] A week later it was Mann's task to advise her of the fate of her bill. He wrote the Rev. Mr. S. J. May in Boston:

> Poor Miss Dix, her bill has failed this morning in the House; or at least it has been referred to the Committee of the Whole on the state of the union, from which it can not be returned should the session continue for a year. I went to carry her the news but she has not come up to the library today.

> Yesterday when her bill came up, men were starting up on all sides with their objections; but today the point under discussion is to pay an additional sum to the soldiers in the Mexican War . . . and almost all are in favor of it. It is amazing how war-mad all the South and Southerners are. Conquest and numbers constitute their idea of glory. Christianity is 1900 years distant from them.[24]

Two days later, Dorothea broke the news to Ann:

My bill has been deferred to the first month of the next session, the second Monday. Pray that my patience may not fail utterly. I go to Maryland on Tuesday and directly to the interior of Pennsylvania.[25]

When Congress assembled the first Monday in December, Miss Dix was back in Washington. The earnest woman at the little walnut desk near the window was beginning to be a familiar figure about the Capitol. At each session she won more friends to her cause. When the bill came up in the Senate again in February 1851, there were excellent prospects for its passage. Miss Dix was elated; it looked as though the great dream of her life was about to be realized. Her thin lips parted into a radiant smile. Soon someone, perhaps Mr. Mason or Mr. Pearce, would be bringing the news. She found it difficult to settle down to work; to walk up and down the corridor would be an open confession of nervousness, and she determined to remain to all appearances as calm and unperturbed as New England granite. She decided to write a letter to Ann while she waited.

> Washington, D. C.,
> February 11, 1851

My dear Friend:

My bill is up in the Senate. I am awaiting the result with great anxiety, but with a calmness which astonishes myself.—

A motion to lay on the Speaker's table is just lost, 32 to 14. It is said that this is the test vote. They are speaking on amendments.—The danger is from debate.—I dread Chase of Ohio.—

Mr. Mason of Virginia sends me word the bill will pass.—

Mr. Shields just comes to say the bill will pass.—You do not know how terrible this suspense!—I am perfectly calm, and as cold as ice.

4 P. M. The bill passed the Senate beautifully. A large majority, more than two to one!—thirty-six yeas to sixteen nays.[26]

With joyful heart she hurried from the Capitol. At home in the quiet of her room she repeated softly, "My cup runneth over. Surely goodness and mercy shall follow. . . ." She paused. A victory had been won in the Senate but before a bill could become an act it had to pass both houses during the session and be signed by the President. At the last session the House of Representatives had approved the measure; surely it would sustain its previous action.

The next morning Miss Dix began inquiring of members of the

House if it would be possible to suspend the rules and bring the 12,225,000 acre bill to the immediate consideration of the House. The action of the House at the preceding session, she thought, was fairly indicative of what its present attitude would be. It was doubtful if there would be any debate; a roll call there and the bill could be sent to the President for his signature. Of Fillmore's sanction Miss Dix was already assured. It seemed only a question of time; meanwhile there were so many hospitals, prisons, and charitable institutions that were soliciting her attention. She had been in Washington so long; she felt that she should be going on, doing other things.

To Miss Dix's surprise there suddenly arose in the House a cry for the rigid enforcement of rules. The hospital bill would have to take its turn. Petty political controversies were consuming the attention of the House. Weeks passed. The first of March came. The session was nearly ended. Would the bill never come up? Would it be delayed and delayed, until finally it would lapse? The thought struck terror to her heart. She began to groom herself for disappointment.

Congress adjourned. The House had not acted. Her bill had suffered a second defeat.

From Washington Miss Dix turned southward, focusing her attention on state legislatures, and bringing about signal hospital victories within the southern, middle, and western states. On several of these "between session" trips, already described in a previous chapter, Miss Dix was accompanied by Fredrika Bremer, the Swedish novelist who visited America in 1851. Miss Bremer met Miss Dix in the Capitol and expressed an appreciation of the fine work that she was doing in behalf of the unfortunate. Miss Dix was pleased with Miss Bremer's interest, and availed herself of the opportunity to inquire as to the care and treatment being given the mentally ill in the Scandinavian countries, the progress being made in the education of the deaf, dumb, and blind children, and of the social responsibilities assumed by the state. Of Dorothea Dix, Miss Bremer heard only the highest praise. Statesmen, physicians, men of letters, and school children spoke of her admiringly, even reverently.

Here was a woman whose life was far more intriguing than the fiction for which Miss Bremer was internationally famous. Some great motive must have inspired her to make those long journeys. "How I should like to hear her story from her own lips," mused Miss Bremer. To her niece in Sweden she wrote:

She is one of the most beautiful proofs of that which a woman, without any other aid than her own free will and character, without any other power than that of her purpose and its uprightness, and her ability to bring these forward, can effect in society. I admire her, admire in particular her courage and perseverance. In other respects we hardly sympathize but I love the place she occupies in humanity, love her figure sitting in the recess of the window in the Capitol, where amid the fiery feuds, she silently spins her web for the unfortunate, a quiet center for the threads of Christian love which draws across the ceaseless contests, undisturbed by them, a divine spinner is she for the House of God. Should I not kiss her hand? I did and do it again in spirit, with thanks for that which she is and that which she does.[27]

When Miss Bremer returned to Philadelphia in July, she was accompanied by Miss Dix as far as Baltimore. Dorothea Dix had come to feel a strange kinship with this literary woman, this ardent feminist from across the seas. She shared her desire to know the finest and noblest minds of other lands. She recalled the splendid vistas that a visit to England had brought to her own hungry soul. They seemed to have so much in common, this vivacious Swedish woman, and this active American; one had already forsaken literature for philanthropy and the other was soon to consecrate her literary talents to reform. As they sat alone in the moonlight on the balcony of General Steuart's villa overlooking the broad Chesapeake, Miss Bremer asked Miss Dix to tell her what it was that directed her into the path which she was then pursuing as "the public protector and advocate of the unfortunate."[28] Dorothea Dix seldom talked of herself except to her closest and most intimate friends. Still, this Swedish woman might understand. She answered slowly:

It was no remarkable occurrence nor change in my inner or outer life, it was merely an act of simple obedience to the voice of God. I had returned from England whither I went on account of my health which had obliged me to give up the school I had kept for several years, and I now lived in a boarding house without any determined occupation, employing myself in the study of various branches of natural history to which I had always been attached, but yet some way depressed by the inactivity of my life. I longed for some nobler purposes for which to labor, something which would fill the vacuum which I felt in my soul.[29]

Then followed the simple story of her visit to the Cambridge jail, the account which she had written for the paper, the Massachusetts survey and the passage of the bills to improve the prison, and to erect a hospital. "That was the beginning," said Miss Dix. "Thus I saw the path marked out for me, and it, and that which I have done in it have, as it were, been done by themselves." Miss Bremer was deeply moved, and wrote

Washington lay behind me, with its political quarrels, its bitter strife of state against state, man against man, its intricate relationship and unsatisfactory prospects, its excited chaotic state. And here was a small human life which by an act of simple obedience had gone forth from its privacy, from its darkness extending itself into a great active principle, fraught with blessing for neglected beings throughout every state in the union, like that little river before us, had poured itself into that glorious creek, and in that united with the world's ocean.

To Miss Bremer the comparison was striking. "The resemblance between that human life and the scene before me was striking also, and the peace and beauty of that night and the pure moonlight were like the blessing of Heaven upon them both.[30]

What new field would this zealous woman enter as soon as Congress took favorable action upon her bill? Miss Bremer did not have long to wonder. For many months as Miss Dix had been journeying back and forth from Washington to Canada, and from state to state, a plan had been slowly shaping itself in her mind. When she had finished her immediate labors in America she would go abroad and visit those countries where the insane were most neglected; she would awaken the people of those nations to their civic and moral responsibilities.—She interviewed Jenny Lind, then on a concert tour of America, as to the advisability of such a campaign in her native country. The Swedish nightingale frankly admitted that she thought no good would be accomplished by such a visit from Miss Dix, alleging that it would be impossible for a foreigner without knowledge of the language or customs to awaken the people of Sweden to a sense of responsibility toward any class of the population. Attributing the singer's reply to national pride, Miss Dix next wrote Miss Bremer, who was at that time in Cincinnati. Her answer was no more encouraging.

Sweden lacks neither goodwill nor means. What is wanted there is energy and impulse of will; and *that* a foreigner unknown in the country, and herself not knowing its language and forms of government, could not give. Jenny Lind is right in that opinion. As things now stand, it would be easier for you to climb to the Chinese Wall than to work any good *personally* for the unfortunate insane in Sweden.

But believe me, dear Miss Dix, what you have done, what you are doing in America, will, when properly disclosed,—as it ought to be, and must be, to Sweden,—work more for a bettering of the insane asylums there than a gift of ten millions could in their behalf. The power of the Idea, and the power of example, are the greater movers of our time, and go forth from heart to heart, from land to land, with electric shock.[81]

Perhaps Jenny Lind and Fredrika Bremer were right, but the conquest of Europe was a dream which Dorothea Dix did not readily relinquish. Suffering is no respecter of persons; it knows no national boundaries, she argued with herself. But the bill before Congress was her immediate concern and for the time being it must overshadow and eclipse any project for world-wide philanthropy. Victory in the Senate was followed by delay in the House. Finally the bill lapsed, but Miss Dix did not despair. Hospitals projected by her memorials to state legislatures were opening their doors all over the country, heralds of a new day in the care and treatment of the insane. "Eventually Congress will take action, in the meantime, patience," she counselled herself. Medical superintendents were writing such encouraging letters, asking her advice about certain details of administration, and inviting her to be present at the opening of their institutions, and to address their officers and attendants. Seldom did she refuse such a request if it was possible for her to attend.

On her tour of southern prisons and hospitals in the summer of 1851, Miss Dix was accompanied by Miss Bremer. Through the Carolinas, Georgia, and Florida, the two women traveled for several weeks. Fredrika Bremer was amazed at Miss Dix's indefatigable energy and the tender solicitude which she had for the sick whom they encountered. It seems incredible the way she could forget self so completely in her devotion to the poor and needy. Miss Bremer was distressed at the poor accommodations afforded travelers in this part of the country, and the extreme discomfort which they frequently experienced, especially on the Savannah River. After they changed boats at Pulaski, they found so many mice and cockroaches in their cabin that they could not sleep. The Swedish woman was greatly annoyed; it was bad enough to be compelled to drink dirty river water but to have mice scampering across one's pillow and to know that giant cockroaches were making inroads on one's luggage was too much. "What will we do?" she asked of her companion. Miss Dix arose, lighted a candle, moved their bags to safer quarters and prepared to make the best of a situation she had had to cope with many times before.

As soon as the boat would draw up to the wharf, Miss Dix would tie her bonnet strings, grab her portmanteau, and be the first person to cross the gangplank. A prison, a poorhouse, or a hospital had to be visited while the captain unloaded his barrels, staves, and salt pork, and took on molasses, rum, and tobacco. In two minutes Miss Dix would be on her way afoot, in a two-wheeled cart, or a hansom. Off to the sick, the criminal, the afflicted. To each she brought some message of hope and cheer, "seeds of spiritual culture," as Miss Bremer described them. "She scatters about her like morning dew as she goes along her way little miniature books called *Dewdrops,* containing religious proverbs, and numbers of small tracts. . . ."[32]

Miss Dix left Miss Bremer and her party to spend some time at Ortega Plantation in northern Florida, and hurried on to St. Augustine to inspect the prisons and charitable institutions there. Miss Bremer missed her companion; she knew no one in Europe who could compare with Dorothea Dix; even Mrs. Fry, the English reformer, could not equal her in fearlessness and self-denial. She shuddered to think of the trip they had just taken down the river; physical danger did not seem to daunt Miss Dix. This very hour she might be crossing one of those terrible dismal swamps.

The year 1852 found Miss Dix again in Washington busy with renewed efforts to get the 12,225,000 acre bill before Congress. Each time she came back she asked for an additional appropriation. She now sought in addition to the 12,225,000 acres of land, $100,000 for a hospital for the relief of the insane of the army and navy and the District of Columbia. The matter of a "lunatic asylum" for the District of Columbia had several times been brought to the attention of Congress. Since 1841 about thirty or forty persons from the District of Columbia had been cared for at government expense, at the Maryland Hospital for the Insane, then located on Broadway at the present site of Johns Hopkins Hospital.[33]

The Maryland Hospital was taxed beyond capacity and these patients were about to be crowded out; Miss Dix was especially concerned that provision be made for their care. Late in August Congress passed a bill appropriating $100,000 for the hospital. For a few hours Dorothea Dix rejoiced, and then the land bill came uppermost in her mind. If only the action taken by Congress on the Government Hospital might be indicative of the outcome of the 12,225,000 acre bill. At last the House voted in favor of it, 98 to 54; in the Senate the same old story of delay was reënacted. It appeared that her bill would be carried over to the next session. He sent for her friend, Horace Mann. Hopes had been so high when the session began but the outlook now was dark indeed. They talked the situation over, Mr. Mann was confident that the land bill would be passed the next session. He did not think it would be necessary even to refer it to the House unless amendments were made. Miss Dix was undecided as to the policy she should pursue. Prospects of a presidential election were beginning to monopolize public attention and interest in philanthropic measures was bound to subside; perhaps it would be well to wait until political scores were settled and a new Congress sworn in.[34] She decided to wait.

For eighteen months she devoted her energies to work in Maryland, Canada, the Middle West and the South, securing extensive appropriations for state hospitals, and adding prestige and moral ascendancy to the cause. Now and then she made a trip to Washington in order to remain in touch with affairs and to keep the issue of a federal grant before the members of Congress. In addition to the land bill, she always had two or three smaller pet charities that she was advancing; sometimes it would be a library for a seamen's home, or subscriptions for an orphanage. In February 1853, Horace Mann wrote:

I saw Miss Dix this morning. She is an angel. She has got two or three hundred dollars out of the government for a library in the District. She has induced Mr. Corcoran to give a bit of land, $15,000 for a building, and $10,000 for a library to be called the "Apprentices' Library" here. Mr. Corcoran came in here the other day and he was overwhelmed with solicitations for money. "But you," said he, "have *carte blanche.*" Isn't she a woman's rights woman worth having, going in for their rights in the right way?[35]

Horace Mann was a true friend. For fourteen years he had been following her efforts at philanthropy, encouraging and advising her. At every turn of the way, he had been ready to sympathize, console, and assist. He had been to her in Washington what George Emerson had been in Boston—"faithful," "loyal," "a tower of strength."

When Congress assembled for the first session of 1854, the excitement in the Democratic party over the land issue had subsided and more interest was manifested in Miss Dix's projected measure than had been shown for four years. Medical men, hospital superintendents, educators, and humanitarians urged upon the members the value of the plan to posterity. Letters and petitions poured into Washington. Newspapers published lengthy accounts of Miss Dix's work in the states and endorsed her present appeal to the federal government. Victory seemed in the offing. Five thousand copies of the memorial were printed and placed in circulation. A bill was introduced which proposed to distribute 10,000,000 acres of the public land among the states of the union, of which 100,000 was first to be given to each of them and the remainder to be distributed among them upon a compound ratio of geographical area and representation in the House. It looked as though Miss Dix's labors of fourteen years were about to culminate in the creation of an endowment that would forever safeguard and provide for the indigent insane.

The bill passed the Senate on March 9, 1854, by a large majority. Miss Dix dashed off a note to tell the good news to Ann.

Washington City, March 9

My dear Annie:

Yours received this morning just when I was putting pen to paper to tell you that my Bill has passed the Senate by more than two-thirds majority. Had every senator been present the vote would have been maintained exactly the same. It is now before the House and Congratulations flow in. I in my heart think the very opponents are glad. And as I rejoice quietly and silently, I feel it is *The Lord who has made my mountain to stand strong.* . . . As for myself longing now and then for rest and truly, it is pleasant to think of the time when labor will not be associated with pain and weariness.[36]

Word came that the House had passed her bill. Her heart filled with thanksgiving, and a jargon of holy thoughts ran through her mind. "I have lifted up my eyes." "My cup runneth over." "The Lord doth build up Jerusalem." Never in all her life had she known such exquisite happiness, exaltation, peace. Esther had redeemed her people. The summit had been reached. Plaudits and congratulations poured in. Dr. Kirkbride, with whom she had planned so many hospitals, wrote, "A thousand congratulations on the success of your noble and disinterested and persevering efforts! There is some virtue yet in Congress and a large hope for the Republic."[37] Ann Heath rejoiced that Dorothea's labors were over, and that there would be no more need of those long exhausting journeys, no more "explorations of the depths of human misery in remote and hidden places," no more "long and weary wrestling" with successive legislatures. Now perhaps she would return to New England. Luther Bell of McLean Hospital hoped that she would find time to write the story of her work for the insane. The Rathbones were inquiring if she would not be visiting the British Isles again.

For six years Dorothea Dix had been appealing to Congress to make provision for the indigent insane; at last a bill had been passed, and all that remained to make a perpetual endowment for the mentally ill a reality was the President's signature. Of that she had not the slightest doubt until one day a friend carried to her a rumor that President Pierce was beginning to question the constitutionality of eleemosynary grants outside the District of Columbia. Miss Dix was startled by this news. President Pierce had personally expressed his interest in the project; surely this was only an idle rumor. Time however confirmed it; President Pierce was considering vetoing the bill. To Miss Dix it seemed incredible that he should think of such a thing. Had not the bill twice before passed both the House and the Senate?[38]

As soon as news of the impending veto reached the press, Miss Dix began to receive letters of indignant sympathy. Ann Heath, fearful of the awful consequences of a veto, hastily dispatched a note to Dorothea bidding her to keep her courage up, and to remember that the President's veto was not final, and that it could be over-ruled by a two-thirds vote. Dr. Kirkbride declared that if Franklin Pierce vetoed the bill, he deserved to see the ghosts of insane people hovering around his bed at night for the rest of his life. Wrote Ann Heath:

There is a remedy. You are not in subjection to Franklin Pierce, the rather obscure New Hampshire man. The flavor of life he has not yet taken from you. . . . I am ashamed of Congress. At this distance they seem a lawless, vagabond set. Is Everett infected? Does he stand idly talking with the rest, and interrupting any general good that might be achieved?

It can not be true. Pierce would not veto a bill on the same day it passed. I shall (not) believe the telegraphic report until I hear from you.[39]

Dear, devoted Ann. Quietly back in Brookline all these years she had been sharing her friend's dream for the mentally ill. She too would feel the weight of this veto. Dorothea wrote to tell her that it had not come yet but that she expected it any day. She quite agreed with Ann concerning Franklin Pierce. "Poor weak man, it will be a bad day's work for him," she prophesied. "How he is to get out of the fetters this will (fasten) upon his freedom, I can not misgive. A storm impends which he little dreams of,—it will shape his very life.[40]

A week later Dorothea Dix assured her friend that the bill was not necessarily lost even if the veto fell upon it, but she feared the Senate could not pass it over the veto without a full house. Miss Dix was frantically interviewing congressmen, and pleading the cause of the mentally ill. Never before had she lived at such high tension; she scarcely took time for sleep or meals, to say nothing of a spring wardrobe for which the warm weather was beginning to create an imperative demand. Would Ann please see if last year's spring bonnet were worth whitening, pressing, and lining with light green silk. Silk tulle trimming around the face, a little green ribbon, or a bit of lace, Dorothea thought would look very well. "I really have not time to consider the subject," she wrote, "you will think for me, my dear."[41]

The veto came, accompanied by a statement of the President's objections. He declared he had been "compelled to resist the deep sympathies of his own heart in favor of the humane purposes sought to be accomplished" by the bill and to look to the larger issues involved. Congress, he said, had the authority to make grants to eleemosynary institutions within the District of Columbia but that it had transcended its power on two previous occasions in granting aid in Kentucky in 1826, and in Connecticut in 1819 for the indigent blind, and for the indigent deaf and dumb. These were unsafe precedents and were not to be followed. "If Congress have power to make provision for indigent insane *without the limits of this district,* it has the same power to provide for the indigent who are not insane and thus to transfer to the federal government the charge of *all the poor in all the States.* . . . The fountains of charity will be dried up at home, and the several States, instead of bestowing their own means on the social wants of their own people, may themselves become humble suppliants for the bounty of the federal government, reversing their true relation to this Union."[42]

The President's veto was protested. For twelve years Dorothea Dix had been rallying friends to the cause of the mentally ill. Pierce had scarcely affixed his veto when she began a program of action by which she hoped to win sufficient support in the two houses to overrule the veto. Her most powerful friends promised to lend their influence, but they would give her no encouragement. It was doubtful if a two-thirds majority could be secured. Members and press of the Democratic party which had not long before praised Miss Dix, now rallied to the position of the President and endorsed his action as evidence of rare constitutional insight and personal courage. An epidemic of scruples seemed to have suddenly attacked Congress. Miss Dix's friends made no effort to conceal their reaction to what they considered political subservience. William Darlington of Pennsylvania wrote:

My sympathies have been so long and so fervently enlisted in behalf of your great philanthropic enterprise—now so cruelly thwarted by the Executive—that I find it difficult to express my sentiments in reference to that procedure in terms of moderation. I have lost all patience with those narrow-souled, caviling demagogues who everlastingly plead the Constitution against every generous measure, and recklessly trample it under foot whenever it stands in the way of their selfish purposes and foregone conclusions. . . . Had the bill been permitted to become a law, no doubt it would have been pronounced and claimed by the despicable echoes of the presidential will and pleasure as one of the noblest acts of work more for being tired. I am not *naturally* very active and *never* do

The debate in the senate was long and bitter. The President was alternately praised and censured. Franklin Pierce as a "northern man with southern principles" had always been a strict constructionist; he always tried to divorce sentiment from legislation.

The refutation following his remarks on the veto were both pointed and caustic. Albert G. Brown, senator from Mississippi, said:

> I have a better opinion of the states than is here indicated. In my opinion "the fountains of their charity" are not more likely to be "dried up" by grants of land for the benefit of the insane than is their passion for learning to be extinguished by similar grants for school purposes; nor is a state more likely to become "an humble suppliant for the bounty of this government" when she receives a small quantity of land for the relief of suffering humanity than she is when she receives a larger quantity for internal improvements and other purposes. We have seen that grants of land for school purposes have not "dried up" the passion for learning, but have stimulated it, and caused it to flow in a steadier and broader stream.
>
> To my mind, this is the first land bill ever brought forward in the true spirit of the deeds of cession. It is the first bill that ever proposed to divide the lands among the states having in them a common interest, share, and share alike. . . . I am a new state man, and I am a just state man. And I now say to the new states, You have no right to take from the common fund for colleges, for schools, for railroads, for swamp drainage, and for other purposes, and for other special purposes of your own, and then say to your older sisters, You shall have no part for any purpose of yours. Can we receive for our schools and deny to the old states for their asylums? . . . Unless it shall be shown that it is unconstitutional to endow a lunatic asylum per se, it will follow that if you can give to an asylum in Alabama from the common fund, you may give an asylum in Delaware from the same fund.[44]

Senator Foot of Virginia could not agree with President Pierce on the point of constitutionality. He stated that there were on record one hundred acts in fifty years where grants of land had been made for education, fifty acts for internal improvements, twenty-five for state and county seats, and others to individuals and private corporations. In support of his argument he quoted from the Constitution. "Congress shall have power to dispose of and make all needful rules and regulations respecting the territory and other property belonging to the United States."[45]

William H. Seward of New York labeled the veto message as "desultory," "illogical," and "confused."[46] On the other hand R. M. T. Hunter of Virginia supported the President's position and maintained that the bill would involve an unwise extension of federal power and an incursion on the rights and privileges of states.

"Ours, sir," he said, "is no government of traditions. It takes none of its authority upon the vague title of precedents." He believed Pierce manifested true courage when he vetoed the bill.[47] C. C. Clay of Alabama opposed the bill because he did not feel Alabama would have a fair share in the distribution and "was grateful to the President for vindicating the true principles of the Constitution and upholding the rights of the states which are the bulwarks against centralism, and the safest guarantees of popular liberty."[48]

Thus ran the argument of the opposition. Cass of Michigan believed it unwise to pass the bill over the President's veto.[49] Senator Broadhead of Pennsylvania agreed with the President in resisting one of the great evils of the times—the tendency toward consolidation.[50]

Valiantly Miss Dix's friends tried to rally support to the bill. Senator Solomon Foot, in his second veto speech, went back of the Constitution to the western lands cession deeds as further evidence of the constitutionality of the hospital bill.

I am unable to perceive, that by any provision of the bill the federal government is made to dictate, or assume any control whatever in the affairs of the states. It in no manner interferes with or encroaches upon the political sovereignty of the states. . . . The bill simply proposes to place in the hands of the state for a specific object, a portion of the public lands, in order to aid them in the maintenance of an unfortunate class of persons who are a proper object of their care and support. The states are in no way relieved from their obligation. The federal government assumes no agency in any matter or duty which devolves upon the states. It does not assume to be the almoner of public charities.[51]

The senator was indignant. "Millions for speculation and monopoly, not one dollar for benevolence and humanity, is the practical maxim which rules in the high places of power in our day." With every nerve strained and taut Miss Dix awaited the outcome of the debate. On May 18 she had written:

The debates are sustained by my friends with great spirit and ability, and in this controversy I am waging with the President thus far I hold all advantage. The last vote against closing the debates, on my side 34, that of the administration 13, but I can not bribe or threaten.

I can not control so a final vote on the question may not give me two-thirds. I would certainly not exchange either mental, moral, or social state with the President. Poor man! I do not know when I may find myself at liberty to leave Washington.[52]

She longed to leave Washington, to get away from the petty quibblings and chicanery of politicians, and from the "weak vacillating executive" as she called Franklin Pierce. "The poor, poor President." How she wished she might go quietly away and shut herself off from the world with Ann for a month. Long talks with that calm, sweet soul would do much to refresh her tired spirits, renew her faith in mankind. No, thank God, all men were not like Franklin Pierce. "Poor, poor man." Pity rather than contempt was what he deserved.

March, April, May, June. Now it was July. Four long months these had been, from the raw, cold winds of March to the blistering heat of a Washington summer. "How much longer?" Dorothea asked herself.

On July 6, the vote was taken. Yeas 21, nays 26. In March the vote had been, "Yeas 25, nays 13." With trembling hand Miss Dix scanned the list, "For," "Against." Everett had not been present. Oh, so many absent. Where was Foot? Fish? Houston? Morton? Sumner? Yes, he had been there and voted to overrule. What! Rusk and Dodge of Iowa had changed sides! Her eyes blurred.

The land bill was irrevocably defeated.

CHAPTER VIII

THE PHILANTHROPIST ABROAD

AFTER THE President's veto, Miss Dix's first impulse was to leave Washington, to go away where she could forget her disappointment. On second thought, she decided she must not give way to her personal feelings; there was still work for her to do in Washington. The Government Hospital across the river was in the process of construction, and she had promised to go over further plans with Dr. Nichols. Miss Dix's physical strength was too far spent to permit additional strain. Medical friends became insistent that she take a real rest. Why not go to Europe? There at least they felt reasonably sure she would not be spending her days and nights preparing memorials, and urging upon parliaments the need of government aid for hospitals.

She was too weary to plan. As early as February 1854, Miss Dix had been invited to join Senator and Mrs. Dix and their son on a tour of Italy, but at that time she had not been inclined to go.[1] Now she realized she must get away from the scenes of the past two years. The suggestion of a trip to Europe had its redeeming features. She could visit her English friends, the Rathbones, and then resume the continental journey that her illness had interrupted twenty years before. After she had rested at Greenbank she could go on to the great cities of France, Austria, and Italy, and visit the asylums and hospitals there.

Of late years many of her medical friends had been studying in European hospitals and bringing back ideas to be applied to American institutions. Dr. Isaac Ray had gone to Europe in 1846 to survey hospitals before assuming management of the new Butler Hospital in Providence, Rhode Island. Dr. Pliny Earle, who had gone to Europe after graduation from the University of Pennsylvania in 1837, returned for further study in 1852. Dr. Earle was one of Miss Dix's most faithful correspondents, and one of the few trusted physicians to whom she went for advice and instruction regarding the insane. Until Dr. Earle's visit to Europe, except for a volume of Heinroth translated into French, little information had reached America about the research being carried on in the hospitals of Prussia, Austria, and the other German states. From these friends Miss Dix learned much of the hospitals of Schleswig, Vienna, and Prague, of the cottage asylums at Gheel in Belgium, and of the nursing schools of Pastor Fliedner at Kaiserwerth.[2] Would she not like to visit these places and see for herself since she had for years been advocating a system of training for hospital attendants?

She decided to go to England. She longed for the peace and restfulness of Greenbank, the great mansion with its wide verandas and broad acres. It would be pleasant to walk across the closely cropped grass down to the lake and watch the ducks. She would forget, if she could, the wrangling of congressmen and her disappointment over the veto; she would think only of the flowers that grew at the water's edge, and the beauty of friendships. What a wealth of them she now enjoyed.

It would be good to see William Rathbone and his wife again. She wondered if he would be so deeply immersed in politics as he had been before. She recalled his election as Mayor of Liverpool in 1837. His demands for political and religious reforms and his sarcastic tongue had made him unpopular at times; but what a genial host he was. He and his wife had made their home in Liverpool a general rendezvous for visitors who had "some especial opinion to propagate, or philanthropic scheme to advance." His grandchildren often remarked that "if the visitor happened to be obscure, or in bad health, or regarded with suspicion by the rest of the world as a heretic or faddist, his welcome was all the more sure."[3]

Miss Dix smiled at the motley succession of guests who had hovered about the pianoforte with the wreath of sweet peas around its maker's name, had read aloud in the parlors, conferred in the library, or taken tea on the veranda. William Roscoe, Henry Fothergill Chorley, and Robert Owen, socialistic founder of New Lanarck, came and went; among others were Lady Byron, Father Mayhew, the temperance reformer, Blanco White, the former Spanish priest and author of *Doblado's Letters,* and John Hamilton Thom, the Unitarian preacher who married the Rathbones' daughter. Audubon, the naturalist, the Channings, and Dr. Tuckerman's daughter from Boston were among the other Americans who spent considerable time at Greenbank.

Early in September 1854, Miss Dix secured passage on the "Arctic," bound for Liverpool. On the day of sailing an incident occurred which illustrates the veneration and affection in which she was held in her native country. When Miss Dix went to the office of the American Steam Packet Company to pay for her ticket the clerk instead of accepting her money gave her a receipt saying that the owners of the ship had instructed him to take no money from her, and that her passage was the gift of Mr. E. K. Collins, president of the steamship line. She acknowledged her gratitude with much emotion, and said with this sum she could carry into effect a plan which she had very much at heart.[4] For a long time she had been wanting to insure her life for the sum of $4,000 and to secure this sum, under the trusteeship of the governor of the state, to the institution at Trenton, her first-born child, as she so fondly designated the New Jersey Hospital for the Insane. The price of the passage returned by Mr. Collins would pay the first year's premium on the policy.[5]

On board the ship she found that she had still more for which to thank Mr. Collins. He had arranged that no one else should be assigned to her stateroom, thus in fact presenting her with two passages. Mr. Collins was on the deck when she arrived. She went forward at once to thank him but he silenced her. "The nation, madam, owes you a debt of gratitude it can never repay, and of which I, as an individual, am only too happy to be thus privileged to mark my sense."[6]

Miss Dix had made no definite plans for a European tour. On board the "Arctic" she wrote Ann:

I have not the slightest interest in going into France or even Italy. In contrast with the aim of my accustomed pursuits it seems the most trivial use of time. I should like to have some person take my place who would fancy it if I could receive in exchange a good amount of working strength.[7]

She found it impossible to change her rôle from that of a philanthropist to that of a tourist and sight-seer. She was annoyed because the roughness of the sea compelled her to pass the time "with such a measure of listlessness as afforded but few results which told for others' good. One incident she did relate to Ann. On Sunday night she observed several persons betting on the steamer's run. She waited until the bets were decided and then solicited the winner for the money to be placed in the captain's care for the "Home for the Children of Indigent Sailors" in New York. Since the passengers felt so free with their money in gambling, she hit upon another scheme for aiding this new philanthropy. That night she would ask each passenger for a donation to the Children's Home as a thank offering thus far on their voyage. She estimated that a hundred and fifty dollars, certainly one hundred, would be secured.[8]

At Liverpool, Miss Dix was met by her friends, the Rathbones, who took her at once to Greenbank. She promised that for a month she would do nothing but rest and renew old friendships, and take easy excursions into interesting parts of the country. In less than a fortnight, however, she was writing back to Boston.

I am still here with dear friends much occupied with charitable institutions and the meetings of the British Scientific Association. All this tires me sadly but I shall take things easier in a week. It is my purpose to go to Scotland to see the hospitals in ten days.[9]

In company with Dr. Hack Tuke she visited a number of the English hospitals. Many changes had come about in the twenty years that had passed. The Earl of Shaftesbury, Dr. Conolly, Dr. Charlesworth, and Dr. Hill had worked unceasingly to make life for the insane more livable. Shaftesbury had helped to sponsor every bill in behalf of the insane that had come up in Parliament since he had given his maiden speech in 1815. In 1842 he had assisted in the organization of the "Society for Improving the Condition of the Insane," and had become its first president. Its object was to interest physicians and to diffuse information concerning the nature and causes of mental diseases. Public meetings were held monthly and prize essay contests were held. A very good idea, thought Miss Dix. Dr. Tuke reviewed the strides that had been made in English institutions since his pious old grandfather had withdrawn his support from public charity and established York Retreat as a protest against restraint in the care of the mentally ill.

He had seen just such conditions in England as Miss Dix described as existing in Massachusetts when she began her work in the early forties. Not all of them were eradicated yet, but he hoped that they would be soon. "In Scotland, however. . . ." Dr. Tuke shook his head sadly. Things were very bad there. He thanked God that Bedlam and Colney Hatch were gone forever. He spoke of the Victoria Fund which had been established by Queen Victoria in 1849 to aid the restored poor on leaving Colney, and he glowed with pride as he told of recent legislation in England, and as he recounted the work of Hill, Conolly, and Charlesworth, and his own relatives, William Tuke, and good old Samuel Tuke who now lay dying at York. These were pioneers of the new day in the treatment of the insane. They were to England what Pinel and Esquirol had been to France.

Miss Dix's friends protested against the idea of an immediate journey into Scotland to investigate social conditions there; first she should see some of the beautiful parts of the British Isles before immersing herself in prisons and slums. For four weeks she toured Ireland; the insane hospitals and the workhouses there were well directed and she spent more time enjoying the beauties of nature than she ordinarily allowed herself.[10] . She loved the quiet peace of "cloud-canopied skies," the thatch-roofed and whitewashed cottages, and the smoke curling upward and mingling in the haze above. It was pleasant to stop and talk with some kerchiefed old woman at her spinning wheel, and buy a piece of lace for Ann or Abby. There was no hustle or bustle in Ireland; and despite its poverty she found a happy, even tenor. Nor were all her days spent in wayside cottages. In a letter to Mrs. Rathbone from Ballinsaloe, Ireland, she told of a visit to the castle of Lord Rosse, and of looking through his telescope, then the largest in the world.[11]

Miss Dix was delighted upon her return to Liverpool to receive word from Hugh Bell that the lifeboats which were repaired, had finally reached Sable Island. On October 26, the day after the arrival of the last and largest lifeboat (the "Reliance"), a large American merchant ship, the "Arcadia," bound from Antwerp to New York and carrying about 160 passengers had run aground on a sandbar off Sable Island in a dense fog about six o'clock in the evening. The sea was so heavy and the storm so violent that none of the island's boats could reach it. As soon as the report came in the next morning, a relief crew set out in the "Reliance" for the wreck. The ship lay two hundred yards off the beach, "head to the southward, settled deep in the sand, and listed seaward with her lee side under water, main and mizzen masts gone by the deck, and a tremendous sea running and sweeping over her bows." After contending with strong currents, high winds, and rolling sea the lifeboat finally got alongside the wreck and managed in six trips to bring ashore eighty persons, men, women, and children. Two other attempts were made to reach the vessel, but the cars and thole pins were broken by the force of the sea; an attempt to send a warp from the ship to the shore likewise failed because of the strength of the current. The following morning as soon as it was clear enough the "Reliance" was sent out again and by ten o'clock the crew and the remaining passengers were landed. Two days later the ship was broken into a thousand pieces and only a few boxes of the cargo were recovered. The Francis metallic lifeboat, "Reliance," had done what no other lifeboat at Sable Island had ever done.[12] Bell wrote Miss Dix:

> Your *Reliance* rode over the waves, as the sailors said, like a duck, and with her and two of your smaller boats, the *Samaritan* and the *Rescue,* the whole of the passengers were safely landed; poor things almost in a state of nudity, not being able to save anything from the ship. Will you not rejoice at this result of your bounty?[13]

With Bell's letter came others of congratulation and appreciation. From Castine, Maine, came a letter from a mother whose son, a member of the crew of the "Arcadia," had been saved through her instrumentality. Miss Dix took pride in the sturdy "Reliance," but more in Captain McKenna who manned her and in Captain Jordan and First Mate Collamore of the "Arcadia." She immediately called their heroic conduct to the attention of the Mariners' Royal Benevolent Society and asked that gold and silver medals be presented to them. Some months later she was to forward the medals from Switzerland to Captain McKenna, together with personal letter of her appreciation of their services.[14]

Miss Dix could not make up her mind to go on to Europe despite letters from American friends insisting that she spend some time in merely sightseeing on the continent. She wrote Ann to the effect that

> Few traveling parties would suit my tastes or habits, and I as little should suit theirs. In fact the institutions of England do interest me, both literary, scientific and humane, and in becoming familiar with them I shall acquire much to remember with pleasure and advantage during the year I propose to complete this side of the Atlantic.[15]

As on her visit in 1835, Dorothea Dix revelled in the intellectual and social contacts which Greenbank afforded. This time she enjoyed meeting the Rathbones' friends more than ever because her enriching experience of the past twenty years now enabled her to make a distinct contribution to the little groups of earnest souls that congregated in the library and discussed philosophy, literature, and philanthropy as they sipped their afternoon tea. About Miss Dix gathered like-minded humanitarians, William and Beason Rathbone, John Hamilton Thom and his wife, Hannah Mary. They talked of the changing Liverpool, the rising tide of industrialism, and the evils in the wake of the factory, the need of uniform hours and wages, the undesirability of child labor, and the miserable housing conditions in Leeds, Manchester, Birmingham, and Liverpool. Miss Dix told about the New England mills and the great flood of immigrants to America. They discussed abolition, the peace movement, woman's rights, the Oxford Movement in the Church of England, and the war in the Crimea. Florence Nightingale, friend of the Rathbones, was doing such splendid work there in the hospitals, and in enforcing sanitation in the British camps. Miss Dix noted the anxiety in families of soldiers and the serious consequences which were pressing additional demands on hospitals for mental diseases. She wrote, "There is little prospect of the soon coming of the Kingdom of Heaven on earth, and the peace which is of Christ and His doctrines." She was also distressed at the spiritual warfare being waged by the Romanists and Anglicans. To Miss Dix it seemed quite as intense as that being waged in the Crimea.[16]

As late as December 1854, she had not thought of going to the continent. In answer to Ann's suggestion that she visit the prisons of Italy, she replied,

I could not but smile at your idea of my visiting the prisons of Italy, an idea, certainly that you have the whole merit of suggesting, for it had not occurred to me for any purpose to penetrate into those places of so many bitter memories and horrible sufferings. What should I gain or would others gain by my passage through those dreary dungeons and under the Piombini? Where I do visit prisons, it is where I have before me a rational object and a clear purpose.[17]

Although Miss Dix went to Scotland originally for the purpose of observations and sightseeing, she remained to launch a crusade for reform. She was delighted with the people that she met socially in Edinburgh, but the condition of many of the public institutions detracted from the pleasure of her visit. Private hospitals for the mentally ill were badly in need of reform. In less than a fortnight she wrote American friends, "I am confident this move is to rest with me and that the sooner I address myself to this work of humanity the sooner will my conscience cease to suggest effort, or rebuke inaction."[18]

"It is true," she said, "I came here for pleasure but that is no reason why I should close my eyes to the condition of these most helpless of all God's creatures."[19]   Her English friends protested when she told them of her plans to survey the institutions of Scotland as she had done those of Massachusetts and other American states. It would do no good, they said. She would be regarded as an impertinent stranger; even Mrs. Rathbone, who had always been so sympathetic, tried to dissuade her. "Your prospects for future usefulness will be endangered." To which Miss Dix replied with deep feeling:

I am not so very ill, only very variable, and I assure you, do not work more for being tired. I am not *naturally* very active and *never do* anything there is a fair chance *other* people will take up. So, when you know I am busy, you may be sure it is leading the forlorn hope—which I conduct to a successful termination through a certain sort of obstinacy that some people make the blunder of calling zeal, and the yet greater blunder of having its first inciting cause in philanthropy. I have no particular love for my species at large, but own to an exhaustless fund of compassion.

It is pretty clear that I am *in* for a serious work in both England and Scotland. I do not see the *end* of this beginning, but everybody says, who speaks at all on this question, that if I go away the whole work will fall off. So I pursue what I so strangely commended.[20]

Miss Dix promptly enlisted the support of prominent persons, editors, and members of the nobility. Physicians welcomed her efforts to promulgate reform and to aid in a cause in which they had long been interested but had been unable to advance. Dr. Simpson in his earnestness, and forgetful that Miss Dix had come to Scotland primarily as a tourist not a philanthropist, unwittingly introduced her one day as "our timely arrived benefactor and reformer." Such a thought was far from Miss Dix's mind when she entered Scotland, and she quickly commissioned Dr. Traill to correct the impression. She knew that sooner or later opposition to the proposals of an outsider would arise and she wished to postpone the evil day as long as possible, but secure reform for Scotland's mentally ill she must. It was with her "a question of conscience, not a self-indulging and indulgent pursuit." "I have here at all events 'passed the Rubicon'," she wrote Mrs. Rathbone on February 20, 1855, "and retreat is not to be thought of."[21]

In broad outline, the history of the care and treatment of the mentally ill in Scotland varied little from that in other parts of the world previously considered. As late as the middle nineteenth century the mentally ill of Scotland were the victims of superstition and neglect. Dr. Hack Tuke, in his *History of the Insane in the British Isles,* asserted that "judging from the records of the past as given or brought to light by writers like Heron, Dalyell, and Dr. Mitchell, no country ever exceeded Scotland in the grossness of its superstition and the unhappy consequences which flowed from it."[22]

The first efforts to secure an institution for the mentally ill in Scotland were made in 1792. Dr. Duncan, President of the Royal College of Physicians of Edinburgh, proposed a plan for establishing a "lunatic asylum" in the vicinity of Edinburgh. Sufficient funds could not be obtained to start the project in a rational way and it had to be temporarily abandoned; however, in 1807 a royal charter was obtained, and in 1813 East House was opened. £2000 was appropriated from surfeited estates, and subscriptions were raised not only in the British Isles but in India, Ceylon, and the West Indies. The management of the hospital was wise and from the beginning attendants were taught something of the nature of mental diseases as well as modes of treatment.

A significant piece of legislation relative to the conduct of "insane asylums" in Scotland was enacted on June 7, 1815. It provided (1) that sheriffs should grant licenses for asylums, (2) that no person could keep an asylum without a license, (3) that license money should be converted into a fund to enforce the law, (4) that inspectors were to inspect asylums twice a year, (5) that sheriffs were to ascertain whether patients were properly confined, (6) that sheriffs should make an order for the reception of lunatics upon a statement signed by a physician, (7) that sheriffs should set at liberty persons improperly detained.[23] A bill proposed in 1818 by Lord Binney and Mr. Brogden and agitated by J. J. Gurney and his sister, Mrs. Elizabeth Fry, for the erection of district asylums in Scotland met with opposition on the grounds that it would be too costly, and at the same time might discourage private philanthropy. Until 1839 there was not a single hospital or retreat for the insane in Scotland south of Glasgow or Edinburgh except six squalid stone cells attached to the public asylum at Dumfries. The Dumfries Asylum had been established in 1839 as a memorial to Dr. Crichton by his widow. At the time of Miss Dix's visit it was a very progressive institution under the direction of Dr. W. A. F. Browne.[24]

Legislation in behalf of the indigent insane was first brought forward in 1848. Although there were several excellent private institutions for the mentally ill in Scotland, as yet no provision had been made for the insane poor. At this time a bill designed not only to regulate existing private institutions but to establish asylums for "pauper lunatics" was brought forward by Lord Advocate Rutherford, Sir George Grey, and the Secretary of War. The same old objections were raised; petitions came in from every shire, and the bill was withdrawn. This was the status of legislation for the indigent insane when Miss Dix visited Scotland in 1855.

Seven asylums had been erected in Scotland under royal charters. These so-called royal asylums were local philanthropic enterprises and were in no way subject to royal control nor did they receive government subsidy. No local taxes were raised to meet their construction; after completion they took in private patients who paid their own expenses or such pauper patients as were cared for by their parishes. There were also many privately owned institutions where both indigent and well-to-do patients received care. The poorhouses and prisons too had their share of mentally ill inmates. There simply was no central authority in the kingdom whose duty it was to exercise a general supervision over the mentally ill or their guardians.[25]

Despite the excellent legislation of 1815 providing for inspection, enforcement was lax. Miss Dix found all of the public institutions in the seven principal cities[26] to be "good, very good," but she also visited thirteen private institutions which were so badly managed that she felt that the "only hope for redress must come by personal effort."[27] The weather was very cold, and hundreds of poor patients were suffering. She discovered that eleven private establishments in Edinburgh had been granted licenses by the sheriff of Mid-Lothian without regard to the necessary qualifications. Ignorant people of the lowest character had been accepted upon their application to open houses for all classes of patients. "Her intrepid raid upon the dwellings where lunatics and idiots were stowed away, her visits to workhouses, and to some asylums where paupers were confined," said Dr. Tuke, "confirmed her worst misgivings and her revelations took many of the Scotch themselves by surprise."[28]

The patients at Musselburgh, six miles from Edinburgh, were so ill-ordered and the proprietors so irresponsible that Miss Dix took decisive steps and brought the matter to the attention of the Lord Prevost, the chief justices, Dr. Traill, and other influential citizens. According to the English law, no one would be admitted to these places without the consent of the proprietors except the sheriff who might bring a physician of the Medical College on his semi-annual visitation.[29] The medical inspections did not involve any direct supervision. By law the physicians were required to report any abuses if they existed, but their pecuniary interests counselled silence; thus the proprietors, bent on making money, had things their own way.[30]

When Miss Dix was denied admission at Musselburgh, she appealed to the sheriff of Mid-Lothian. He tried to joke with her, prevaricated, and was most unaccommodating. She had never tolerated such conduct from an officer in her own country and she refused to condone it in Scotland. She wrote to Mrs. Rathbone:

> The sheriff is a bad man, wholly despotic, and ridicules the entire idea of reform; the Procurator Fiscal is not like the sheriff, a dissipated man, but a member and elder of Dr. Guthrie's church . . . tied with red tape to the sheriff; the Lord Advocate is . . . a selfish man so that I have an odd sort of work on my hands. But ultimately good will result from this. I certainly hold myself much better occupied in doing this work than in strolling about Rome or Florence.[31]

She consulted the Justice, three physicians, Sir Robert Arbuthnot, Mr. MacKenzie, and several others. They reached the conclusion that there was nothing to do but to demand a commission of investigation of the Home Secretary in London, Sir George Grey. Then the question arose, "Who should go?" One was an invalid, the doctors could not leave their practices, and others had urgent business. Why could not Miss Dix herself go? The Lord Prevost was not too favorable toward the idea of an investigating committee.

It became clear to Miss Dix that if she wished this thing done she must go at once.

As soon as she learned that the Lord Prevost contemplated a trip to London, obviously to have the first word with the Home Secretary, she looked into her purse, counted time, and for a brief moment considered her health, for she had not been feeling well for several days. Her conscience, however, quickly pointed the way to duty, and wrapping some warm traveling garments about herself, she called a cab, and at a quarter past nine that evening she was seated in an express train direct for London, expecting to arrive there in twelve hours. She had taken time to telegraph Lord Shaftesbury, asking for an interview at three o'clock the next afternoon, and naming King's Cross Station as the point of her arrival.

Anthony Ashley Cooper, Seventh Earl of Shaftesbury, had been one of the prime movers in the agitation for reform in England and now Miss Dix sought his assistance in obtaining a commission to investigate conditions of the mentally ill in Scotland. In his preface to the two bills for the "Regulation of Lunatic Asylums and for the Better Care and Treatment of the Insane in England and Wales," he had said, "I wish that circumstances enabled me to extend the bills to Ireland and Scotland, for I believe that not in any country in Europe, nor in any part of America, is there any place in which pauper lunatics are in such a suffering and degraded state as those in her Majesty's Kingdom of Scotland."[32]

While Miss Dix was on her long journey to London that night, the Lord Prevost, unaware of her departure, was leisurely having his trunk packed prior to taking the day trip. At nine o'clock the next morning and just thirty minutes out of London, an accident occurred which delayed Miss Dix's train until eleven. There was not a minute to lose after she arrived. She had never been in London before and she did not know a single location. As she stepped from the royal mail carriage, a man came forward and asked if she were Miss Dix. He then announced himself as a messenger from Lord Shaftesbury, informing her that His Lordship would see her at three o'clock that afternoon at 19 Whitehall Place.

Miss Dix looked at her watch. It was then eleven o'clock. She did not have time to go to a hotel and dress for presentation. She took a cab and inquired the distance to Kensington where the Duke of Argyle resided. She learned that she could reach it in an hour.

Discreetly she pulled the curtains of the cab, threw off her traveling coat and exchanged it for a velvet one which she carried in her hand, folded on a fresh cashmere shawl, and concluded that she did not appear "so much amiss as one traveling so far might look."

Just as the clock struck twelve, the cab drew up in front of Argyle Lodge. Presently Miss Dix was conducted to the library where she found the Duke. She explained her mission. Would not His Grace give immediate sanction to the Home Secretary for a commission to investigate conditions of the insane in Scotland? A little later the matter was settled and the Duke agreed to call for Miss Dix at Whitehall Place and to go with her to Downing Street.

At half past two she appeared at Whitehall Place, and Lord Shaftesbury, who had anticipated her coming, had the Board in session. They talked the matter over and decided that no time should be lost in urging the "usually tardy" secretary to appoint a commission. The Duke of Argyle arrived and reported that Sir George Grey had been summoned to a council at Buckingham Palace. "You shall see him yourself," he said to Miss Dix, "but I shall see him at the palace and will state what you have said."

It was then four o'clock and being unable to accomplish any more that day, she sent for a cab and went directly to 38 Gloucester Square, where her banker, Mr. Morgan, lived. Late that evening she received a message from the Duke of Argyle saying that the Home Secretary doubted his authority to appoint a commission for Scotland and that the Lord Advocate must be consulted. Miss Dix did not wish this as she feared social and political interests would influence Lord Moncrieff's action. The next morning she again went to Argyle Lodge for another interview with the Duke. He reported that Sir George expressed a "willingness to comply but hesitated to act." Meanwhile Miss Dix conferred with the Earl of Shaftesbury and got forward some affairs respecting English hospitals.

On the following day the Duke of Argyle sent word that the Home Secretary had taken up the matter with the Lord Advocate in Edinburgh. Did this mean further procrastination and possible failure? Dorothea Dix made no pretense at interpreting English law, but she did know the frailties of human nature. She would take no chances on a decision from the Lord Advocate. She wanted action; Grey was the man to act. She took a carriage and drove to Downing Street to talk with Sir George himself. She hurried up the steps and hastily scribbled a request for a personal interview in the reception room of the Home Department. In a few minutes she was ushered up with some state, and presented to His Lordship, who received her courteously. She stated her object. Grey replied that he had already consulted the Chancellor and that he doubted the Secretary's power to issue warrants without the concurrence of the Lord Advocate.

Grey had telegraphed the Lord Advocate and he was expected to be in London on Monday. The Home Secretary graciously thanked Miss Dix for her efforts, and she in turn expressed appreciation for his early attention to the matter. She next approached Sir James Clark, personal physician to Queen Victoria. She laid before him the startling data that she had obtained and the plan which she had in mind for initiating reform. He heartily approved both the plan and method and promised to lend his influence wherever possible.

Monday came but the Lord Advocate had not arrived from Edinburgh. Tuesday, then Wednesday. On Thursday he arrived and sent a note to Miss Dix, making an appointment for the following day. She was apprehensive of the interview. Would the Lord Advocate quote verbose passages from English law? Would he regard her as an "American Invader" as Dr. Browne of Dumfries had done, or would he be sympathetic as she revealed conditions as she had seen them? The conference was a long one. In the end Miss Dix obtained from him a promise that a commission for the reform of all Scotland would be appointed.

In less than a fortnight, Dorothea Dix had entered London, unheralded and unannounced, had gone straight to the most important officials in the kingdom, laid before them the deplorable condition of Scotland's insane, and secured the appointment of two commissions, one of inquiry for the whole of Scotland, and the other, a special committee for investigating the abuses in Mid-Lothian. She wrote Mrs. Torrey on March 8, 1855:

> This assures, first, reports into the condition of all the insane in Scotland. Next the *entire* modification of the Lunacy laws, the *abrogation* of all *Private* establishments; the establishment of two or three new general hospitals.[33]

Miss Dix returned to Edinburgh to gather data to be submitted to the royal commission and to outline the survey which it should presently undertake. Her health was considerably impaired by her strenuous labors in London, and exposure brought on by a hurried visit to Westminster Abbey and St. Paul's on a cold, damp, wintry day, and as soon as her report was ready for the commissioners Miss Dix left Scotland and sought rest in the milder climate of England. Dr. Tuke would not hear of her staying alone in a hotel in London, and he brought her to his home at York Retreat. The order of commission was issued by Queen Victoria on April 9, 1855, and in less than a week after the appointments were confirmed, investigation of the insane of Scotland was begun.[34]

It was weeks before Miss Dix was able to be about again, but her mind was not inactive. As she lay in her room at York Retreat, she read reports of the commission's progress in Scotland and made plans for the future. While calling at Dr. Simpson's home in Edinburgh she had by accident met a lady from the south of England who asked her if she had ever visited the islands of Jersey and Guernsey. Miss Dix replied that she had not; whereupon the woman proceeded to tell her of the abuses to which the insane were subjected, and pleaded that she go there. A trip to the Channel Islands was impossible at that time, but she had not forgotten the incident.

One day not long after Miss Dix's return to York, Dr. Tuke came to her room with some pamphlets and inquired if she read French, saying, "Here is an interesting report from Dr. Van Leuven of Jersey." During the day she read the article telling of the work which a young Dutch physician had undertaken in behalf of the insane of Jersey. When the doctor returned that evening, Miss Dix said, "I see a movement is made in Jersey; if it has led to no result beside employing Dr. Van Leuven to visit and report on hospitals abroad, my going to Jersey would be quite a work of supererogation, for which I have, I assure you, no inclination. Do write to the doctor for information."[35]

Dr. Van Leuven was prompt to reply. All that Miss Dix had heard of the terrible conditions of the mentally ill in Jersey was true, and what was worse, the legislation recently passed affecting the insane in England and Scotland made the situation worse. The keepers of private institutions who could not qualify under the new and more stringent regulations now threatened to invade the islands and carry on their lucrative and nefarious business there.

Dr. Van Leuven welcomed support of his efforts to reform conditions in Jersey.

Island of Jersey
May 8, 1855

My dear Tuke,

I have your welcome letter and hasten to answer you about Miss Dix's visit. Strange to say, it was only last Saturday . . . that I had a proposal from Mr. Isaac Pothecary of Grove Place near Southampton (well known for its inhuman treatment and dealings in lunatics, . . .) asking if I would give him information and assistance in establishing a private asylum for the insane in Jersey—he could not go on in England since the commissioners [there] were so severe, the laws so stringent, and the formalities for the reception of patients so embarrassing—"to escape or avoid all this nonsense in England, he intended to transport not less than twenty private patients (of whom some paid £500 and more per annum) to Jersey, where even no license is required" and "he had come here to look out for two or more fit places for their reception." "I would then," so he writes, "have you visit my asylums twice a week, and be well paid."

I could not help, my dear Tuke, thinking of cattle and horses and slave-dealers, and of York asylums in 1816 and of Bethlem Hospital in 1852. What had I to do? Mr. Pothecary was decided about coming over with the poor patients next week. I could not check him. Ought I to withhold my assistance? Well, I thought, I do not assist the mercenary interests of Mr. Pothecary, but I may assist his unhappy patients. If I withdraw entirely, I leave the poor sufferers at the mercy of their *owner,* and of some of the many doctors in Jersey, who do everything for money.

So the matter stands in an island whose government does not care one bit for its own pauper insane, and much less for those imported from England. Could Miss Dix persuade the English government to admit *no* asylums in Jersey, Guernsey, or Wright, but under the same laws as exist in England? This would be the proper thing. If Miss Dix will come to Jersey, I will give her a hearty welcome that she may counterbalance the odious *Insanity Trade* now begun. Please communicate to Miss Dix my most respectful regards. And let me hear soon.

Yours very truly,
D. H. Van Leuven.[36]

"There, my friend, this must help me get well," she wrote Dr. Buttolph telling him of Dr. Van Leuven's proposal. As she sat in Lindley Murray's wheel chair in the garden of York Retreat, still very weak and feeble, she visualized the work that she would do for the poor "demented souls of Jersey." "Leads of Providence," she designated these calls of duty that came to her. "I shall see their chains off," she wrote Ann. "I shall take them into the green fields and show them the lovely little flowers and the blue sky, and they shall play with the lambs and listen to the song of the birds, ... This is no romance," she confided. "This will all be, if I get to the Channel Islands, Jersey and Guernsey, with God's blessing."[37]

Ann read this paragraph over again. Between the lines there was something that gave her comfort. Dorothea was not well but in her compassion for the neglected insane of the British Isles and in her zeal for reform, she had forgotten her grief over the defeat of the land bill. Dorothea was too noble to bear a grudge, Ann reflected, too generous to let disappointment interfere with her usefulness.

While at York there came to Miss Dix a note from William Rathbone, a note which she treasured to the end of her days. In her estimation the testimonials of twenty legislatures, the Congress of the United States, and the British Parliament could never supplant the approbation of her friends. Mr. Rathbone wrote from Greenbank on Sunday, July 8, 1855:

My dear Friend:

Not being inclined to sleep, I have thought that a quiet hour before breakfast could not be better employed than in saying, God bless my valued and loved friend and speed her successfully in her progress—so far as is consistent with the scheme of His inscrutable yet ever beneficent Providence. He has tried you in the success of what you have undertaken beyond what I (have) ever known, or, as far as my recollection serves me, have ever read of any other person, male or female—far beyond that of Howard, Father Mathew, Mrs. Chisholm, or Mrs. Fry. I speak now of the entirety of the success as much as of the extent, and it has not turned your head, or as I believe, led you to forget the source from which your strength has been derived.

In the most tender love, therefore, to a faithful and self-sacrificing minister to His designs, He may fit the burden to your strength, and not try you too far by allowing you to carry the *World* before you. That your head has not already been, as we say, turned by the magnitude and vast extent of your success, is, as much as the many other parts of your character, the subject of my respectful admiration. These thoughts have been suggested by the *check so far* you have met in your efforts to supply the wants of the insane in Newfoundland.

Your affectionate friend
W. Rathbone.[38]

It was the middle of July before Miss Dix was able to proceed to Jersey. The trip was typical of so many in her life. She left London late Friday, was detained off Guernsey by fog, barely escaped sunken rocks, and did not arrive at the Jersey pier until late Saturday afternoon. Sunday she rested, but early Monday morning she was on her way with Dr. Van Leuven to visit the hospital. There she saw forty insane in a horrible state, "naked, filthy, and attended by persons of ill character committed to this establishment for vice too gross to admit of their being at large."[39] After a careful inspection of the cells and yards Miss Dix took Sir George Grey's letter of introduction and drove to the Government House. She approached the Governor's mansion not as an "American Invader," dependent on her own resources but as one who had not only the approval of the Chancellor and the Home Secretary but the "prestige of parliamentary success." The Governor was not at home but Miss Dix left a note asking for an interview. She then went with Dr. Van Leuven to look at a possible site for a hospital— les Moraines, the escheated property of an insane woman who had died without heirs, and one from which the crown received a substantial annual rent. She approved the location if the property could be. obtained as a gift, and then proceeded to visit several mentally ill persons who were kept in private homes. "A very sad scene," she commented in her notes.

On Wednesday following, Miss Dix went with General Touzel to see the Governor. She told him of her objective and recounted her visits to the mentally ill of Jersey; she then told him of Mr. Pothecary's purpose in moving his establishment to Jersey. The Governor received the evidence which she presented, summoned the attorney-general, and promised to take up the matter. They next considered the plan for a hospital for Jersey. The Governor pledged his support but warned Miss Dix that she would have to fight her way with three dozen members of the local governing body—twelve rectors, twelve yeomen, and twelve constables.

The next few days were spent in surveying farms, visiting the mentally ill throughout the islands, interviewing members and appearing before various boards.[40] The officials of the island paid the usual deference to Miss Dix's suggestions. They quickly promised remedial action because they were jealous of their local autonomy and feared that if she reported the abuses she had seen their powers would be abridged. In a short time, Miss Dix had Mr. Pothecary in custody of the High Constable of Jersey, while the patients he had transported were placed under the protection of the law.[41] Meanwhile, she had selected a site for the hospital, La Maison de l'Esperance, that she hoped would be established, and was feverishly writing to Dr. Buttolph for "hints, plans, and specifications by return steamer . . . without cost." "I must push these people," she said, "or the building will not be finished till next century."[42]

True, it was 1868 before the hospital was completed, but Miss Dix had brought the islanders to a sense of duty. The good work was begun and when she returned to Greenbank, Dr. Tuke wrote, "You have good reason to be satisfied with the results already apparent, and with Dr. Leuven left on the spot, there is probably less danger of the thing being lost sight of. There will be nothing more needed, I believe, but keeping up a brisk fire."[43]

American friends were watching with unfailing interest reports of Miss Dix's humanitarian ventures which reached them from time to time. The Association of Medical Superintendents at their annual meeting in the summer of 1855 voted to invite her to "favor" them at their next meeting with an account of her observations and investigations abroad. This account would be read in private session and regarded as strictly confidential if that should be Miss Dix's wish. Dr. J. H. Nichols, Secretary, and Superintendent of the Government Hospital for the Insane, Washington, D. C. wrote:

Our association has never met without many grateful recognitions of your invaluable services, and though, at the last meeting you and ourselves were much more widely separated than ever before since we became an organized body, I can assure you that you never held a higher place in our respectful consideration. And while on the one hand we felt with much fraternal solicitude on account of your continued feebleness, it on the other afforded us the liveliest satisfaction to learn that our Mother Country men have received you with that eminent consideration and personal kindness which are so fully accorded to you everywhere at home.

We miss you from the country, and especially do those of us miss the great benefits of your personal encouragement and coöperation, who are the immediate masters of those "many mansions" of beneficence which owe their existence under Providence to the extraordinary success of your appeals to humanity in prosperity in favor of humanity in adversity. We pray for the renewal of your health and strength, and shall hail with gladness your return to the scene of your widest and most fruitful labors.[44]

Rest had been no more possible for Dorothea Dix in England than in America, after she had heard "the suffering cry aloud for relief." She had been ill five months out of the ten that she had been abroad, but in the five that she was convalescent she had visited dozens of hospitals, poorhouses, and private homes where insane were confined, secured a lunacy commission for Scotland and instituted reforms in the Channel Islands. At last she told Mrs. Rathbone, "I must turn a deaf ear to the cries and go beyond the reach of the sound of the many afflicted ones, till I have gathered up force to renew—should it please God that I work longer—the work whereunto I am called."[45]

The Rathbones were spending a couple of months in Switzerland and insisted that Miss Dix join them as their guest and see the Alps. She decided to accept their invitation, but ignored their suggestion that she should bring a maid with her. The visit to Switzerland proved to be a real vacation. There with the Rathbones, she closed her ears and eyes to suffering and for one brief holiday as she said "drank in the splendor of the Alps." For Dorothea Dix, mountains had an unfailing charm; she found a certain spiritual exaltation in beautiful scenery. She described to her friends in America, the "snow-clad peaks, mantled with their regal robes of pasture and forest, as a sublime cathedral anthem to God." No other place in all the world, she thought, could be so reassuring, so inspiring as "those glorious Alps." The wails of the insane did not penetrate those mountain fastnesses; one heard only the rush of water, the tinkle of cowbells, or the voices of the herders as they yodeled back and forth across the narrow valley.

Miss Dix was so much improved by her visit to Switzerland that she decided after accompanying Mr. and Mrs. Rathbone back to England, she would make a tour of the hospitals, prisons, and insane asylums of Europe, extending her journey as far as Turkey and perhaps making a long-desired trip to the Holy Land. She did not know when she would be able to visit Europe again, and it did not seem right to return to America without having personally seen what was being done for the mentally ill on the continent. The fact that she spoke only English and a little French did not deter her in any way from her proposed plans. "I will make myself understood in some way," she told her friends. "I will manage to see the things that I want to see."

France lay first in her path, and for three months she made excursions from Paris, as her health permitted, to Quilly, Rouen, St. Yon, Orleans, Nantes, and Tours. Paris with its historic associations was especially interesting to her. Here the movement for civil liberty had begun, and it was here that Philippe Pinel had applied the philosophy of the Revolution to the science of medicine and instituted a régime of non-restraint and humane discipline in the hospitals of Salpetiere and Bicetre, and released mental patients from the bondage of iron fetters. Marvelous strides had been made in medicine since that memorable day when Pinel, fresh from Gheel and the medical schools of Paris, had stricken the chains from the limbs of a madman and bade him respond to faith and kindness. By 1855 non-restraint was the rule of the better hospitals, and drugs were prescribed less and less in mental cases. Even the use of calomel and quinine was being more restricted. Careful diet, hydro- and occupational therapy were being substituted for drugs and restraint. Hundreds of hospitals, as Miss Dix learned, had not yet reached this high state, and thousands of mentally diseased persons did not enjoy hospital facilities. Nevertheless a good beginning had been made.

After consulting nine officials in turn and explaining her mission in detail to each, Miss Dix became the possessor of a full police and magisterial sanction under seal, which gave her permission to enter all of the prisons and hospitals of Paris without exception.[46] She found that all the charitable institutions in Paris, liberally supported as they were by the government, possessed "in a large measure great excellencies" but also two faults which she could not tolerate. The first was a general want of ventilation and the other was the experimental character of the treatment administered by the internes. In all these establishments, Sisters of Charity, Dominicans, and other religious orders worked side by side with other employees. Miss Dix admired some of the nuns for their gentle, altruistic mien, while she criticized others as being selfish, ignorant, and lacking in regard for their unfortunate patients.

Late in January 1856, she set out for southern Italy. The bad weather which she had experienced all fall in France seemed to follow her to Naples, which made visiting out-of-the-way places all the more slow and difficult. Thirteen days were spent in Naples. Miss Dix did nothing for the hospitals there; to her surprise she saw a better institution for the mentally ill in Naples than she was to find in all northern or southern Italy.

Traveling northward to Rome she was shocked at the conditions abounding in the shadow of the Vatican. One of the institutions was so terrible that she started immediately on the difficult task of securing reform. It mattered not to Dorothea Dix that she was a woman, a Protestant, and a foreigner unable to speak the language of the country. She had gotten along very well so far; she had suffered no more inconvenience traveling alone in Italy than in England or America, and she regretted that she had not come before. Without delay she would secure an audience with Pope Pius. Surely the Supreme Pontiff would not knowingly tolerate such cruelty as she had seen meted out to his afflicted subjects within the confines of the papal states. Miss Dix made the acquaintance of Cardinal Giacomo Antonelli, the Papal Secretary of State, and secured his enthusiastic approval of the project which she wished to present to His Holiness. Through his good offices she was granted an interview with the pope. Pius IX had an excellent command of English and Miss Dix had no trouble in making her mission known. As she afterwards remarked to a friend, "the pope was benignity itself." Once in his presence, she forgot the gulf that separates a Unitarian from a Catholic. Pius IX showed visible emotion as she portrayed the miseries to which the unfortunate insane of the Eternal City were subject, and promised to make a personal investigation of the hospitals in Rome and invited her to return for a second audience. The next day he drove unannounced to the asylum of which Miss Dix had told him and personally inspected the wards. When she came again to the Vatican, Pope Pius confessed his distress at the state of affairs which he himself had observed and thanked her, both as a woman and as a Protestant, for crossing the seas and calling his attention to the miseries of the mentally ill of his flock. "A modern Saint Theresa," he remarked to Cardinal Antonelli as she departed.

"And did thee really kneel down and kiss his hand?" asked a Quaker friend, upon her return to America. "Most certainly I did," she replied. "I revered him for his saintliness." Of the bureaucracy of the papal government she was less trustful. After fourteen days in Rome she proceeded north but not without promising some of the citizens and physicians that she would return in a couple of months if no action were taken. "I fear I may find it my duty to return to Rome in May," she remarked in a letter to Ann. "In that event I shall not, I suppose, be able to embark for the United States till late in the summer or in the autumn. You must expect me only when you learn I have taken passage for New York."[47]

Tales of the horrible suffering in the Turkish prisons and hospitals had come to Miss Dix. She wrote to Mrs. Torrey:

> You need not be much surprised to hear of me in Constantinople. . . . Till quite lately I have not had a thought of personally undertaking anything in that quarter; but recent political and social changes, joined with information had from Sir Charles and Lady Hamilton, recently returned from the East, have led me to believe that something might be commenced in the way of reform. . . . My work seems to me to be indicated by Providence, and I cannot conscientiously turn away from attempting, as far as possible, to alleviate miseries wherever I find them.[48]

The general hospital in Genoa, as those in other Italian cities, was very good, but the hospital for the insane was so bad that Miss Dix felt she must take steps toward securing its reorganization. She made an appointment with the chief doctor and the Protestant minister in an effort "to represent the importance of entire change for the patients." "I do not think it will do much good," she wrote Mrs. Rathbone, "but it is my duty to try. I shall appeal in writing to the king. Leave for Milan tomorrow." Later she added from Turin:

> My plans appear to be about as stable as spring breezes. After the meeting touching hospital affairs yesterday and which only served to establish my opinion of the melancholy defects of the institutions in question, I was invited to visit today the five prisons of Turin, and to join in my application for hospital reform some remonstrance against the pernicious arrangement of these establishments. I have not to convince officers of government alone, but to make stand against the *priests,* who interfere with everything that is done or to be done. I never felt anything more difficult than this work in Italy. In Rome I found government and the priestly office united, and the very shame of foreign and Protestant interposition quickened them to action or promise rather

than humanity; but in Florence, Genoa, and here it is a fact that changes are coming over the old rule, and one must wait a little where so much is doing, and to be done. I will now make no more plans for going or returning, so many things constantly occur to change or hinder my intentions.[49]

News from Constantinople continued to move her sympathy for the mental defectives of Turkey. Many innovations were taking place in Turkey and Miss Dix was hopeful that the hospitals would share in this advance of civilization. She recalled Dr. Earle's description of Timar-havé as a place of torment, when he had visited it in 1838. She "would love to do something for those demented souls, rend chains asunder and lead the poor hapless creatures out of the dungeons into the warm sunshine."

So busy had she been in Florence, Naples, Genoa, and Milan that she had scarcely had the leisure to visit the works of art which these cities afforded. "Yet I saw," she hastened to explain to Mrs. Rathbone, "a good deal considering the claims of the hospitals and the short time I spent in each place." The proposed reforms in Rome occupied much of her thought and correspondence. The appeal to the Pope had involved "care, patience, time, and negotiation." She was indignant to think that "6000 priests, 300 monks, 3000 nuns, and a spiritual sovereignty joined with temporal powers had not assured for the miserable insane a decent, much less intelligent, care."[50] Nor was her anxiety relieved when word reached her from one of the officers of state that land had been bought and architect's plans had been submitted. She had witnessed so many delays in her life and had seen brightest hopes resolved into disappointment through procrastination. "Now if these *are not carried out*," she wrote Dr. Buttolph, "I do *not return* to the United States but go to Rome and stay till they do that which is needed. . . . I have the idea of removing these mountains (of difficulty) and seeing if Protestant energy cannot work what Catholic powers fail to undertake."[51]

Not until she was given definite assurance that a tract of land near Villa Borghese had been purchased and that a special physician had been sent to Paris to study the organization and methods of the best hospitals did she make any plans. She then decided to go to Constantinople as fast as possible, making stops only at those cities which she felt it absolutely necessary to her survey of European prisons and hospitals or those that were ports of call en route. She carried with her no letters of introduction but was always fortunate in meeting some person who would give her the assistance which she desired. "You will not be more surprised than I am that I find traveling alone perfectly easy," she wrote American friends. "I get into all the hospitals and prisons I have time to see or strength to explore. I take no refusals, and yet I speak neither Italian, German, Greek, or Sclavonic."[52]

"Providence graciously protects me," she wrote the Rathbones from the Island of Corfu, "and I am in no respects thus far impeded in my great objects of seeing the prisons and hospitals."[53] It was all very indefinite, this journey of Miss Dix's. She scarcely knew from day to day what would be her next destination or how long she would stay in any locality. Constantinople was her principal objective and the bent of her spirits urged her on. As she approached the Near East and the theatre of war, she became grieved at the news of terrible slaughter, and the merciless ravages of death and plague. It was offset only by reports of the splendid effort of Florence Nightingale and her gallant English sisters to alleviate the miseries of the battlefield and hospital. If she could get a pass she wanted to go over to Scutari and observe the hospitals and the work being done by the British Sanitary Commission. By good fortune she met a physician attached to the suite of Archduke Maximilian, at Trieste, and he promised her entrance to all of the Austrian hospitals if she went on to Vienna.

On April 2, while waiting at Piraeus, Greece, for a steamer from the Peloponnesus, word came by a French boat that peace had been declared and that the Crimean War was at an end. "We give devout thanks that the hours of warfare are ended," she wrote her friends at Greenbank, "but how long it must be before the wounds which have been inflicted on our social and domestic happiness are healed or forgotten. . . . I feel that Miss Nightingale will have a great work still in the East. God bless her."[54]

The journey to Constantinople went through a part of the war zone. Despite the announcement of peace, all was in readiness for attack and throughout Greece there was an air of military expectancy. After crossing the isthmus, Miss Dix wished to visit Corinth, but the captain would not consent to her leaving the protection of a powerful guard of a hundred soldiers which surrounded the transport carriages. About three weeks before, a band of robbers had attacked the carriages and succeeded in carrying off all the luggage and money of which a large amount was being conveyed to pay the soldiers at Athens. In each carriage there now sat an armed soldier, while on either side in close file rode a bodyguard. Mounted soldiers galloped hither and thither, and hidden in the bushes at intervals were small groups of soldiers.[55]

Miss Dix reached Constantinople the second week in April, having made most of the landings en route. At Smyrna, she found a good English hospital for sailors, and also one for the Greek and for the Dutch. It was characteristic of Miss Dix to lose no time in starting on her hospital tours; she learned to find her way quickly about by noticing the flagstaffs before landing. Shortly upon her arrival in Constantinople, she set out for Scutari. At the wharf she approached two rowers in a caique and spoke but two words, "Hospital, Scutari." They nodded and half an hour later she was landed at the wharf of upper Scutari. After discharging the boatmen she inquired of an English sailor the way to the nurses' quarters. She hoped to meet Miss Nightingale who was then completing her own mission of mercy in the Near East. Miss Dix inquired for her at once, but to her disappointment was told that she had been at Balaklava for over a month, whither she had been called by a great deal of sickness among the English and French troops. Miss Dix then visited the chief hospitals, asking many questions regarding the organization and management, the commissary, the diet kitchen, laundry facilities, and water supply. She was pleased to find the hospitals, now filled chiefly with convalescents, in such excellent order.

In Constantinople Miss Dix visited all of the hospitals and prisons. Of these were a large number as each nationality, Armenian, Greek, Catholic Armenian, Slav, and Turkish, had its own hospital and prison. Dr. Cyrus Hamlin, President of Robert College, in whose home Miss Dix resided during her stay in Constantinople, secured for her admission to the great Greek hospital at Ballocli. She was politely treated in both the Greek and Armenian institutions and with the exception of "Bagnio," the Turkish penal prison, she gained access to every institution that she expressed a desire to visit. Although the general prison seemed to be very well regulated, she was not at all pleased with the management of the psychopathic departments of either the Greek or Armenian hospitals. The Turkish debtors' prison was filthy and badly in need of ventilation. Her severest criticism, however, was called forth by the English prison. Dr. Hayland, the physician, regarded her visit as an intrusion. This attitude she resented very much, and in the report which in every case she addressed to the heads of the institutions that she visited, in which she pointed out desirable changes, she expressed the caustic opinion that she had expected to find the English prison the best conducted institution in the city and had found it the worst.

She was greatly surprised as well as gratified to find in the Turkish quarter a very well directed psychopathic hospital. For years, said Dr. Hamlin, "[she] had read these high-wrought descriptions of expelling the devils of insanity by alternate tortures and generous treatment, and was prepared for anything."[56] Instead of dungeons, chains, and brutal treatment she found light, cleanliness, ventilation, order, clothing, careful diet, and intelligent physicians. Sulieman's Mosque and Hospital she declared was the very best in the city of Constantinople.

The director of the hospital was a native Turk from a wealthy and influential family. He had been educated in Paris. While a student, he had become interested in the new methods that were being employed in the famous French hospitals for mental diseases. He conceived the idea of returning to his native city and establishing a similar institution. As he studied the system, methods, and organization of the French hospitals, he was generously aided and encouraged by Parisian physicians. Upon his return to Constantinople he established the institution which Miss Dix now praised so highly, when she wrote:

The insane of Constantinople are in far better condition than those of Rome or Trieste, and in some respects better cared for than in Turin, Milan, or Ancona. All the patients were Turks, fifty-two men, twenty women, eighteen servants and attendants, three physicians, one resident director, and night watchmen. . . . The provisions for the comfort and pleasure of the patients, including music, quite astonished me. The superintendent proposes improvements. I had substantially little to suggest and nothing to urge.[57]

After three weeks in the Turkish capital[58] Miss Dix continued her journey, hoping to meet Miss Nightingale en route. Aboard the steamer, "Franz Joseph," on the Danube, bound for Pesth, May 1, 1856, she wrote Ann of her travels.

My dear Annie and Miss Greene:

I do not know when this letter may reach you, but I write on the chance it may survive the perils of indirect posts and direct but danger encompassed steamers. Look on a map and you may trace my route from Venice, whence I last wrote, to Trieste, Ancona, Molfetta, Brindisi, Corfu, Cephalonia, Zante, Patras, Missolonghi, Mycenae, Corinth, Piraeus, Athens, Syra, Tinos, Andros, Mytilene, Gallipoli, Marmora, Constantinople, Bosphorus, Varna, Sulina, mouth of the Danube, Galatz, Balaka, Assoria, whence the boat is bound up this grand river to Pesth and Vienna. . . .

I have the strong hope that I shall not need to return to Rome, for a letter from my banker there acquainted me that the Pope had listened to my remonstrance and intercession and restored Dr. Guildini to the charge of the hospital which augurs well for the residue of my petition, and the fulfillment of the distinct assurances I received before I left Rome. I have as far as at present practicable effected the objects of my visit to Constantinople but it has opened to me work for the future. So far as the Christian hospitals are concerned those the Mohammedans are better, to my surprise.

I do not see anything to hinder my embarking for the United States within three months. I am likely to be at Vienna two or three weeks, for the government had very courteously given me beforehand the entree of the prisons and hospitals, and if I do not see too much to mend, I may discover something to copy for application at home.

I find traveling here alone no more difficult than I should do in any part of America. My usual experience attends me. People are civil and obliging, who are treated civily. . . . I am the sole representative of England and America on the boat. There are besides, people of many tribes, and persons of far distant English possessions, affording a singular association of oriental costumes and occidental attire. As for speech Babel is illy illustrated. You will wonder that I give so meagre descriptions of persons and places, but if one is busy examining while pausing for a few days or hours in a city, there is little time for putting on paper in an interesting way details worth sending so far.

I have resisted the very great temptation of going to Palestine which I desired more than anything besides, because I could not afford the expense, though only twelve days from Jerusalem. All my life I have wished to visit the Holy City and the sacred places of Syria. As yet I have confined my journeys to those places where hospitals or the want of them have called me. I trust my observations may be applied to some good uses.[59]

Only fragmentary bits of Miss Dix's correspondence during the next three months is extant and it is with difficulty that the rest of the narrative of her journey on the continent may be reconstructed. The few letters to Ann Heath and Mrs. Rathbone deal largely with the state of her health, over which her friends were ever anxious, brief references to the beauties of the scenery, and her desire to be home again. She spent considerable time in Vienna, visiting hospitals and prisons, and was on the whole much impressed with what she saw. Maximilian Jacobi and other physicians had revolutionized the hospitals of Vienna during the past generation and had built up institutions that were to serve as models for others. While in Pesth and in Vienna, Miss Dix pressed the need of a new asylum in Dalmatia on the east coast of the Adriatic. It is not known how long she remained in Vienna, but events of subsequent years indicate that she stayed long enough to make many friends and valuable associations. On the margin of her Bible she wrote before a favorite passage the date, "May 18, 1856, Vienna." Later there is another entry, "July 4, 1856, Stockholm, Sweden." It was August first before she reached London. Meanwhile she had visited Russia, Sweden, Norway, Denmark, Holland, a part of Germany, Belgium, and France. She wrote from London, August 1, 1856:

I have been greatly blessed in all my travels. In Russia I saw much to approve and appreciate. As for the hospitals in St. Petersburg and at Moscow, I really had nothing to ask. Every comfort and all needed care were possessed, and much recreation secured—very little restraint was used.[60]

Miss Dix rested at Greenbank for a few days before sailing for America. There in the mansion that she had come to regard as her English home, she recounted for the Rathbones the story of the journey that had taken her through fourteen countries and into hundreds of institutions for the poor, afflicted, and criminal. What a long journey it had been, Paris, Naples, Rome, Florence, Trieste, Turin, Venice, Cyprus, Constantinople, Budapest, Vienna, Moscow, St. Petersburg, Christiana, Stockholm, Brussels, Amsterdam. "Will thee never rest?" asked a Quaker friend who had dropped in for the evening. "Will thee not retire upon thy return to America?"

Dorothea Dix only smiled. She liked to think that at fifty-four life for her had just begun. Two years abroad had erased from her mind all thoughts of weariness and disappointment. She was going back to America not to retire from her labors but to begin them anew. Across the fly-leaf of her Bible she had written Wordsworth's "Ode to Duty."

CHAPTER IX

ODE TO DUTY—AN INTERLUDE

IT WAS THE last of September 1856 before Miss Dix reached America. She always felt relieved when an ocean voyage was over. The "Arctic" on which she had crossed two years before had since gone down with several of her dear friends on board, and this made her more wary of the Atlantic. "I do not fear the sea," she had written Ann, "but I never for an hour forget the vicinity of the presence of danger, and in the event of accident the almost certain loss of life."[1] The voyage was smooth and uneventful, yet it was with grateful heart that she set foot upon her native soil once more. "I have been brought home safely for some good purpose."

Letter after letter awaited Miss Dix's arrival in New York. Some bore congratulations of friends upon her safe return and invitations to visit in their homes; hospital superintendents urged her to make inspections and to assist in legislative campaigns. Hospitals were overcrowded, extensions were necessary, larger appropriations must be made. "Can't you come for just a month and help us? Without your help we cannot possibly secure additional funds." "Must have another hospital in this state, how shall we proceed?" "Having difficulty with Board of Directors, need your advice." So much work lay ahead and here was a note from dear Annie, pleading with her to come to Boston for a few weeks at least. Miss Dix shook her head benignly. How different was this from her homecoming twenty years before! Then she had wondered where she could go, now she could not decide where to go first, to visit the hospital at Trenton, the new government hospital in Washington, or the prison at Sing Sing.

There was yet so much to be done for the hospitals. It was not sufficient to carry a bill through a state legislature, help draw up plans, select a site, supervise construction, and finally see the hospital completely staffed and in operation; difficulties between the staff and the public had to be ironed out and friends of the hospital had to be found among legislators and philanthropic persons, who would see that its interests were not neglected. Superintendents were constantly soliciting her assistance for one project or another. On her desk lay a dozen requests that it would be impossible to refuse.

Before a month had passed she had made out an elaborate schedule and was busily hurrying from hospital to hospital and from prison to prison. On December 26, she wrote Ann from New York:

I arrived safely and without accident on Monday night. Tuesday spent at Ward's, Randall's, and Blackwell's Islands, Wednesday up the Hudson to Sing Sing prison, on Thursday (today) High Bridge, to juvenile asylums and reformatories; tomorrow to Bloomingdale; Saturday, hospitals in the city, and Saturday evening to Trenton, New Jersey. Thus you see the progress of my doings. I now think I shall go to Philadelphia on Tuesday, on Wednesday make the purchases for the hospital at Harrisburg, on Thursday go to Harrisburg, a day's journey; see the patients Friday; return to Philadelphia Saturday, spend Sunday at the hospital; Monday, almshouses; Tuesday, Trenton; Wednesday set out for Buffalo, Geneva, Canandaigua, etc., to explain anew the miseries of their almshouses so if you do not hear from me, please do not consider yourself forgotten nor even unbeloved.[2]

Suddenly her plans were shifted and a week later she was writing to Ann from Toronto, Canada, whither she had been called to visit the poorhouses. Without thought of self she had rushed northward, where she believed her services to be of the most immediate value. Perhaps no other letter that Miss Dix ever wrote expresses quite so forcibly the depth of compassion which she had come to feel for the poor and unfortunate as one which she wrote to Ann Heath from Toronto, December 30, 1856.

It is truly sorrowful to find so much suffering through neglect, ignorance, and mismanagement, but I hope for better things at no distant time. The weather has been severe and stormy, but in proportion as my own discomfort has increased, my conviction of necessity of search into the wants of the friendless and afflicted has deepened. If I am cold, they, too are cold. If I am weary, they are distressed; if I am alone, they are abandoned.[3]

As the years went on, the more Dorothea Dix did for the sick and indigent, the more she saw to do; the more hospitals there were established, the more manifold their demands on her time and the more opportunities for service. No one could get to the root of a controversy so quickly, so quietly, and so fearlessly as she. Superintendents who were having difficulty with boards of trustees or among their personnel frequently sent for her to help them solve their problems.   Experience and common sense soon taught her that no institution could so quickly become the object of scandal and malicious gossip as a hospital for mental diseases, and none could be so quickly wrecked by political avarice.   How well she knew the part that diseased imaginations of patients and criminal motives of discharged attendants played in bringing accusations against the most conscientious and honorable of superintendents. How often in model institutions had she not been approached by apparently rational persons who tearfully told lurid and gruesome tales of how unfairly they were confined by designing relatives and conspiring physicians and how brutally they were treated, often displaying self-inflicted bruises as evidence against heartless attendants.   There were men who believed they were being slowly poisoned by jealous nurses, and women who imagined their chastity had been violated by physicians or employees.   It was sordid and heart-rending at best to visit one of these institutions with its myriads of reincarnated Cromwells, Wesleys, Virgin Marys, Cleopatras, and Napoleons, but let one of them gain the sympathetic ear of a few outsiders ignorant of the nature of the disease and the true conditions in the hospital, and a great furore would result.   Letters would be deluged upon Miss Dix and the board of trustees.   Local newspapers, often without investigating the source, would publish sensational reports which had not the slightest foundation of truth.

Miss Dix had learned never to place any weight upon the testimony unless it was supported by careful and impartial investigation. In her long career she saw many a conscientious superintendent lose his position and the hospital a splendid executive, because of the distorted imagination of patients and the wagging of a few evil tongues.

She disliked being dragged into institutional quarrels and local politics, and had an abomination for publicity, but her sense of duty compelled her to rise to the defense of persons unjustly accused even though it brought her distress and grief.   Once in a conflict of authority between the matron and the steward in the hospital at Worcester, Miss Dix, called in to adjudicate matters, took a very decided stand.   Not satisfied with her decision, the disputants took their controversy outside to the press where her sense of justice was strongly maligned. Ann Heath, who always read the newspapers and searched the columns for references to her distinguished friend, was genuinely perturbed. It was outrageous that any one would say such terrible things about so generous and self-sacrificing a person as Dorothea Dix. She would write her at once and tell her that she for one did not believe the statements true. In reply, Dorothea wrote:

> My dear Annie, do not take too much to heart that which people say in Worcester; it is as the weight of a feather to me. I am *right,* what harm can these do me? The Lord is the strength of my life, whom shall I fear; the Lord is my defense on my right hand, of whom shall I be afraid? I am steadfast in His might.[4]

It was this abiding conviction that she was right and that God would prosper her that had carried her through her labors of the past seventeen years. "My God will not forsake me now," she had repeated in hours of stress and anguish. "Right shall triumph in the end, I cannot fail."

Never did Miss Dix become so absorbed in local affairs that she lost sight of the larger sense of human relationships. The European tour had enlarged her vision of service. She watched eagerly for news from abroad, progress being made on the hospital in Rome, and by the Scotch Lunacy Commission. She was glad now that she had gone on with her inspection of European hospitals; how selfish it would have been to have confined her travels to sightseeing. The Scotch Lunacy Commission alone was worth the trip to Europe. It was interesting to see how the work of the Royal Commission confirmed her own investigation. Its recommendations were most encouraging. "We must have no Colney Hatches in Scotland, huge, overgrown, unmanageable establishments whose interior reveals the gloom and monotony of a prison."[5]

A list of suggested improvements followed. A new day was at hand for the insane of Scotland. She was happy to have had a part in it. Among her papers she treasured a bon voyage letter sent to her by Hack Tuke just before she sailed from Liverpool:

> York, England, September 14, 1856
>
> My dear friend: I have pretty much given up the pleasing illusion of seeing you before sailing . . . I am inclined to envy you the feelings which you must have in the retrospect of what you have been enabled to do since you set foot on British land. I cannot doubt that the day will come

when many, very many, will rise up to call you Blessed. Blessed to them, who, until they have been relieved from their bodily infirmities, cannot thank you for all you have done, and the yet more you have longed to be able to do, for them.

Your truly attached friend,
Daniel H. Tuke.[6]

Close beside it was another letter from Dr. John Conolly, expressing his appreciation of her approval of the work he was doing at Hanwell. "God bless you, my dear lady," he had written, "I honor you and your great labors for the benefit of your fellow creatures in many ways."[7]

These English friendships meant so much—the Rathbones, the Conollys, the Tukes. Five years later when the nation was submerged in civil war and she herself was engaged in ameliorating distress on the battlefield, memories and letters from these "dear ones abroad" alone lifted up her spirits and dispelled the gloom which engulfed her soul. "Your thoughtful care for my gratification in planning that pleasant journey to the Continent has enriched my life for all time," she wrote to her friends at Greenbank in 1862. "I never find the glorious views of the Alps fade from my mind's eye. A thousand incidents recall the memory of those great snow peaks piercing the skies."[8]

The year 1857 was a busy one for Miss Dix. Inspection of hospitals, prisons, and poorhouses, and reports kept her, as she said, swinging like a pendulum back and forth between capitals. A letter begun in Cleveland was apt to be finished in Trenton, or Baltimore, or Washington. Maryland had that year voted an additional appropriation for the insane and the new government hospital in Washington was being put into operation. The hospital for the Insane of the Army and Navy in Washington, D. C., was one for which she was to develop a peculiar affection and for many years it was to be one of her several homes. Letters addressed to Box 27, Washington, were always sure to reach her. With the Nichols and the Goddings of Washington, she was quite as much at home as with the Buttolphs, the Rathbones, the Heaths, and the Emersons. The large northwest room on the third floor of the Center Building was always ready for her. There she was sure to find hooks and eyes, bits of tape, thread, scraps, clippings, and her bottle of smelling salts just as she had left them in the big cabinet with its dozen of carefully labelled drawers. It was pleasant to look across the Potomac and see the great dome of the Capitol rising above the city of Washington. "Not a better setting in all the world for a hospital," she proudly told Dr. Nichols upon her return from Europe.

Miss Dix and Dr. Nichols, who was to become the first medical superintendent of the new hospital, had been asked to make recommendations and to negotiate for the site. They were both greatly impressed with a beautiful estate situated at the junction of the Potomac and East Branch, and commanding a splendid view of the river and the city beyond. It was a fine sloping piece of ground with several good springs and many beautiful trees. "A park in itself," Dr. Nichols had declared the first time that they visited it. "This is the best site that can be found," Miss Dix had replied, "I will be satisfied with no other."

The tract at that time was owned by Thomas Blagden, who asked $40,000 for it and was reluctant to part with it at that price since it was his home and was much beloved by him and his wife and daughters. Congress had appropriated only $25,000 for the site and Mr. Blagden was unwilling to consider less than the price he had originally asked. For two weeks Dr. Nichols and Miss Dix drove about the vicinity of Washington examining farms in Maryland and Virginia but none suited quite so well as the St. Elizabeth tract which Mr. Blagden owned. Dr. Nichols tried in vain to make a proposition to Mr. Blagden. At last he gave up. "There is nothing more that can be done," he told Miss Dix. "We shall have to give the matter up; and it is the best site in the world for a hospital." "I am not ready to give it up," she replied, "I will see Mr. Blagden myself."

She secured an interview and went alone to Mr. Blagden. She told him of the thousands of unfortunate persons who would be affected by his decision, the peace and calm that this beautiful country place would bring to warped and broken minds, tired and broken bodies. Her plea was irresistible and at last Mr. Blagden consented to part with his home for $25,000, the figure which had been set by Congress. That night he wrote his acceptance. It now lay in the locked drawer beneath the first draft of the ill-fated memorial to Congress.

Washington, D. C., November 13, 1852

Dear Madam:

Since seeing you today, I have had no other opinion (and Mrs. B. also) than that I must not stand between you and the beloved farm, regarding you as I do, as the instrument in the hands of God to secure this very spot for the unfortunate whose best earthly friend you are, and believing sincerely that the Almighty's blessing will not rest on, nor abide with, those who may place obstacles in your way.

With Mrs. Blagden's and my own most friendly regards.

Very respectfully,

Your obedient servant,

Thomas Blagden.[9]

The next day when Dr. Nichols brought the papers Mr. Blagden began to feel the significance of his decision. He walked the floor and wrung his hands. "I don't want to part with it! It is dear to me and my family, but I won't break my word to Miss Dix—I told her that she should have it, and she shall have it."

"Surely he can never regret it now," said Miss Dix as she surveyed the grounds and buildings of the national hospital for the mentally ill of the army and navy. "What a majestic memorial all this is to his sacrifice."

To her mind there was no nobler philanthropy than that associated with hospitals. A letter to Mrs. Rathbone, from Zelienople, Pennsylvania, August, 1857, illustrates some of the methods which she used to secure funds for various projects.

Here at Zelienople I am both looking for a farm well situated and well watered, and studying an institution having chiefly the features of the celebrated Rauhe Haus at Horn near Hamburg. It is a new reformatory erected by a noble minded clergyman of the German Lutheran persuasion, one of those men of rare power, Fénelon-like spirit, and Apostolic self-sacrifice whom we occasionally see rising up to show the astonished world how much one man can do . . . without riches, save the riches of a sanctified spirit. . . . I proceed tomorrow to Economy, hoping to secure from the followers of that singular man, Rapp, the Suabian peasant who emigrated with his family to the United States more than fifty years ago, a contribution for hospital uses. . . . The large wealth accumulated by singular skill and industry before the death of their leader and founder, Rapp, is stored in secret and no doubt before many years will escheat to the Commonwealth. They have no

longer hopes or expectations. The prophetic declarations of their
Founder are falsified and now a handful remain where once their name
was "Legion." One seeks of them charities as conferring on their stag-
nant life a real benefit. Lately they gave $500 to the new hospital.[10]

In the years preceding the Civil War, Miss Dix kept an ear close
to the ground as she journeyed back and forth across the country.
East and west, north and south, strife was brewing. She was invited to meetings everywhere. Religious zealots, abolitionists, free
traders, political leaders of all stripes and colors were bidding for
her interest if not her support. Dorothea Dix had deep convictions
on social questions. She abominated slavery, like the Unitarian
and good New Englander that she was; but there was another
aspect to the question. She refused to take sides protesting that
surely in the mercy of Providence things would somehow work out
peacefully. After all, her mission was to the insane, the poor diseased minds north and south, and she could not afford to commit
herself. Save with her English friends and a few intimates she
rarely discussed politics in America, yet her letters to Mrs. Rathbone
during those years indicate the serious interest which she took in
the national welfare. Early in the spring of 1858, she wrote from
Conshohocken, Pennsylvania:

I have paused today from traveling to write letters and the first will
be for your reading. You will perhaps have remarked in the American
papers notices of spontaneous revivals in the religious world—the multi-
plication of social and public meetings for prayer and exhortation, a
movement including all classes, ages, and conditions likewise an impulse
pricking the conscience of the western world, north and south. I do
not see in this age evidence of a millenium. This is peculiarly the age
of impulse and we must esteem it happy for those whose impulses are
directed to good and not evil acts. I remark that nearly all forensic
speaking, popular lecturing, and legislative utterances are in the mass
declaratory and chiefly composed of appeals to the emotions and feelings
rather than set forth argumentatively and gravely as lessons embodying
sound doctrine. What are your views on this question?

I am coming to look with much composure on the public affairs of
the world—having ceased to look for peace, repose, political tranquility,
and harmony among the nations. I will not permit myself to be distressed at what I cannot help to an end. Some honest patriots I may live
to see command the issues of government but it is not probable.[11]

Another time she wrote:

> Our new President, Buchanan, has commenced his administration
> under favorable auspices with the most ill-considered acts—his cabinet
> appointments are confessedly little creditable or satisfactory even to the
> party which he represents—and ill augury attests some following pro-
> ceedings such as the appointment of Robert Walker to the government
> of lands. As for his ruse in bringing out the decision of the supreme
> court concerning the Dred Scott case, it is a total failure—and so far
> from satisfying any parties creates distrust in all.[12]

A year later she writes in an almost bitter vein. Mr. Buchanan
had greatly disappointed most of his political friends in the northern
states and fallen below the measure of ability generally accorded by
his political opponents.[13] Sectionalism was growing rampant and
civil strife lay in the offing. With almost maternal instinct Dorothea Dix hurried about looking after institutions, seeing that their
houses were in order and that the indigent and sick of mind were
being provided for.

January found her in upper New York with snow two feet deep
and the temperature below zero. In July she was in the middle
west. In that month, she wrote Ann Heath from Nashville:

> I do not know whether you have followed my devious journey, but
> if you look on the map for Philadelphia, Baltimore, Washington, Chesa-
> peake Bay, Norfolk, Williamsburg, York, Hampton, Portsmouth, Ral-
> eigh, N. C., Weldon, Petersburg, Richmond, Charlottesville, Trenton,
> Rockbridge, Central, Va., Salem, Abington, Bristol, Va., Dalton, Geor-
> gia, Chattanooga, and Nashville, Tennessee, you will follow my devious
> course.[14]

October found her in Boston. In March she went from Georgia to
Texas. Texas was then thought to be on the very outskirts of
civilization, the routes of transportation were difficult and primitive,
and Miss Dix's friends questioned the advisability of her making
such a trip. Again the tonic of opposition urged her on. There
were mentally diseased persons in the newer states as well as in the
older ones, and they needed to be looked after. Texas had abundant
resources in land with which to endow eleemosynary institutions;
some advance had already been made in this direction and she determined to see for herself how far-sighted and provident the legislators were with regard to the mentally ill. She wrote Ann:

My visit to Texas was called for. The people are generously disposed to do their duty toward the insane, the blind and deaf mute and they have appropriated 3,000,000 acres for educational purposes. Their schools are thriving, their churches increasing, their vast territory filling up with industrious people. The (lawless) still find hiding places there or stalk in public as elsewhere but Texas is not the Alsatia of the United States now as it once was but a great and soon to be influential state. Some of my journeys are perilous, all very fatiguing but kindness, good will, and welcome meet me everywhere when three thousand miles from New England.[15]

Miss Dix did not expect any one in Texas would know her but on the contrary people were constantly taking her by the hand and acknowledging her as a beloved friend in such a manner as to make a lasting impression on her mind and heart. Her eyes, she said, often filled with tears at the "homely, heart-warm welcome, the confidence, the cordial good will, and the succession of incidents" which proved how very much she dwelt in the hearts of her countrymen. "I am so astonished," she told Mrs. Hare, "that my wishes in regard to Institutions, my opinions touching organizations are considered definitive."[16] One of the state officials said, "You are a moral autocrat; you speak and your word is law."

One day while Miss Dix was eating her dinner at a small public house on a wide and lonely prairie, she observed the tavern-keeper standing with the stage list in his hand reading, and from time to time gazing critically in her direction. She thought this was because she was the only woman passenger, but when she took out her purse to pay for her meal as usual he protested, "No, no, by George! I don't take money from you; why I never thought I should see you and now you are in my house. You have been good to everybody for years and years. Make sure now there's a home for you in every house in Texas. Here, wife, this is Miss Dix. Shake hands and call the children."[17]

"Don't think me conceited in relating this incident," she said to Mrs. Torrey. "It is only one of a hundred in Texas, one of a thousand this winter all through the South. I am constantly surprised by spontaneous expressions of the heartiest good-will, and I may well be careful what I demand for hospitals etc., for my work is unquestioned, and so I try to be very prudent and watchful."[18]

In 1859, in addition to her journey to Texas, Miss Dix made an extensive trip through the South and up and down the Mississippi. That winter she asked more than a third of a million dollars from the legislatures in the different states.[19]

She was given a public ovation at Columbia, South Carolina, early in December. "I am very happy in knowing I am much beloved by my fellow citizens in this part of the Union," she wrote Ann. "We will prove our regard for you by our acts in behalf of those for whom you plead," promised a senator who spoke in behalf of that branch of the legislature. "Our state will always welcome you as to a home, and so will our firesides among the wives and children," said another. "Yes, yes! That we will," spontaneously responded others who were present. "Egotistical lines," she told Ann, "keep them to yourself." It was gratifying to this New England woman to be so graciously received in a land that was so rapidly developing a Yankee complex, a distrust of all things northern.

What was all this unrest and friction coming to, Miss Dix asked herself. Was there not danger that all this controversy over state's rights, tariff, and threats of secession might precipitate civil strife? Sometimes it made her heartsick, weary, and she wished that she might go away, back to England until all was peaceful and calm again.

But from England also came news that exacted its toll of pain from Miss Dix. She was distressed to hear how the private houses for the insane in England had been overlooked by the Lunacy Commission. She could neither excuse nor forgive them for their neglect:

They surely should know their duty, if they do not; but their dull eyes and sluggish, far-separated visitations have revealed something of the dreary horrors of those heathen receptacles sustained by a Christian people. . . . They are too indolent to exert the influence which their official station gives to remedy . . . what their criminal sufferance made them participants in maintaining.

Given that same authority herself, Dorothea Dix would not have "let one circling moon pass her changes" as she said, before she would have been again upon that field of labor, nor would time or money have been spared in the service.[20]

Another trip abroad, especially at the present time, was out of the question. Too many bills were pending, too many insane hospitals as well as other charities were demanding her attention at home. Mental diseases in America seemed to be increasing at an alarming rate.[21] So the story of the next two years of Miss Dix's life is still the record of social developments in the United States. Hospitals for the mentally ill always commanded her first attention. They were overcrowded and in some instances superintendents, overtaxed with details of administration and of securing appropriations from the legislature, had allowed unpardonable practices to enter into the care and treatment of their patients. Conditions at Blockley Asylum were very bad. Dr. Smith reported to the Medical Superintendents of American Institutions for the Insane in 1859 that the hospital was in a most unhealthy location for in the vicinity were offensive and pest-breeding water-closets, sinks, and sewers; that the water supply was deficient, heating and ventilation were bad; that rations were inadequate and that the institution was generally mismanaged.[22] The absence of epidemics, according to the report, was uniquely attributed to the hypothesis that "derangement of the mental faculties renders the system less vulnerable to the ordinary causes of diseases and death."[23]

A digest of the reports of asylums for the year 1859 indicated that the most important topic for the concern of the medical superintendents was the imperfect and insufficient provision for the care of the public patients in the several states. "This is so strikingly the case," commented the editor of the *American Journal of Insanity,* "that a stranger would be ready to conclude, upon a careful perusal of these documents, that the decent and humane care of the pauper insane is the exception rather than the rule throughout the land." Lack of enlightened sentiment rather than defects of any one system of charity was held to be responsible for the condition.

Miss Dix took up the situation of the Pennsylvania hospitals. She urged the legislature to make such reforms and appropriations as would relieve congestion in the Philadelphia hospital and other institutions. As a result of these efforts on the part of Miss Dix and the coöperation and assistance of men like Thomas Bakewell and John Harper, Dixmont Hospital was established.[24] In 1860 Miss Dix again appeared before the Pennsylvania legislature and solicited aid for the insane of the state. By April she was able to write Ann and ask her congratulations on being through with the legislature for that season and quite successfully. $55,000 was appropriated for the Western Hospital, $20,000 for the Old State Hospital, and $23,000 for the institution at Media.[25]

In addition to provision for the mentally ill, Miss Dix was now recommending special training for idiots and feeble-minded children. There were already several institutions giving this training in the United States, namely in Boston, Syracuse, and Columbus, Ohio. The work which Miss Dix observed in these schools and in those which she had visited in Europe convinced her that this class of defectives required special attention and that definite harm resulted when they were confined in the same institution with deranged persons and adults. She believed that feeble-minded children need not be helpless burdens on society for she declared that they could be taught trades. Institutions for their care might be made in part self-supporting, but she bitterly opposed their labor being exploited for profit. The sight of a roomful of these defective children being taught music, reading, arithmetic, and simple handicrafts always brought to mind her own schoolteaching days in Orange Court where the brightest boys and girls in Boston came to her for instruction. It gave her pleasure to see some child's face light up as she told a story, or passed out picture cards or toys that she had solicited from more fortunate children.

Meanwhile she continued to travel night and day. In November 1860, she learned that the hospital bill in South Carolina was at a standstill and likely to die for lack of agitation. She promptly closed up her business in Mississippi where she happened to be, and rode three days and nights without stopping. Within a month Miss Dix had secured the unanimous passage of a bill involving an appropriation of over $155,000.[26]

The same winter she secured an appropriation for the construction of a new hospital to be located at Knoxville, Tennessee, and an addition to the old one at Nashville. The year 1860 was a memorable one for Miss Dix and for the mentally ill. "Providence seems leading me on," she wrote Mrs. Rathbone, "and He, by whose mercy I am preserved, blesses all my labors for the afflicted."[27]

In Washington for Christmas, she became more alarmed than ever for the fate of the nation. "I can do little more than send you a line of remembrance from this city of present disloyalty and anarchy," she wrote Ann.

The public papers will give you an account of what is passing. We illustrate a national contagious frenzy; it is downright madness. I have never read anything in history of any people more extraordinary than that which is characterizing the people of the gulf states, but South Carolina in particular. Now, in the national capitol there one cannot discern that the government which has been, is not, stone dead. The poor vacillating weak president has no sincere admirers and few friends, the secretaries have with all faced dishonesty squandered on the South money, munitions of war and such helping to stimulate secession, as has no doubt quickened the insane proceeding of the Palmetto State. The treasury is clean swept but a desire is left and now yesterday loans were taken at 12, 15, and finally 30%. The country has been left to the rapacity of the low, the avaracious, and the traitorous; an example illustrating the fact that without religious education a people may plunge in a moment of hot-headed excitement to verge of ruin.

It is not possible to predict what the next three months may bring forth from the misty future but I am rather hopeful that the worst is past and that we may trust a reflex movement is about to turn the woes of loss and destruction back. The lessons people now are learning may be wholesome and permanently instructive but the Democratic party dies hard and in its frantic efforts to readjust the shaken fragments of its power is capable of real mischief. There is amidst the amazing change of the past few weeks a singular tranquility, little or no excitement, in fact the seat of government that was is all but a city of the dead, not literally a shrouded corpse but dead in action,—intellectual force of resources.

I shall be here for a few days longer and then proceed to Harrisburg. Trenton is always my post office address. While the public affairs are so greatly confused I shall not attempt to do anything in Illinois and Missouri so now I can tell you only that I await the coming revelations and results, so (do) others.

My love to your sisters, J. Green
Affectionately yours,
D. L. Dix.

A postscript follows: "Be of good cheer for sadness cannot heal the national wounds. . . ."[28]

In the South there were dire rumors of what would happen if Lincoln became president—the whole situation would collapse, the Union suddenly so dear to the North, particularly New England, would be dissolved. His election had been a defeat for southern sectionalism, his inauguration would seal the doom of the South, economically and politically. Defeat came hard; too much of American tradition had its roots below the Mason-Dixon line for the South to withdraw without a heartache. There had been a time when the Union was sacred to southerners, too; but now, so many other things hung in the balance. As state after state seceded, a panicky feeling ran throughout the country. People stood about in anxious groups, North and South. Fear gripped the strongest hearts in the South, prejudice against Lincoln mounted daily. His advent to the presidential office seemed like an evil portent. If only the inauguration might be stayed. Fanatic schemes of how tragedy might be averted were being evolved in dark and hidden places. Half-mad men plotted against the very life of the incoming president.

Of one of these grim and daring schemes Dorothea Dix heard in some mysterious way. It was said that an extensive, organized conspiracy aimed to seize Washington with its archives and records and then declare the Southern Confederacy the *de facto* government of the United States. At the same time all lines of communication between Washington and the north, east, and west were to be cut off, thus keeping troops from being brought to the defense of the city. If Lincoln's inauguration were not prevented in this way, his life would fall a sacrifice.

Miss Dix went at once to the office of Samuel Felton, president of the Philadelphia and Baltimore Railroad. Through her charitable work she had met Mr. Felton just as she had met hundreds of influential people throughout the nation. She asked for a private interview, saying that she had an important communication to deliver.[29] Mr. Felton listened attentively for more than an hour as Miss Dix put into tangible and reliable shape facts which he had already heard in numerous detached fashion. Troops, she said, were at the very moment drilling along the lines of the Baltimore and Philadelphia, the Washington and Annapolis, and other railroads. These men were being drilled to obey the commands of their leaders and those leaders had as their objective the city of Washington.

President Felton was so impressed that he immediately took steps to investigate; he hired detectives to enlist as volunteers among the squads of men secretly drilling along the right-of-way from Harrisburg and from Philadelphia to Baltimore and Washington.

They became familiar with certain plans and as a result, on that memorable night a few weeks later, Lincoln was safely smuggled into Washington. Miss Dix's rôle in saving the life of the president-elect may have been a minor one, but knowledge of the plot opened her mind to a world of seething possibilities and made her fearful of events to follow.[30]

Called back to Springfield, Illinois, by telegraph to save a bill, she hearkened once again to duty. She tried to forget affairs in the capital and plunged into her work for the mentally ill. A letter from St. Louis asked her to go to Jefferson City to look after bills there. "I thank God I have such full uses for time," she wrote Ann, "now that the state of our beloved country would crush my heart and life. I was never so unhappy but once before, and that grief was more selfish, perhaps, viz: when the 10,000,000 acre bill was killed by a base man in power."[31]

A few days later she was able to write to Ann, "All my bills have passed. My winter has been successful. I have had great cares, greater fatigues, countless blessings unmeasured, preserving mercies, and am joined to all occasions for thanksgiving, well, and still able to work very satisfactorily. God spare our distressed country."[32]

Those were anxious days in March 1861. Seven states had already seceded. A confederacy had been formed. The peace conferences of February had failed. There was a tense calm throughout the land—the lull before the storm, as the nation waited for the new administration to take up its work.

CHAPTER X

THE SUPERINTENDENT OF NURSES

SIX WEEKS later Miss Dix was resting at the home of Dr. and Mrs. Buttolph of the State Hospital at Trenton. It was not feasible to launch new projects when affairs of the country were so unsettled. All eyes were focused on Washington. Events followed thick and fast since Lincoln had taken his solemn oath on the east steps of the Capitol. With the firing of Fort Sumter the clash of arms was inevitable. Quickly there flashed across the wires the President's stirring call for 75,000 volunteers. "That means civil war," remarked Miss Dix as Dr. Buttolph read aloud the headlines from the daily paper. Flags were unfurled the next morning and the city of Trenton took on a martial air. The streets were full of carriages and people were hurrying about from one place to another. Groups stood on street corners and conversed in excited tones. Temporary recruiting headquarters were set up in vacant buildings, and by evening men were drilling—laborers, mechanics, business men, college boys and their professors. Troops must be sent at once to defend the nation's capital.

Miss Dix's native state, Massachusetts, quickly responded as did other northern states. President Lincoln issued the call for volunteers on Monday and by Thursday two regiments of Massachusetts troops, the Sixth and Eighth, were well on their way.

Meanwhile events transpired which augured ill for the safety of Washington. On Wednesday, April 17, the state convention of Virginia, by a vote of 103 to 46, resolved to submit the question of secession to the people. Secessionists in Baltimore had suddenly become active. If Maryland seceded, communication with the north and east would be seriously imperiled if not entirely cut off. Breathlessly the North waited to hear of the safe arrival of reinforcements in Washington, and to see what would be the next move of the secessionists. It did not have long to wait: On April 19, the anniversary of the Battle of Lexington, the Sixth Massachusetts Regiment, marching through the streets of Baltimore on the way to the Washington station, was attacked by a mob. Brisk fighting followed, in which a number on both sides were killed and several wounded. The main body of troops, however, managed to cross the city, boarded the train, and reached Washington that afternoon. News of the attack was immediately telegraphed, and in a couple of hours bulletins appeared on the streets and newsboys were crying that the Massachusetts soldiers had been attacked and that the first blood of a mighty civil war had been shed. Exaggerated accounts of the dead and wounded poured into Trenton. Hospitals were reported filled to their utmost capacity, and the dead and dying in the streets.

Dorothea Dix consulted no one: Here was a work for her to do. Inquiring of Dr. Buttolph when the next train left for Baltimore, she ordered a carriage, quickly gathered a few personal effects into her handbag, instructed Mrs. Buttolph to send the remainder to her later, and departed. Three hours after the riot in Baltimore Dorothea Dix was on the train en route to see that adequate provision be made for the wounded. She found crossing the city difficult but refused to turn back. By the time she reached the scene of the fighting, hospitals had been improvised and the wounded were being given medical attention. There being nothing further to do in Baltimore, she took the late afternoon train to Washington.[1]

There were rumors that the city might be attacked that night. It was reported that fifteen hundred men were gathered at Alexandria, seven miles from Washington, and that a vessel had been seen unloading men on the Maryland side of the Potomac. There were between four and five thousand men under arms in the city of Washington. The White House was turned into barracks. Jim Lane had that day marshaled his Kansas warriors at Willard's and placed them at the disposal of Major Hunter, who had assigned them to the East Room.[2] Washington, inert and colorless when last visited by Miss Dix, was now wide-awake, feverish, animated, and bristling with crisp sentinels who halted strangers. Everywhere could be heard the tramp, tramp of marching men and the rumble of moving vans.

Miss Dix went straight from the station to the War Department where she offered herself and some nurses to the surgeon-general for free service in caring for wounded soldiers. It was the sort of thing one would expect her to do. Late that night John G. Nicolay, one of President Lincoln's secretaries, wrote:

The organization of militia and the late arrivals of troops have been making things seem quite warlike for a few days past; but we have been much impressed with the conditions surrounding us by the arrival this evening of Miss Dix who comes to offer herself and an army of nurses to the government gratuitously for hospital service.[3]

John Hay, the other secretary, commented, "She makes the most munificent and generous offers."[4]   To Ann, Dorothea wrote briefly:

I think my duty lies near the military hospital for the present. This is not to be answered. I have reported myself and some nurses for free service at the war department and to the surgeon-general wherever we may be needed. I am preparing work, etc., so I can not write but this I think you ought to know.[5]

On April 23, Secretary of War Cameron accepted Miss Dix's gratuitous services to select nurses for the Union army, and on June 10 she was granted her commission as "Superintendent of United States Army Nurses," the first of its kind ever issued. The morning after her arrival in Washington, she set out to learn the status of the medical department and what were the facilities for military hospitals. She found the Medical Bureau in a deplorable condition; organized to care for an army of 10,000, it became pitifully inadequate when the forces were suddenly increased to 85,000; and it was to be still worse when additional enlistments brought the total up to half a million.

The medical corps of the United States Army on January 1, 1861, had consisted of one surgeon-general, thirty surgeons, and eighty-three assistant surgeons. Of this number three surgeons and twenty-one assistant surgeons were to resign and serve in the Confederate forces. Prior to the Civil War there were no general hospitals in the army. The military hospitals were all post hospitals. The largest of these, located at Fort Leavenworth, Kansas, had a capacity of only forty beds. Emergency hospitals would have to be set up in Washington and the vicinity, Georgetown, Alexandria, Baltimore, and Philadelphia.[6]   The surgeon-general, Dr. Lawson, was slowly dying at Roanoke, and the burden of meeting the increased demands upon the Medical Bureau, fell to Dr. R. C. Wood, acting surgeon-general. Dr. Satterlee, Medical Purveyor for the Army, was in New York purchasing supplies and Dr. Wood welcomed Miss Dix's offer to supply nurses. On April 23 he appealed to her for further aid.

Dear Madam:

I called to see you yesterday and also spoke to Mr. Cameron. A very large quantity of medical supplies has been ordered from New York and will ultimately come through. We are deficient in lint and bandages. I would most respectfully suggest that you institute preliminary measures for these important items of surgical necessity. I have the honor to be,

> Most respectfully
> Your obliging servant,
> R. C. Wood
> Acting Surgeon-General.[7]

The next day Dr. Wood wrote again, suggesting that she arrange for 500 hospital shirts to be made "long and of common cotton material."[8]

With her customary dispatch, Dorothea Dix began to prepare for emergencies which must soon arise. Soldiers, regulars and raw recruits, were daily streaming into Washington. Often they arrived at the capital after riding thirty-six hours in cattle cars, with little food or sleep. Sometimes they were compelled to stand on the streets from twelve to eighteen hours in the hot sun or drenching rain, while the colonel or quartermaster rushed frantically about trying to find out where or how a requisition for food could be obtained. Herded into insufficient and unsanitary quarters, there was increasing danger of epidemics.

No sooner had President Lincoln called for volunteers than groups of loyal women met and formed societies with vague ideas of contributing in some way to the relief of the soldiers. The response was spontaneous and widespread. That very afternoon of April 15, societies were organized in Charlestown, Massachusetts, and in Bridgeport, Connecticut. A few days later, women in Lowell, Massachusetts, proposed to "supply nurses for the sick and wounded and to bring them home when practicable, and to purchase clothing and other provisions not supplied by the government." They also planned to send books and papers to camp, to keep a record of each soldier, and to be in constant communication with the officers of each regiment in order that they might be kept informed of the condition of their friends. Before a week had passed, Boston schoolteachers had formed a unit to sew for soldiers, and students in the Girls High School and Normal School spent their spare time scraping lint from old linens to be used in hospital dressings. On April 19, a similar society was organized in Cleveland, Ohio. A few days later some prominent women of New York met at the Infirmary for Women to discuss tentative plans for a soldiers' aid society. To this meeting Rev. Dr. Henry Bellows and Dr. Elisha Harris were invited. Both were enthusiastic over the projected organization, and Rev. Dr. Bellows issued a call for a general meeting to be held at Cooper Institute on April 25. At this meeting the Women's Central Relief Association of New York was formed.[9] In this organization lay the genesis of the United States Sanitary Commission.[10]

Although the army did not at first look with favor upon these civilian organizations, Miss Dix was quick to avail herself of their services in the preparation of lint, bandages, and hospital garments. The *Boston Transcript* of May 4, carried the following news item under the heading, "What Women Can Do."

The ladies at Union Hall received an order for 5000 cotton shirts, for our troops at the South this week and in a few hours commenced delivering the goods, completed at the rate of 1000 a day. On Thursday Miss Dix made a requisition for 500 hospital shirts, and on Friday they were ready. And the women do all this not merely by converting Union Hall into a bee hive but by summoning to their help all the busy swarms every where around. Every church in the city lends a hand. All our sister churches in East Boston lend one with 500 needle-women detailed by the Catholic priest.

A pile of shirts came in from Bunker Hill, marked in indelible ink,

> The lowly bed
> The humble prayer
> Will gain the battle
> For God is there.[11]

Thousands of women all over the North volunteered not only havelocks,[12] bandages, and hospital garments, but offered to come to Washington and nurse the sick and wounded. At the time of the Civil War, there were still no "trained nurses" in the present sense of the term. There were women who had had hospital and practical nursing experience, but their numbers were limitd. Hospitals were still generally regarded as places of refuge for sick strangers or people who were without homes, and as isolation camps during time of pestilence. It was not until some time after the discovery of anesthetics and the advent of modern surgery that hospitals were patronized extensively by persons who could "afford to be ill at home," and there was no attempt to institute a curriculum or course of training for nurses in any American hospital before 1870.[13] Miss Dix was deluged with letters as soon as it became known that she would have charge of the employment of women nurses. Women of all ages offered their services; some were middle-aged with practical experience in caring for the sick in their own homes, others were sentimental young girls without the slightest knowledge of how to attend the sick, while still others were adventuresome women eager for change and excitement.

Although not a nurse herself and without definite hospital experience, Miss Dix had profited much by observation. She knew only too well that an army hospital was no place for a young girl or woman who did not possess good health, courage, and substantial character; hence in her bulletin on the qualifications for nurses, she spoke plainly and tersely! "No woman under thirty need apply to serve in the government hospitals. All nurses are required to be plain looking women. Their dresses must be brown or black, with no bows, no curls, no jewelry, and no hoop-skirts."

In *Our Army Nurses,* Mary Holland gave an interesting account of how she became an army nurse. She had read Miss Dix's circular carefully. It was very fashionable then to wear hoop-skirts and Miss Holland was loath to part with hers. She felt she could meet other requirements but that she could not walk without a hoop. Yet the urge of patriotism was too powerful, compelling. "Well, if I can't walk without it, I will crawl; for I must go and I will do the best I can." She wrote Miss Dix:

I am in possession of one of your circulars, and will comply with all your requirements. I am plain looking enough to suit you and old enough. I have no near relative in the war. I have never had a husband and I am not looking for one. Will you take me?[14]

The reply was, "Report at once to my house, corner of Fourteenth Street and New York Avenue, Washington."

Such rigid regulations were not destined to make Miss Dix popular with romantic young women, but that did not deter her. She was a woman who did her duty fearlessly; she commanded respect but she did not court popularity. Her inflexible standards were to bring her much grief before the war was over. In the end, she was to say, "This is not the work that I would have my work judged by."[15]

Miss Dix's own qualifications for the important work that lay before her were twenty years experience in public life, and a passion for efficiency and humanity. She was quite familiar with hospital administration. For years she had been an unofficial adviser to scores of hospitals, she had visited the military hospitals at Scutari and she was familiar with the work of the British Sanitary Commission during the Crimean War. She was a keen judge of character and was better acquainted with hospital organization than almost any other person in America. She was called hard-hearted because of her contempt for vanity, selfishness, and greed, and because she was inexorable in her decisions. The office of superintendent of women nurses was one which, by its very nature, had to be filled by a woman. There were many women in America who aspired to public service and who would willingly have served in this capacity had they been asked, but there were few who were so well prepared.

Dr. Elizabeth Blackwell, of New York, was an exception. Miss Blackwell was the first woman to graduate from an American medical school. She took graduate work in Paris, and while abroad became interested in nursing schools. She met Florence Nightingale in England and learned first hand of the work that she was doing in this field. In 1859, Miss Blackwell and her sister, Dr. Emily Blackwell, had incorporated and built the New York Infirmary for Women and Children in order to give opportunity to medical women who were hard pressed for clinical experience. Shortly before the outbreak of war in 1861, she had just returned from England where she had been discussing hospital plans with Miss Nightingale. She at once placed her services at the disposal of the Medical Bureau of the army and the Woman's Central Relief Association of New York. Her professional activities, however, had aroused considerable jealousy among medical men and she soon withdrew from all administrative circles rather be the cause of friction which might hinder war service. She did offer to give volunteer nurses a month's hospital training before they took up their work in military hospitals, and throughout the war she labored devotedly in the selection and instruction of candidates at Bellevue Hospital.

About a hundred of these hastily trained women entered the army hospitals, many of them remaining until the close of the war.[16]

More women volunteered to serve as army nurses than could be accepted, and soon strict orders had to be issued forbidding women from coming to Washington who did not have official permits. Many came because of their desire to be near relatives in the army; others came from the highest and most disinterested of motives; but there were also those who came from love of adventure. By the last of May, Miss Dix felt compelled to issue the following timely caution:

All persons are respectfully and earnestly requested not to send to army headquarters, or moving stations, women of any age in seach of employment, unless the need is announced by either letter or advertisement, there being no provision made by the government or otherwise for such persons. There are many who are anxious to join their friends who believe they will readily find remunerative employments. They arrive without means either of support or defraying return expenses, and so far from meeting fathers, brothers, or husbands may learn that their regiments are on the march to distant stations. The expense for providing these ill-counselled but well-intentioned and helpless persons in Washington falls inconveniently on individuals who are not willing to witness needless exposure or suffering.

D. L. Dix.

Washington, May 29, 1861.[17]

Seldom did one pick up a paper in the first months of the war but to read of two or three women stowaways with some regiment, bent on getting to the front and there doing service as nurses.[18] This created an additional problem for Miss Dix. There were wives who insisted on following husbands, and mothers who desired to be near their sons in case of injury or death, meanwhile ministering to other wounded soldiers. The war department was firm. No women were to be admitted beyond the lines. Women nurses were to be employed solely in the base hospitals. According to an order from Adjutant General Thomas, women nurses were not to reside in the camps nor to accompany any regiments on the march.[19] Women found in the camps without passes were promptly sent back to Washington. Although impatient with their indiscretions, Miss Dix tried to look after these women and to see that they were properly cared for in Washington and sent home as soon as possible.

In addition to selecting nurses, Acting Surgeon-General Wood asked that Miss Dix establish a receiving station for such hospital supplies, shirts, sheets, bandages, and lint, as might be sent in by the various aid societies and such gifts of special articles of diet, delicacies needed in individual cases as jelly, eggs, milk, chickens, canned fruit.[20] She took up her residence at 500 Twelfth Street between E and F, but before long these quarters were inadequate and she took over another house on H Street. Here Miss Dix, at her own expense and on her own responsibility, provided temporary quarters for newly recruited nurses and stranded women until they could be sent elsewhere. Here rest and refreshment for weary nurses and convalescent soldiers might be obtained without cost. Two secretaries were kept busy with correspondence, the filing of applications, and the distribution of circulars.

Washington was alive with excitement; no one knew when the hostilities would begin. Daily some move was expected on the part of the secessionists. Regiment after regiment might be seen marching up and down Pennsylvania Avenue. Flour suddenly jumped to $18.00 a barrel and housewives began to fear famine. Willard's Hotel, according to John Hay's diary, prepared for war by eliminating *cartes* from the menu and "the tea table was reduced to the severe simplicity of pound cake."[21] The lobby was as usual the center for rumors of all sorts. In and out of its doors passed civilians, soldiers, brokers, statesmen, politicians, officers in blue uniforms with scarlet lined capes and swords, and excited women in stiff crinolines and hoops. Mounted officers rode up and down the avenue, their horses' hoofs clattering over the stone paving. Workmen were busy putting up temporary barracks and hospitals.

By May 1, the East Street infirmary was ready for occupancy. In a short time the Union Hotel in Georgetown was opened. Dr. Howe of Boston, who visited the C Street infirmary the middle of May commented on the quiet, earnest, and business-like manner in which the Sisters of Charity went about their work of nursing. "The ladies of Washington," he reported, "visit the infirmary frequently and Miss Dix, who is the terror of all mere formalists, idlers, and evil-doers, goes there, as she goes everywhere, to prevent and remedy abuses and shortcomings."[22]

Clubs, warehouses, and lodge rooms were in a few weeks converted into hospitals or workrooms where patriotic women sewed from early morning until late at night, making uniforms and hospital garments, and scraping the lint which was then regarded as so necessary in dressing wounds. Before twelve months had passed nearly every church in Washington had been commandeered for one purpose or another. Temporary hospitals were also set up in the Capitol, in the Patent Office, in St. Elizabeth's Insane Asylum, and in private homes.[23]

Similar though not such extensive use was made of schools, warehouses, arsenals, and churches of other cities. There were few extemporarized hospitals north of Philadelphia. In Rochester and Buffalo, contracts were made by the government with local hospitals for fifty and seventy-five cents a day per bed. Mason Hospital was the only hospital established in Boston by the government during the war. In the western army, temporary hospitals were set up in schoolhouses, depots, warehouses, hotels, and cotton presses.

Dorothea Dix was responsible for the nurses in all these hospitals. As she viewed the matter, her duty did not stop with their appointment, she must also see that they did their work honorably and efficiently. She was willing to sacrifice every bit of energy that she possessed in the work that she had undertaken and she demanded as much of others as she did of herself. During the four years of the war she did not take a single day off from her work; although ill and confined to her room for some weeks in August 1861, she directed activities from her bedside. When well, she visited hospitals far and wide, inspecting wards, kitchens, sanitary facilities, and inquiring into the needs and wants of patients, carrying with her always an ample supply of reading material for convalescents, together with the jellies and other delicacies sent to her by private benevolence to be given to the very sick; she adjusted differences where nurses were concerned. She took long journeys from Washington both by land and by water. Through her years of travel she had learned to transact business quickly and to make the best of transportation facilities, and although she was often seen elsewhere, she was seldom missed from her office. Hospital business might take her one week-end to Baltimore, another to New York, and still another to St. Louis, but most of the time she was working in and about Washington. In the west, Miss Dix soon found it necessary to appoint special agents for the hospitals in that region; and for this purpose she named Mr. James E. Yeatman of St. Louis, and Mrs. D. P. Livermore, of Chicago. They detailed nurses who were sent to hospitals on the requisition of post surgeons.[24]

In these stirring times, Miss Dix had little time for private correspondence. Her letters to Ann Heath and to Mrs. Rathbone are in the main brief, usually involving some personal request as the making of a simple dress for street wear, or the purchase of waterproof alpaca, a kind of material not to be found in America—and one that was of great service in disagreeable weather. A letter to her friend, Miss Heath, written on Sunday evening, May 26, 1861, however gives an intimate glimpse into her activities during the early part of the war.

My dear Annie:

My life is so filled with crowding cares that I do not recollect what time passes between letters received or sent to my friends. I know certainly that I have written since I heard and that since I last wrote to Miss H. Guild to whom I am much indebted for a substantial . . . new dress exactly what I needed and which is finished precisely as I like, plain and substantial as well. I never had so few moments for myself. I went three or four days ago to the Relief House to see and arrange for some sick soldiers of the Massachusetts Sixth and Eighth, and while I was in Colonel Jones' tent your brother, Fred, came in looking much better than I ever saw him and truly I should imagine he has found his true calling. . . .

I have written to the Secretary of War for a pass to Fortress Monroe where a hospital must be organized. There is soon to be active service, I fear, and our brave men must be provided for if wounded. I have but one difficulty which is the chance of remaining longer than I desire, but it would be better to be there during the battle if there is one, since then we could do the most good. These are strange times and this war truly seems now not unreal. Our soldiers behave nobly. Do write. . . .

Your friend affectionate and truly whatever befalls.

D.[25]

Hurriedly constructed barracks with inadequate provision for bathing, laundry, and sewage, carried in their wake a train of vermin and disease. Lice, dysentery, measles, and malaria among the soldiers added to Miss Dix's anxiety. The sanitation of the army camps was deplorable. Dr. Elisha Harris, Rev. Mr. Henry Bellows, Dr. W. H. Van Buren, and Dr. Jacob Harsen, who had been sent down by the Women's Central Relief Association of New York to confer with President Lincoln and the Medical Bureau regarding the establishment of a Sanitary Commission, had pronounced conditions in the campus a reflection on modern civilization.[26]   Dr. Harris declared the whole aspect of the Medical Bureau as one of "dignified routine and Rip Van Winkle sleepiness."[27]

Apparently nothing could be done about the matter.   The Medical Bureau insisted that it was doing everything possible and protested against the "unnecessary intrusion of petticoats and preachers."   Even Miss Dix was beginning to get on the nerves of some of the surgeons, "prying and poking about," as they said, and "exceeding her authority."   President Lincoln listened attentively to the plea of the New York delegates that a commission be appointed to inquire thoroughly into the matter of diet, camp equipment, ambulance service, precaution against infection, the organization of military hospitals, and the routine through which the assistance of patriotic women might be made available as nurses; but he doubted the advisability of setting up what he feared might turn out to be a "fifth wheel to a coach—not only needless but embarrassing to the indispensible running gears."[28]

The delegates entreated the government to require more rigor in the inspection of volunteer troops, as they believed under the existing conditions many underaged and unsuitable persons, such as were likely to swell the bills of mortality, were encumbering the hospitals and embarrassing the columns.   They also stated the urgent need of better cooks and conveyed the offer of the Women's Relief Association to assume the duty of selecting cooks, instructing and registering them; and lastly reported that the Association was already selecting out of several thousand candidates one hundred women suited to become nurses in the general hospitals of the army.

The efforts of the delegates were not entirely fruitless.   Finally on May 22, Acting Surgeon-General Wood wrote the War Department of his approval of a sanitary commission which would serve as a committee of inquiry and advice.   Such an organization, he said, must not interfere with but must strengthen the existing organization of the Medical Department and its activities should be confined to the volunteer troops.   The following day the delegation presented a draft of powers which they wished to obtain from the government.   On June 9, Secretary Cameron issued an order for the commission and on June 13 it was approved by the President. Thus came into being the United States Sanitary Commission, which was to render invaluable service in the camps and on the battlefield, and to relieve Miss Dix of much stress and strain despite the fact that she often clashed with its agents and resented certain infringements on her authority. That she was not popular with the Sanitary officers is attested by the fact that none of the so-called official histories of the commission or the Medical Department of the Army devote much space, if any, to the work of Miss Dix as superintendent of nurses. Lengthy tributes were paid to heroic and picturesque volunteer nurses, such as "Mother" Bickerdyke, and Mrs. Annie Wittenmyer, but not a word for their self-sacrificing and untiring superior.[29]

A further view of the progress of events as it appears through the experience of Miss Dix proves revealing indeed. In the spring of 1861, the general consensus of opinion was that the war would not last long. Lincoln on April 15 had asked for only ninety day volunteers. Moreover, there was much confusion in the North as to the real cause of the war, so strong had been the preaching of abolitionists. Hawthorne voiced the sentiment of many when he wrote a friend, "We shall be better off without the South,—better and nobler than before." It was thought that after one or two hard battles the Confederates would be begging to come back into the union or that the North would decide to let them go in peace. As a result, the Medical Department was slow and cautious in its expenditures, and when the first clash of arms really came at Bull Run, on Sunday, July 21, it was sadly lacking in efficiency. This disastrous engagement confirmed the report of Dr. Harris and Mr. Olmstead of the Sanitary Commission when they had stated the weakness of both the military forces and the medical corps.[30] There was nothing in the army in 1861 which corresponds to the modern field hospital; each regiment had its own hospital consisting of three hospital tents, and certain medicines and surgical supplies.[31] Each regiment was allowed one surgeon and two assistant surgeons. There was no ambulance corps and the only detail for this duty was the drum corps.

After twelve hours fighting, the battle became a rout. The Union forces were panic-stricken; some of the soldiers never stopped running until they reached the Potomac. As news of the battle reached Washington, Miss Dix, her faithful corps of nurses and servants, agents of the Sanitary Commission, together with hundreds of public spirited citizens, redoubled their efforts to make places for the wounded. There was no sleep in the capital that night. Messengers galloped through the streets and wagons rumbled past with their loads of lumber and provisions. By morning a score more of warehouses, churches and lodge rooms were flying flags of yellow bunting, indicating that units of the general hospital had been established there, awaiting the wounded to be brought back from Virginia.[32] The word from the front was most distressing. Over 10 per cent of the federal troops had been either killed, captured, or wounded. An improvised hospital had been set up in Sudley Church in the vicinity of Bull Run, and 300 of the 1124 wounded had been taken there. The pews had been hurriedly torn out and the men were laid on piles of straw covered with blankets. Late that night the church, supplies, and medical staff were captured by the Confederates. All night long the doctors extracted bullets and performed amputations. The next morning a drizzling rain set in and the men who had been sweltering in the heat the day before now lay shivering on their blood-soaked pallets. Because of insufficient clothing, food, and stimulants, most of the cases proved fatal within twenty-four hours. The rain did not stop for three days and wounded men still lay drenched on the battlefield or in the bushes to which they had dragged themselves. When it was reported that there were still men on the battlefield at Bull Run, Medical Director King came out with a train of thirty-nine ambulances, but General McDowell could not get the consent of the Confederate authorities to remove the prisoners; the ambulances had to return to Washington empty.[33]

At news of the battle, Miss Dix had dispatched nurses to Alexandria. So urgent did she feel the need for nurses now that she asked but one question of volunteers, "Are you ready to work?"[34]

The North was horrified by the battle of Bull Run. When Miss Dix learned of the shortage of ambulances, she purchased one out of her own personal funds. In all her travels and surveys of prisons and asylums she had seen few sights more pathetic than those that greeted her as she went about her visits to the military hospitals, and few ever excited her righteous indignation more. McDowell's army slunk back into Washington, clad in the garments of dead soldiers: some had no coats, others had no shoes; none had complete uniforms; all were dirty and unshaven. They sat on the edge of the curbing, cooking their meals in discarded cans over fires made from boards wrenched from fences or wandered about begging food from house to house. Here and there one might be found lying full length in the gutter or crouched against a doorway half-asleep, dejected, hungry, sick. They were without leaders, the officers having gone to Willard's where an equally untidy and indifferent lot of men had congregated to talk over the battle.

Miss Dix shook her head woefully. In another week every available bed would have to be commandeered unless something were done to provide decent food and shelter for these men. On inquiry she learned that the War Department was short of tents, cooking equipment, and uniforms. Scurvy, dysentery, and fever threatened the well-being of the army. Together with the Sanitary Commission, she pleaded for a change in the soldiers' diet—more green vegetables and fruits, and less meat. To the many aid societies over the country she sent out appeals not only for hospital garments and bandages and rolls of old linen, but for jellies, jams, preserves, dried fruit, anything that would help prevent scurvy. Loyal was their response: Baltimore, Boston, New York, Cincinnati, Chicago, and thousands of smaller cities and villages sent in their full quotas of garments and old linen and preserved fruits. In Philadelphia, the Girard House was converted for the time being from a fashionable hotel into a workshop where from morning until night, weekdays and Sundays, one could hear the whir of sewing machines and the conversation of a hundred busy workers. Every woman who could use a needle found employment, and those who could afford to donate their services worked quite as incessantly.

The outbreak of hostilities increased Miss Dix's labors. Boxes of hospital supplies and canned fruit soon began to arrive at her door in great vans. With the battle of Bull Run, hospital accommodations at Alexandria had to be increased. Temporary hospitals were set up in private homes; among them were the Hallowell House on Washington Street, the Tibbs House previously known as the Belle Haven Institute, a female seminary, the Fowle and Johnson homes on Prince Street, the Methodist Church, two houses on Wolfe Street, the Grosvenor house on Washington Street; the Fairfax Theological Seminary was converted into a hospital for Kearney's division.[35] More nurses were employed and more calls for supplies had to be filled, but through the Sanitary Commission

Miss Dix was relieved of much of this responsibility. A number of aid societies which she had organized continued to send their donations of hospital garments, jellies, jams, and pickles, directly to her for distribution among the sick; and throughout the war she continued to maintain both the house on H Street and the one on the corner of Fourteenth and New York, and hired her own staff to assist in sorting and distributing the boxes that were daily addressed to her care.

Over the women nurses, Miss Dix kept as careful and maternal watch as her manifold duties permitted and much more than many of them desired. Her home was always open to them for rest and recreation in the few hours they were off duty, and when they were sick, she tried to see that they had special care. Women who came to her well recommended were given the most cordial welcome and gracious consideration, but for the romantic adventuresome women she had neither time nor patience. She took particular notice of Louisa May Alcott, the talented daughter of Bronson Alcott, the Boston schoolmaster, when she arrived in Washington, and in Miss Alcott's *Letters and Journals* there is a priceless picture of Miss D. L. Dix, Superintendent of Nurses.

Daily our Florence Nightingale climbed the steep stairs stealing a moment from her busy life, to watch over the stranger of whom she was as thoughtfully tender as any mother. Long may she wave.[36]

Miss Alcott spent six weeks nursing in the Union Hotel, Georgetown, before she became ill with pneumonia. Although she spent only a short time in hospital service, few nurses who kept records of their war time experiences left more vivid or sparkling accounts of an otherwise drab and sordid picture. Her first hospital experience began with a death, and owing to a defalcation of another nurse, she abruptly plunged into the superintendence of a ward of forty beds. "I spent my shining hours washing faces, serving rations, giving medicine, and sitting in a very hard chair, with pneumonia on one side, diphtheria on the other, two typhoids opposite and a dozen dilapidated patriots hopping, lying, and lounging about."[37]

Up at six, dress by gaslight, run through my ward and throw up the windows though the men grumble and shiver; but the air is bad enough to breed a pestilence; and as no notice is taken of our frequent appeals for better ventilation I must do what I can. Poke up the fire, add blankets, joke, coax, and command but continue to open doors and windows as if my life depended upon it. Mine does, and doubtless many another, for a more perfect pestilence box than this house I never saw—cold, damp, dirty, full of vile odors from wounds, kitchens, wash-rooms, and stables. No competent head, male or female, to right mat-ters, and a jumble of good, bad, and indifferent nurses, surgeons, and attendants to complicate the chaos still more.

After this unwelcome progress through my stifling ward, I go to breakfast with what appetite I may,—find the inevitable fried beef, salt butter, husky bread and washy coffee. . . .[38]

When Miss Alcott became ill, the matron, Mrs. Ropes, wired at once for Louisa's father; meanwhile Miss Dix came and insisted that the patient be removed to Willard's. Miss Alcott refused to be moved and not until after Mrs. Ropes had died of the same disease did she consent to go home. Before she left Miss Dix brought "a basket full of bottles of wine, tea, medicine, and cologne, besides a little blanket and pillow, a fan and a Testament." "She is a kind old soul," Louisa May wrote in her journal, "but very queer and arbitrary." Nevertheless, she had a deep and lasting affection for Miss Dix. In *Hospital Sketches,* published in 1863, Miss Alcott wrote:

Whatever others may think or say (of Miss Dix) Nurse Periwinkle is forever grateful, and among her relics of the Washington defeat, none is more valued than the little book which appeared on her pillow, one dreary day; for the "D. D." written on it means to her far more than Doctor of Divinity.[39]

Women nurses were employed at the rate of one to every two male nurses. Medical officers desiring women nurses appealed to Miss Dix, and no nurses were to be accepted at any army hospital "without her sanction and approval, except in cases of urgent need." Women nurses were under the control and direction of the medical officer in charge of the hospital to which they were assigned, and might be discharged by him if they proved incompetent, insubordi-nate, and otherwise unfit for their vocation, but no nurse was to be discharged without full particulars being given Miss Dix.

For their services at the outbreak of the war, women nurses re-ceived forty cents a day, their rations, quarters, and transportation,[40] while male nurses employed in the United States hospitals received $20.50 per month besides rations, clothing, and medical attendance.

Clothing was computed at $3.00 a month and $2.00 each month was retained and entered on the payroll as credit. Later the wages of both men and women nurses were slightly reduced.[41] The army regulations permitted one woman nurse to every ten beds in a general hospital, but it was seldom that a nurse did not have many more patients than the allotted quota which was later raised to thirty.[42]

Although it was the original plan of the Medical Bureau to restrict the 'employment of women nurses to base hospitals, it was not long before they were rushed on emergency to the temporary hospitals being set up back of the lines. On January 9, 1862, Assistant Surgeon J. R. Smith, at the order of the Surgeon-General, wrote to Miss Dix requesting that twenty nurses report to Assistant Surgeon Clinton Wagner at Point Lookout and thirty nurses to the Assistant Surgeon at Harrison's Landing.[43]

Despite the orders of the Surgeon-General and the Secretary of War, there were in service with the army many women whose names never appeared on Miss Dix's rolls. Following a battle, local women volunteered to care for the wounded, and proceeded without official sanction from Washington. Wives accompanying agents of the Sanitary Commission frequently did duty on the field, as did women employees and workers with the Christian Commission. At the very outset of the war the services of religious sisterhoods, such as the Sisters of Charity, Sisters of Mercy, and the Order of St. Vincent, were promptly placed at the disposal of the War Department, and the first hospitals at Washington and Georgetown availed themselves of their offer.[44] Many of the surgeons preferred nuns to volunteer nurses. Miss Dix, however, was not in sympathy with either the Catholic Church or the object of religious sisterhoods, and whenever possible she discriminated against their employment. Seldom did she approve the application of a Catholic woman to become a volunteer nurse if a Protestant could be substituted. Nevertheless, the Mother Superiors of these organizations offered their services directly to the medical director in charge, and in the pressure of the hour, which was frequently clouded with the smoke of battle and punctuated by the groans and cries of the wounded and dying, he was not only willing to override Miss Dix's authority but thanked God for the gentle dark-robed sisters who had come to his assistance. Numerous convents of the Sisters of

Mercy, Charity, St. Vincent, and other orders were converted into emergency hospitals and throughout the war invaluable service was rendered by the Catholic sisters. Especially distinguished for their labors were Mother Anthony O'Connell of Cincinnati, Mother Francis of Chicago, Mother Angela of Mound City, and Mother Gonzaga of Philadelphia.[45]   At Annapolis and Chester, important work was performed by the Holy Cross Sisters, an Anglican order.

At the time Dorothea Dix received her commission, there was no definite understanding of what her duties should consist. In addition to selecting nurses, she was soon called upon, by virtue of her experience, to assist in the matter of hospital supplies and equipment, and to give advice in so many quarters that her office took on new and, as one of the surgeons remarked, "undreamed of" proportions.   For twenty years, she had been inspecting hospitals, pointing out mistakes, and remedying abuses, and it came to her as second nature to ferret out inefficient management, carelessness in attendants, shirking and indifferent physicians.   She was now past sixty years of age and it was hard to alter habits of a lifetime. She found it difficult to realize that no system organized overnight, as the army hospitals had been, could be perfect, and that it was not easy always to find the same high type of surgeon in the army that she had known in Dr. Hayward, Dr. Woodward, her grandfather Dix, and her Uncle Henry Elijah Dix who had sacrificed his life as an army physician during an epidemic at Norfolk thirty years before.

Nothing infuriated Miss Dix so much as to find a doctor intoxicated on duty; it was bad enough any time, but on duty it was inexcusable, unforgivable, criminal, and not to be tolerated.   There was but one cure for such practice—dishonorable discharge. Straight to the Surgeon-General she would report the facts, demanding an immediate hearing.   Miss Dix had little native tact, and when she became incensed over the conduct of some of the surgeons and nurses, her wrath knew no bounds.   She showed lapses of the qualities she had striven so hard to attain; the soft voice that had calmed the maniac and sick became shrill, sharp, caustic; and she revealed blunt, domineering, and dogmatic tendencies of which under normal conditions no one would have been more ashamed than she.

Army physicians had always had liquor, and they resented any attempt to be reformed along the Puritan total abstinence lines that Miss Dix and the Christian Commission so whole-heartedly endorsed. Many of the army doctors were conscientious and self-sacrificing, but others "failed to carry either skill, morality, or humanity to their work."[46] The latter knew no peace when the superintendent of women nurses was about. They knew that she had won the unqualified approval of Stanton, who had succeeded Cameron as Secretary of War, and say what they would, they could not shake his confidence in her. The minute she descended upon a hospital and found conditions not to her liking, someone in authority would be summoned in to answer charges. An incident is told that complaints had come in that in a certain hospital not far from Washington delicacies intended for the patients did not reach their destination. Jellies, jams, preserves, pickles, and other foods to tempt jaded appetites appeared on the officers' tables rather than on the patients' trays. One day a slender woman of commanding presence came to the hospital. She did not introduce herself, but by her very majesty of voice and manner she secured the consent of the medical director to visit the wards. She suggested change after change in the arrangement of the hospital, and the officer's indignation and irritation became greater every minute.

At last he said, "Madam, who are you that you thus presume to invade my domain and thus dictate to me, the officer in charge?" She looked the surgeon straight in the eye, and raising herself to her full height, answered in that unequalled voice, "I am Dorothea L. Dix, Superintendent of Nurses, in the employ of the United States Government." When she had gone, the chagrined surgeon inquired of an associate who and what this Miss Dix was to speak with such authority. "Why man alive," the officer replied, "don't you know her? Why she has the rank, pay, honors, and emoluments of a major-general of volunteers and if you have got her down on you, you might as well have all hell after you."[47]

To faithful matron and conscientious surgeon her visits inspired courage and strength rather than disdain and ridicule. She realized how pitifully short the army was on medical supplies and how hard these tireless workers tried to ease the pain of fever-tossed patients. She never left them without an encouraging thought, a word of commendation and praise. Whenever possible she walked through the wards, stopping to hand out books, fruit, or flowers from the basket that she carried on her arm. She felt helpless as she passed through the long pain-fraught corridors, and listened to the moans of the suffering men, the shouts of the delirious, and the gasps of the dying. "Every breath is like a stab," whispered a boy from the Massachusetts Eighth. "Yes, I know," she would reply as she smoothed back the pillow and took down his mother's address. "This war in my own country is breaking my heart," she wrote Mrs. Rathbone.[48]

Years later when hypodermic syringes, fever thermometers, rubber ice-bags, metal screens, and antiseptics were but a small part of the equipment of every hospital, she often thought how much suffering might have been spared had these simple aids been available during the Civil War. She shuddered to think how doctors had probed for bullets without sterilizing their instruments and how morphine had been thrust into the flesh on the tip end of a pocket knife. How thankful she had been for anesthetics; they had made amputations less of a butchery. Nothing at the time of the Civil War had been found to prevent gangrene. Sometimes whole wards died of it.[49] "God give us peace," she always prayed on leaving a hospital.

The scope of Miss Dix's work was still to increase. Early in 1862, scurvy broke out in the army in the west, and throughout the spring and summer of 1862 and 1863 it was necessary to send vast quantities of fresh fruits and vegetables to the armies under General Grant and General Rosecrans. Thousands of bushels of potatoes, onions, dried fruits, lemons, and barrels of sauer kraut were obtained and transported to the camps by the Sanitary Commission. The appearance of a disease that threatened the whole northern army increased the need for women nurses.[50] So heavy were the demands in the east on the Sanitary Commission that late in 1861, Miss Dix's friend, William Greenleaf Eliot, and General Fremont, together with some other public-spirited citizens of St. Louis organized a Western Commission having as its immediate object relief supplies to be sent to the troops in the vicinity of St. Louis and the west where many of the soldiers were suffering from lack of medical attention. Dr. Eliot appealed to Miss Dix in the matter of nurses, and she hurried west to help organize the local hospitals, to the chagrin of the commanding officers. The Western Sanitary Commission had no auxiliary societies. Conditions in Missouri were such that the Ladies' Union Aid Society had to work in secret. Nine-tenths of the people, said Dr. Eliot, looked on the work with contempt and it was necessary to appeal to Eastern friends for support. Miss Dix wrote to many people whom she knew in Boston, New York, and other cities, commending Dr. Eliot's project. Advertisements placed in the *Boston Transcript* and other papers yielded handsome returns. In all, Boston alone sent $200,000 and New England a total of over $500,000. One of the chief reasons for their prompt response to this appeal was the New England antipathy for the extension of slavery and the close interrelation of the Unitarian and merchant groups of the two localities.[51]

The war continued much longer than any one had anticipated and each year the friction between the Medical Bureau, and the Sanitary Commission and the superintendent of nurses became more and more intense. The surgeons resented the intrusion of the Sanitary Commission's experts, "meddlesome sentimentalists," as they called them. Miss Dix's nurses were criticized and discharged and others were employed without advising her of the reasons. The surgeons declared she exceeded her authority and some of them even went so far as to ask the Secretary of War to remove her from office; however, most of the regular officers were loyal to her and on more than one occasion supported her position much to the disgruntlement of the medical officers. The story is told that once while visiting Hampton, she came upon three convalescents who for some offense were being punished by hanging from the thumbs. "Who has ordered this?" she sharply inquired. She soon found the officer in charge and demanded that the proceeding stop. The officer went into a rage. That was his business, he would tolerate no interference, especially from a woman. She should respect his authority. Miss Dix did not linger to hear the rest of his tirade; she went at once to the department commander, who at that time happened to be General Butler. She asked which of the two, she or the surgeon, in that branch of the service outranked the other. The answer was, "Miss Dix, of course." The men were then released and the officer discharged.[52]

Secretary Stanton finally consented to the reorganization of the Medical Bureau. Surgeon-General Finlay, who had succeeded Acting Surgeon-General Wood, was now retired, and Dr. William A.

Hammond, who had been engaged in organizing the general hospitals at Hagerstown, Chambersburg, Baltimore, and Wheeling, was appointed to take his place. Dr. Hammond was inclined to be more friendly toward the Sanitary Commission than his predecessors had been; subordinate officers, however, still continued to resent the visits of the inspectors; at the same time they most readily accepted the Sanitary's liberal gifts of ice, medicines, and fresh fruits and vegetables.

It was all a tremendous strain on the superintendent of nurses. Surgeons complained that the nurses she selected were too old, incompetent and insubordinate, and appealed to the surgeon-general for the authority to employ their own nurses. They declared that Miss Dix had made most of her rejections on account of youth and beauty rather than because of lack of ability to care for the sick. Such accusations were false. She did reject many young girls who applied for service in the nursing corps, but it was not because she had a grudge against youth. She may have made mistakes in refusing some women places, but it was through caution and overzealousness rather than personal prejudice. Said Mrs. Brockett, at the close of the war:

> Her nature is large and generous with no room for narrow grudges or mean reservations. As a proof of this, her stores were as readily dispensed for the use of the hospital in which the surgeon refused and rejected her nurses as for those that employed them. She had the kindest care and oversight over the women she had commissioned. She wished them to embrace every opportunity for rest and refreshment, rendered necessary by their arduous labors. A home for them was established by her in Washington, which at all times opened its doors for their reception and where she wished them to enjoy that perfect quiet and freedom from care during their occasional sojourns, which were the best remedies for their weariness and exhaustion of body and soul.[53]

A letter to Ann Heath, dated March 16, 1863, gives a fair idea of what the superintendent of nurses was going through.

> Time rolls on. We still measure its age by the flow and ebb of conflicts and battles, no more by the secession and peaceful objects, aims, and labors of our accustomed life. When shall we have peace? is the cry of our hearts, yet no clear sky is discerned through the dreary cloud of rebellion spread over our beloved country. We must be patient so all may work for our good here and hereafter. I am full of care day by day

within a space of ten square miles. I have nearly 180 nurses to control, besides all at a distance and in Pennsylvania and most of the states I have delegated my authority to parties I have thought to be responsible. I have much to do with the brigade soldiers and ill soldiers at large. As yet I have not been off duty for a day since the rebellion. I trust I have both grace and strength to carry forward my work till the end.[54]

A month later she wrote:

Our times are very sad, and events are hinging on so many uncertainties that I feel the best security from an overwhelming anxiety is in the careful performance of daily duty and daily reference to the precepts of our land. It is strange to pass time as we have counted the past two years. We are hoping, indeed, that so great national trouble will work great benefit to the national character and that the fires of tribulation may act like the reformer's fire and purify from sin and wickedness and elevate and spiritualize.[55]

It was hard to rationalize and see good coming out of anything so disastrous as war, but pious woman that she was, Dorothea Dix tried to see the hand of God at work in all that she could not understand. Out of so much tribulation should come a righteous land, sanctified to liberty and humanity and where "goodness and mercy should dwell forever" in the hearts of men. It was a lovely dream, this Utopia that should come with peace; in the frenzy of devotion to an ideal, men were willing to fight, to give up life itself, that posterity should know no more of strife, and crime, and hate. The Christian Commission was preaching the holiness of the cause. Beside campfires it held services. Men lifted up their voices and thanked God for the rôle that they were privileged to play in the great cosmic drama. A prayer, and then a hymn,

> God moves in a mysterious way
> His wonders to perform.

By 1863, the Civil War had become a holy war. The forces of right were aligned against the forces of evil. It was the era of the mixed metaphor. "The national soul was being baptized with fire and the spirit." It would emerge purified; "graft and corruption, vestiges of a dark past, were about to be sloughed off." The Emancipation Proclamation was the forerunner of a new day, and for a brief hour the erstwhile "railsplitter in the White House" was a hero, the "Gideon" and "prophet of a regenerated America," the land-to-be where all men were brothers, and greed and avarice were no more, and public office was a public "trust" to be served with the true zeal attendant upon "servants of the high calling of God." No one subscribed more prayerfully to the hope that a finer, more Christian America would result from this purification by fire than did the superintendent of nurses. It helped her to bear the assaults that constantly came from the subordinate members of the medical staff and it gave her courage and strength to go on.

In October 1863, an effort was made to clear up the differences existing between the medical staff and the superintendent of nurses. The main point at issue related to the exclusive authority of the superintendent of women nurses. On October 29, General Orders 351 was sent out by E. D. Townsend, Assistant Surgeon-General, by order of the Secretary of War.

The employment of women nurses in the United States General Hospitals will in the future be strictly governed by the following rules:

1. Persons approved by Miss Dix, or her authorized agents, will receive from her, or them, "certificates of approval," which must be countersigned by Medical Directors upon their assignment to duty as nurses within their Departments.

2. Assignment of "women nurses" to duty in General Hospitals will only be made upon application by the Surgeons in charge, through Medical Directors, to Miss Dix or her agents, for the number they require, not exceeding one to every thirty beds.

3. No females, except Hospital Matrons, will be employed in General Hospitals, or, after December 31, 1863, borne upon the Muster and Pay Rolls, without such certificates of approval and regular assignment unless specially appointed by the Surgeon-General.

4. Women nurses, while on duty in General Hospitals, are under the exclusive control of the senior medical officer, who will direct their several duties, and may be discharged by him when considered supernumerary, or for incompetency, insubordination, or violation of his orders. Such discharge with the reasons therefor, being endorsed upon the certificates, will be at once returned to Miss Dix.[56]

A mere cursory reading of Orders 351 reveals nothing more than a reiteration of the substance of previous circulars from the War Department and the Surgeon-General, but a closer study shows the subtle method which was being used to outline the duties of the superintendent of nurses and in common parlance, "to put Miss Dix in her place." The harmless appearing "third section" was the one which struck the blow to Miss Dix's authority. "No females . . . will be employed . . . without such certificates of approval and assignment unless specially appointed by the Surgeon-General." The Surgeon-General was reserving authority to appoint nurses. "In other words," Miss Dix reasoned, "surgeons who do not like me may appeal directly to the Surgeon-General and have nurses sent out by him."

Orders 351 practically abolished the office of superintendent of nurses. Miss Dix's pride was deeply wounded. The Surgeon-General had yielded to the entreaties of inferior medical officers, and the Assistant Adjutant-General, acting under the approval of the Secretary of War, had issued the circular. Had Stanton done this, the man who had approved and supported her all along? Surely he had not known what this would mean. Perhaps the authority had been given by a subordinate in the department. It was betrayal. Surely Stanton would not do that. For thirty months she had worked incessantly, without a single day of rest or holiday, without pay. She had given unstintingly of her private means and solicited from the bounty of friends without reservation. Love of country and compassion for the sick and wounded had been the motives which impelled her actions. Except for visits to a few nearby hospitals for the insane she had abandoned her work for the mentally defective and turned to the more pressing business of providing nurses and certain hospital supplies for the sick and wounded. Was this curtailment or transfer of authority the reward for patriotic endeavor and self-sacrifice? How the conspiring surgeons must be gloating over these orders. Miss Dix had been defeated.

"What shall I do?" she asked herself. "I must think this out carefully before I act." It would be pleasant to leave the bitter scene, to go far away. To Greenbank, perhaps. Oh, for an hour within those friendly walls. Up in her room she softly closed the door. A sob caught in her throat. "No, I must not give way . . . there is but one way out of this, and I must find it."

Miss Dix did not resign; this would have been playing directly into the hands of the medical men who had opposed her, and too, there was still much work for her to do to make the lives of the soldiers happier and more comfortable. But the blow was one that she could not forget. Years later, when she talked over with Horace Lamb the materials that were to be used in writing her biography, she lamented that her Civil War experience had been such an un-happy one. She wished that it might be forgotten entirely. After all, she said, it was only a "brief episode" in her life compared with the other causes that she had championed. She had done what any loyal patriotic woman would have done. Her services had not been appreciated by the medical officers and they had conspired against her. After her death unbiased persons in the Medical Bureau of the War Department began to comprehend the full significance of her labors, but Miss Dix always felt that her war service was not the work by which she wished her life to be judged.[57]

Meanwhile, although Orders 351 had broken her heart, she would not give in. She concealed her sorrow as best she could and continued to go about her duties as though the circular had never been issued. She felt something of the hurt that had come when her engagement to Edward Bangs had been broken, but with it more of the sting that had come when President Pierce had vetoed her twelve million acre bill; it was an old familiar pain. "Must every milestone in my life be marked with heartache?" she asked herself.

From Chattanooga the Union troops were sending out piteous appeals for hospital supplies, nurses, fruits, vegetables. Once more she turned from her own sorrow to minister to the needs of others. Then came the battle above the clouds at Lookout Mountain, with its thousands of slain and injured. Next, Missionary Ridge. It was no time to give thought to wounded pride and the innuendo of petulant physicians when soldiers were shivering in the cold, hun-gry and sick. Reports came to her office of the heroism of Mother Bickerdyke and other nurses during the blizzards that overtook the Union troops, tales of how the tents had blown over in the night and Mother Bickerdyke and a faithful companion, clad only in calico and with light shawls about their shoulders, had heated bricks and crawled under the wreckage of canvas and laid them by the sick soldiers so that they would not freeze before morning. Their chief at Washington could not be less valiant in face of difficulty, and for a time she pushed the humiliation out of her mind.

To the few who comprehended Miss Dix's situation, her courage was remarkable. Her magnanimous conduct toward those who had tried to undermine her position and cast reflection upon her work commanded the respect of many. Stanton gloried in her fortitude, and Surgeon-General Hammond, no doubt, had his own regrets. When it came time to equip the United States General Hospital at Chester, Pennsylvania, and put it in order with the least possible delay it was to Miss Dix that Dr. Crane appealed on order from the Surgeon-General.[58]

By 1864, the government was convinced that a real military hospital program would have to be inaugurated. Makeshift warehouses, lodge rooms, and private homes could be used no longer. With the opening of summer a large number of army hospitals designed along the most modern and scientific lines were in the process of construction. Wards were built to accommodate sixty patients. There were detached buildings for administration, separate dining rooms for patients and officers, laundry, quartermaster's supplies, guard house, "dead house," quarters for female nurses, chapel, operating room, stables. There was no set scheme for the arrangement of buildings, some were in parallel formation, others double cross, or "U" or "V" shape.[59] The War Department had at last listened to the pleas of Miss Dix and the Sanitary Commission. The sick and wounded of the army were to be given decent shelter and sanitation, and the nurses who had lived under the most abject conditions were now to be given suitable quarters. The wards were now to afford the ventilation which Miss Alcott had depicted as so badly needed in *Hospital Sketches;* and the proper sewage that had been the burden of Dr. Harris' incessant letters to authorities was to be provided at last.

The spring campaign of 1864, however, opened before the new hospitals were ready and it was late in the summer before adequate hospital facilities were at last available. The ambulance corps was also deficient and had it not been for the work of the Sanitary Commission in outfitting hospital ships in Chesapeake Bay and transports on the Potomac and Mississippi rivers, the lives of thousands would have been sacrificed. As it was, men frequently lay on the battlefield several days after being wounded. Grant's "hammer" campaign of 1864 brought forth its daily quota of dead and injured, and as the army advanced toward Richmond, emergency stations were set up in the rear of the lines. Miss Dix spent as much of her time as possible at these rude makeshift hospitals. Georgey Woolsey described Fredericksburg station as "hard work, dirt, and death everywhere." Men were continually being brought in and "stowed" away in filthy warehouses where for three or four days no one seemed responsible for them and the only food available was the hard tack and coffee supplied by the government.

A similar report came in from City Point. Miss Dix with Mrs. Annie Wittenmyer set out to investigate conditions.[60] Regardless of her sixty-five years and the fact that she now weighed only ninety-five pounds, she made no effort to spare herself. The trip was a difficult one and when they reached the camp too late to do any work that night, they were unable to find even a place to sleep and were compelled to spend the night on a pile of shavings on the floor of one of the store rooms. Mrs. Wittenmyer was amazed at the daring and resoluteness of her superintendent. The next morning Miss Dix was up early as though she had had the best kind of a bed; a hurried bit of breakfast, taking care not to eat anything that a sick soldier might crave, and she was off to inspect the patients, the kitchens, and the supply rooms.[61]

So the summer past, then winter, and spring again, and at last Lee had surrendered at Appomattox. The war was over, and peace had come. Thunder and smoke ran around the circle of forts, "an improvised salute." Shouts and music filled the air. Men wanted to shout, to sing. It was all over, this bloody strife. That night Dorothea Dix looked out from her window and saw Washington illuminated as it had not been since the war began. On the surrounding hills bonfires leaped skyward, and in the streets below, men and women milled about, singing and shouting.

"Father, I thank thee," she whispered.

———

Time went more swiftly now. Before a week had passed, the joy of peace was clouded by the assassination of Lincoln. Andrew Johnson moved into the White House, and in a few weeks the work of demobilization was begun. There were still hundreds of sick and wounded soldiers to be cared for. They were brought from the field hospitals into the base hospitals. The Christian Commission and the Sanitary Commission began balancing their books and distributing their last stores among the hospital units in Washington. Someone had to assume responsibility for looking after the nurses in these hospitals and of caring for these last remnants of the "boys in blue" during the summer. Most of the surgeons in the Medical Bureau were clamoring to get away for a well-earned vaca-

tion. "I will stay on," volunteered Miss Dix, and so she remained
in Washington during the heat of June, July, and August, visiting
the hospitals daily and carrying on a vast correspondence trying to
locate missing sons, fathers, husbands, and sweethearts, and spreading cheer and comfort. One by one the men were discharged and
the hospitals closed. Ann was begging her to come to New England
as soon as she could and get out of the heat. Early in August, Miss
Dix resigned her commission to become effective in September.
Not until September 11 did a reply come from the office of the
Surgeon-General.

Dear Madam:

I am instructed by the Surgeon General to inform you that by direction of the Honorable Secretary of War, the office of Superintendent of
Women Nurses in connection with the Hospital Service of the Army,
has been discontinued and the Medical Directors have been ordered to
discharge all women nurses remaining on duty at the U. S. A. General
Hospitals in their respective departments, the speedy closure of these
hospitals rendering their service unnecessary.

Very respectfully, etc.,
By order of the Surgeon General
C. H. Crane,
Surgeon, U. S. A.[62]

That night Miss Dix took off a few minutes to thank Ann and
her other New England friends for their kind invitations.

No, I can not come at present, certainly not until the volunteers are
mustered out. I never felt more need of labor in their behalf than now.
I resigned in August the place of Superintendent of Women Nurses to
take effect the tenth of September but did not thereby relieve myself of
labor. I have turned over the house I rented to other parties and become
while I remain here, a boarder. I am resuming care for the insane as
well and find life has its own returning obligation for the helpless and
suffering. I bid you farewell with loving heart.[63]

Secretary of War Stanton had observed Miss Dix as she went
about her mission of mercy that hot summer long after the smoke
of battle had cleared away and the excitement of war time had
subsided. She was among the last to quit her post of duty. One
day he asked her in what way she would prefer to have her services
recognized officially. Would she like a great public meeting pre-
sided over by the highest officials, or a vote of money from Con-

gress. Neither appealed to Miss Dix. "What would you like?" he finally asked. "The flag of my country," she responded, never thinking that the request might be granted.

On January 25, 1867, she received from General Townsend a box containing a stand of the national colors, together with a copy of the order from the Secretary of War.

War Department
Washington City
December 3, 1866

Order in Relation to the Services of Miss Dix

In token and acknowledgment of the inestimable services rendered by Miss Dorothea L. Dix for the care, succor, and relief of the sick and wounded soldiers of the United States on the battlefield, in camps, and hospitals during the recent war, and of her benevolent and diligent labors and devoted efforts to whatever might contribute to their comfort and welfare, it is ordered that a stand of arms of the United States colors be presented to Miss Dix.

Edwin M. Stanton
Secretary of War.[64]

"No greater distinction could have been conferred upon me," she replied, "and the value of the gift is greatly enhanced by the manner in which it is bestowed."[65] "No possession will be so prized while life remains to love and serve my country."[66]

CHAPTER XI

THE CLOSE OF AN ACTIVE CAREER

IT WAS FULLY eighteen months after the war was ended before Miss Dix was willing to release herself entirely from the duties which had fallen upon her as superintendent of nurses. Soldiers dying in the hospitals or camps that she visited had often given her commissions to carry out that involved much correspondence. For wounded men who recovered, as well as for nurses who had become incapacitated through war service and were unable to work, she took upon herself the matter of securing pensions. She spent months in comparing the lists in the War Department and in the files of the Sanitary Commission and trying to bring records up to date.

At last she was able to return to New England for a brief visit. What aspects did life next present to the incessantly active but now ageing woman? Boston had changed greatly during the war, but Brookline and Dorchester where her brother Joseph lived, and Cambridge were much the same. A memorial hall was being projected at Harvard in memory of the men who had given their lives for the Union. Miss Dix had an unwavering affection for Harvard. In her youth social and intellectual life had centered around the college. In later years she had known many of its professors and numbered them among her friends. Her uncle Henry Elijah Dix had graduated from Harvard, and her own father was once a student there. It was to Harvard that she bequeathed her precious stand of the national colors to hang over the portal of Memorial Hall.

Ann was delighted to see her old friend again. Dorothea was the same busy person that she had always been, Ann told her sisters, and it was useless to try to make her stay longer when there was hospital work to do. She had not changed as much as Ann had expected. Although nearly sixty-five, there was scarcely a streak of gray in her brown hair; it was not so lustrous as it used to be, Ann thought, but it was fully as abundant, and combed back as it had always been, flat and loose over the ears and in a large coil on the back of her head. Fashions might come and go, but "Thea" was quite content with a few sombre gowns softened by a fold of tulle about the throat. Ann and Susan, who had made most of her clothes for the past forty years, had seldom been able to coax her into a ruffle or even a lace fichu for trimming. "Furbelows, dust ruffles, crinolines, and stays may do for others," she had remonstrated, "but my clothes to be practical must be simple." And there the matter had ended.

"You do not think I look any older?" Dorothea had repeated. One had to speak a little louder to Ann now, she thought. Susan smiled. Dorothea had not outlived all of her vanity. It was true Miss Dix had kept her age unusually well considering the state of her health and the hard work in which she had always engaged. Her voice was still beautiful, and she moved about as quickly and sprightly as a woman half her age. Her eyes were so bright that one scarcely noticed the fine lines that radiated from the corners and furrowed the thin cheeks and the high brow. The Heath sisters seemed to have grown much older. Ann did not see so well and she walked a little stiffly. Abby was broken with grief over the death of her husband, Mr. Barnett. Ann was sixty-seven. It pained Miss Dix to think that perhaps before very long death would be claiming "dear Annie" as it had claimed so many of her friends— Mr. Rathbone, Francis Lieber, Fredrika Bremer, Horace Mann.

"Will you rest now or will you go back into hospital work?" people inquired of her on every hand. "Rest?" she would smile and repeat aloud the poem she had been quoting to herself for over thirty years.

> Rest is not quitting the active career
> Rest is the fitting of self to its sphere
> It's living and serving the Highest and Best
> It's onward, still onward, and that is true rest.[1]

She would resume her hospital work. She planned an inspection of all the American institutions for the mentally ill, but first she had another project in mind. For some time before she left Washington, she had been interested in the newly established cemetery at Hampton, Virginia, near Fortress Monroe. A monument had been proposed, but the persons who originated the idea had become weary of the task of raising the necessary funds and were about to abandon the project when Miss Dix came along. For Fortress Monroe, she had a certain sentimental regard; there she had bathed so many feverish brows, smoothed so many pain-tossed pillows, and received so many dying messages. Thousands of valiant soldiers now slept in neat rows beneath the shadow of the fort. It seemed ingratitude, a disloyal act, not to go on with the monument and erect a fitting tribute to the memory of those brave men. In a few days she would go up into Maine to the rock quarries and select a granite of such imperishable quality and beauty as would be worthy of the "martyrs of freedom" who lay buried at Fortress Monroe.

In a letter to Mrs. Rathbone, August 1866, she described the progress which she had then made toward the monument:

Lately I have collected in a quiet way among my friends $8,000 with which to erect a granite monument in a cemetery at Fortress Monroe where are interred more than 6,000 of our brave, loyal soldiers. . . . I had especial direction over most of these martyred to a sacred cause, and never forget the countless last messages of hundreds of dying men to fathers, mothers, wives, and children; never forget the calm, manly fortitude which sustained them through the anguish of mortal wounds and the agonies of dissolution. Nothing in a review of the past four years' war, so astonishes me as the uniformly calm and firm bearing of these soldiers of a good cause, dying without a murmur as they had suffered without a complaint. Thank Heaven the war is over. I would that its memories also could pass away.[2]

After Miss Dix took over the work of the monument, contributions came in rapidly and work had so far progressed by the spring of 1868 that its completion by the first of April was assured. This mighty obelisk of syenite, seventy-five feet high, was to rest upon a massive base, twenty-seven feet square; to ships coming in from the sea to Hampton Roads, it would be the first object visible over the low peninsula. About the base of the monument she proposed a circular fence made from musket barrels, bayonets, and rifled cannon set in blocks of granite. In December 1867, Miss Dix appealed to Major General Dyer, who in turn endorsed a letter to General Grant asking for 1000 muskets and bayonets, 15 rifled guns, and a quantity of 24 pound shot with which to construct her fence. The request was granted, and early in May the completed monument, bearing the simple inscription, "In Memory of Union Soldiers who Died to maintain the Laws," was turned over to the care of the federal government. Secretary Stanton again responded with an appreciation of Miss Dix's services.

> War Department
> Washington, D. C.,
> May 12, 1868

Dear Madam:

Inasmuch as by the Act of Congress the National Cemeteries are placed in charge of the Secretary of War and under his direction, I accept with pleasure the tender of this memorial to our gallant dead, and return the thanks of the Department to the public-spirited citizens who have furnished the means for erecting it; and to yourself for your arduous, patriotic, humane, and benevolent labors in bringing to a successful completion such a noble testimonial to our gallant dead who perished in the War to maintain their government and suppress the rebellion.

> Yours truly
> Edwin M. Stanton
> Secretary of War[3]

Those who had envisaged a perfect republic after the "purifying" process of war were doomed to disillusionment. Graft and corruption in high places continued unabated and sectional hatreds were intensified rather than obliterated. It was a sad America that faced reconstruction, and no one was to feel the futility of war in bringing about national regeneration more than Dorothea Dix. The cost of the four years' struggle had been tremendous both in life and money. In the dramatic intensity of the hour, philanthropy had been diverted to the more urgent demands of the war, the Christian Commission, the Sanitary Commission, and tens of thousands of soldiers' aid societies, north and south. By the close of the war such an enormous drain on the finances of the nation had almost "dried up the fountains of charity." Among society's dependents who had suffered were the mentally ill. As was to be expected, the number of insane had increased at a greater rate while the facilities for caring for them remained the same, except in the south, where those in institutions suffered extremely for want of care, food and medicines, and some hospitals had been abandoned.

The year 1867 found Miss Dix again assuming her duties as a self-appointed commissioner inspecting jails, poorhouses, and institutions for the mentally ill. For the next fifteen years, she was to be almost constantly traveling back and forth from New York to California, and from Maine to Florida. Hospitals for the diseased of mind had come to be her "children" and she spent her time going from one institution to another, performing some ministry for each. During the war there had been an increase in population as well as a heavy influx of immigration into the north and west, and the existing institutions were soon found to be inadequate. In 1868, the total number of mentally ill in America was estimated to be 54,285, of whom 7,229 were not provided for. There were fifty-four hospitals exclusively for mental diseases in operation and six under construction.[4] The northern and western states, less hard hit by the war than those in the south, were able to finance new hospitals and poorhouses, and consequently as soon as the real need was made apparent, an effort was made to correct the situation. The Public Charities Commission of Pennsylvania reported that there were twice as many insane in prisons and poorhouses as when Miss Dix made the appeal which resulted in the construction of the second state hospital at Harrisburg.[5] Pennsylvania now appropriated $200,000 for a third hospital. Connecticut likewise increased her hospital facilities, and in 1867 Tennessee became the first state to make separate provision for its Negro insane. In all of these new hospital ventures Dorothea Dix gave support, encouragement, and personal aid. There is an interesting letter from her friend, Professor Silliman, regarding the Connecticut hospital.

It is just two years this month since you came here to move this matter and now the first patients are in the new hospital building. How much we all owe you for your timely aid, courage, and energy, without which this noble work would not have been undertaken, certainly for many years. And it was all done so quietly. The springs of influence were touched in a way which shows how possible it is to do great and noble things in public assemblies without a lobby or the use of money.[6]

The increase of naval and military forces during the war and the aftermath of deranged minds and broken spirits produced an over-crowdedness in the government hospital in Washington. When Miss Dix appealed to Congress for additional quarters, her request was granted almost spontaneously.

Miss Dix did not include the southern states on her first itinerary after the war because she did not know how she would be received there. She also felt somewhat bitter herself as a result of her experiences as superintendent of nurses in receiving under her charge thousands of Union soldiers who had been released from Confederate prisons, mere skeletons, half-mad from the privations they had undergone.

In 1869, Miss Dix wrote Ann from Trenton that she was leaving for California "to execute a long delayed work at Stockton." I can not, of course, say how long I may be absent or how I shall return. Providence permitting the execution of my plans, I may be back before September."[7] In St. Louis, she stopped for a brief visit with the Eliots and with Mrs. Jessie Benton Fremont with whom she had been closely associated during the war. Miss Dix was especially interested in the new states and she was pleased to observe that a state so young as California had made such fine provision for its unfortunates.

It was midwinter before she was able to reach the south, from whence she was now receiving earnest appeals to come and do something for the mentally ill. She was happy to know that the vindictive attitude of most Southerners toward the so-called Yankees did not extend to her personally. She no longer wondered whether she would be able to shake hands with those for whom she had great affection but whom she had lately come to distrust. Quickly she forgot any ill feeling that she might have contracted while in the capacity of superintendent of nurses, and recalled the friendships she had enjoyed in the South before the war, the pleasant visits to Francis and Matilda Lieber's home in Columbia, South Carolina, the Dobbins and the Moreheads and the Swains in North Carolina, and the Clays in Alabama.

At best the annals of reconstruction constitute a sordid tale, but when one considers how the unfortunate, helpless, and afflicted were exploited at the hands of corrupt politicians, "scalawags," and "carpetbaggers," humanity seems more outraged than ever. The treatment of the insane in South Carolina was especially pathetic. During the war, Dr. Parker, faithful head of the hospital in Columbia, had been compelled to dismiss many of the servants and conduct the institution on little or no appropriations and on half-rations. Under the post-war administration, from one-half to two-thirds of the board of regents were Negroes, only interested in the spoils of office. Dr. Parker's position and the whole future of the institution were threatened. The news of Miss Dix's coming brought hope to Dr. Parker. Alfred Huger of Charleston wrote to her upon her arrival at Columbia in January 1870.

My dear Madam:

I have just heard of your arrival at Columbia. The Past, the Present, and the Future, are by this announcement grouped before me. It is the instinct of the afflicted to be aroused and encouraged when your name is mentioned. Ruin and desolation hold their court among us. Our poor little state is sinking under a weight of calamity and woe, our temples are draped in mourning, and our hearts are in the dust. Still we flock to the altar when the High Priestess is there. . . .

I was one of the founders of the Lunatic Asylum. Everywhere and at all times I have watched its progress. During the war I was in daily, almost hourly interchange with our valued friend, Dr. Parker, and with that household of wounded minds over which he presides, and as we believe, doing so with a holy purpose. Dr. Parker is the father, brother, and friend, the very "shield and buckler" of our stricken brethren.

We have heard, like a summons to meet death, of his possible removal, and we have heard also of your providential advent. If the authorities that rule over us select this man as a victim, or if Dr. Parker can endure his surroundings no longer, then there is an agony on us, and may we not appeal to you for succor. . . . We look to you both as the viceregents of "Our Father who is in Heaven" and we will not look in vain! Dr. Parker has no equal in our state for the position he occupies. You have no superior, with your mission signed in the High Chancery of Heaven, and witnessed by angels who do justice and love mercy.

In this hour of our trial, a word of information or of consolation from you would be a boon and a blessing.

Faithfully and with profound respect,

Alfred Huger.[8]

Records do not show how quickly order was brought out of chaos. Dr. Parker retained his position, and it is fairly safe to assume that Dorothea Dix did not leave the state without playing an influential rôle in the adjustment of the institution's difficulties. In North Carolina, the hospital for the insane had suffered privations during the war, but conditions were never so bad there as in states where carpetbag rule was rampant in the post-war period. In Raleigh, Miss Dix was given the gracious welcome accorded an old friend. Special honors were shown her when she appeared before the legislature and she was thrilled with gratitude. Nor had she forgotten the magnanimous treatment accorded her by the North Carolina officers who had halted her train during the war.

In 1871 when she came back to supervise the construction of new additions to the already overcrowded hospital, she wrote:

The citizens and public functionaries in the state have met me with such unmistakable cordiality that I needs must have put out of my mind the terrible past, during the rebellion and take up the line of work where I left it in 1860. Strange to say, none are heartier in welcoming me home to North Carolina than the Democrats and Confederates so that my plans are accepted and acted upon with an alacrity that hourly surprises me.[9]

Throughout the south, as well as in the north and west, institutions for the mentally ill had suffered neglect and retrogression more terrible than Miss Dix imagined possible in five or six years time. It was heart-rending to go through the south and see beautiful buildings lapsing into decay, over-crowded inmates half provided for, the staffs undermanned, and the worst practices entering into common use again. Manacles, chains, and straight-jackets discarded years before were brought back. "It would seem," she told Mrs. Torrey, "that all my work is to be done over so far as the insane are concerned. Language is too poor to describe the miserable state of these poor wretches in dungeon cells."[10]

Miss Dix redoubled her efforts after her visit to the south in the spring of 1870, but the strain of added exertion proved too much. She was compelled to stop in Louisville "to shake off a cough which had become too troublesome to neglect longer" and decided to spend the rest of the season "indoors" in Washington. She suffered a relapse at Columbus, and by the time she reached Trenton, New Jersey, she was desperately ill. "Malaria in the most malignant form," her physician declared. "Her system has been saturated with it for years." She lingered for weeks in the hospital at Trenton, swinging in the balance between life and death. When she was able to go about again, her physicians cautioned her that in the future she must not subject herself to such long journeys and to work at such a pace. She promised and for a while was faithful to these orders, and contented herself with reading, catching up with her private correspondence, and following up various social movements. She was much interested in the newly organized Young Women's Christian Association in Boston, and in the temperance movement. The latter cause, she averred in a letter to Mrs. Rathbone, seemed quite unsteady in 1870, "Now advancing with potential influences for good, now swept aside by a wave of reactionary forces very difficult to control in large committees." As she looked about her, she thought "on the whole good in all and everything predominates though the reader from the journals would suppose evil alone was in the ascendant."[11]

Once more in Washington, she answered Ann's query of what she found to do by enumerating a list of tasks and errands that would have been staggering even to a well person.

Mail brings requests from ex-soldiers to look after their back pay and pensions, requests from seven persons who have lost money registered and not transmitted by mail through various post offices, to present their cases to the Depredation Bureau of the post office. One case of an effort to sell counterfeit money makes a communication to the assistant secretary of state necessary; a request to get three children, one an infant three months old, into the Foster Home; a request for a contribution to the Young Men's Christian Association; another for clothing for two families; another to aid a foreign mission, the last being declined having no cash on hand; a request to examine and present a petition for a Revolution claim to be paid; opinions on the Woman's Rights and their fitness for the learned professions, etc., and the best method for organizing and sustaining reform homes for fallen women, etc.

Now if you think I am idle any part of the working time for the twenty-four hours, you are mistaken. I have all the time and have always as much as I can do.[12]

To go into Miss Dix's travels for the next ten years would be but idle repetition of details that had already marked her interviews, journeys, inspections, and surveys. The value of her later work was not impaired by age. In 1877, when Miss Dix was seventy-five Dr. Charles Folsom, in his book, *Diseases of the Mind,* asserted that "her frequent visits to our institutions of the insane now, and her searching criticisms, constitute of themselves a better lunacy commission than would be likely to be appointed in many of our states."[13] A national figure was this little old woman in her dark dress, shawl and bonnet, who wore a bit of red, white, and blue ribbon upon her breast as proudly as any soldier wore his army button. She still gathered up wherever she went collections of stuffed animals, clothes, stereopticon views, toys, and magazines, for the entertainment and employment of the patients in various hospitals.

In her later years she was to devote her time to a wide range of philanthropies and nothing gave her more pleasure than to go about and personally see her work bearing fruit. When the fire in Boston left so many Portuguese homeless and destitute, she was among the first to offer assistance in gathering up food and clothing. In this connection there is among the Dix-Heath Manuscripts a sequence of letters which illustrates the peculiar methods which she sometimes used to further her pet charities. When in Edinburgh in 1855, Dorothea had purchased a shawl as a gift for Ann. For some reason Ann never wore it, nor did her sisters. Miss Dix knew this, and, liking the shawl and having a need for it herself, she wrote to Ann and offered to buy it. "Now if you can use $20 for something you can use or wear any way as a little token of remembrance from me, I should be glad to make the exchange. Consider this and give me your decision. I am in real earnest."[14] Ann was willing that Dorothea should have the shawl, but she disliked to take the money and suggested that it might be spent more profitably in connection with some of Thea's charities. Miss Dix was insistent and Abby and Ann finally agreed to accept the money and keep it until she should find a use for it. In less than a fortnight, Miss Dix wrote suggesting that Mrs. Caswell, in charge of the relief work among the unfortunate Portuguese, would find the twenty dollars useful in providing garments for some of the two hundred and twenty-five destitute women who were about to be confined. In the next paragraph she appealed to Ann and Abby for baby clothes, and in the last thanked them for the "promised" twenty dollars. "I never had as much real satisfaction in relieving people," she told Abby, "as in helping these Azorean Portuguese islanders."[15]

Her travels were less extensive now. She spent more time "at home" in the institutions at Trenton, at St. Elizabeth's as the government hospital in Washington was now called, and in the Pennsylvania Hospital at Dixmont. Next to Trenton and the Army Hospital, she loved the institution at Dixmont. And for Miss Dix the superintendent and trustees of Dixmont had a similar regard. Here they looked forward to her visits. When a portrait of Miss Dix was presented to the hospital by an unknown citizen of Pennsylvania, the treasurer, Mr. John L. Harper, wrote the donor:

You know, sir, in the olden time, each institution sacred to charity had its patron saint. The Dixmont Hospital, notwithstanding our Protestant and iconoclastic ideas, has a patroness whom we respect and love; indeed who is canonized in our affections as strongly as were saintly ladies in the Mediaeval Age. The mission of "Our Lady" is to create those noble institutions which aid in the restoration of the dethroned reason, and Dixmont Hospital is one of the jewels which will adorn her crown hereafter.[16]

Miss Dix was especially fond of the Army Hospital. She had selected its site and it was upon her recommendation that Dr. Nichols had become its first superintendent. Mrs. Nichols set aside a room for her in the building in which the superintendent's apartment was located, and when Dr. Godding succeeded Dr. Nichols, his wife kept the same room always ready for Miss Dix's unexpected visits. Sometimes she stayed only overnight and again she might remain for two or three months. She liked to come back to her room in the Centre Annex, where everything was sure to be found just as she had left it, not a pin or a chair out of place. On warm afternoons, when her health permitted, she delighted in walking about the beautiful grounds and watching the boats on the Potomac, and passing a word with the strolling patients, or examining new shrubs and plants. Every unusual bit of shrubbery or foliage excited her interest.

Knowing her lifelong interest in botany, Dr. Nichols and Dr. Godding called her attention one day to a particular tree and asked her if she could give its botanical name. To their surprise and her own, she was unable to identify the tree, which happened to be a black haw. She assured them she would look it up and let them know the next day. Unable to find the information in the rather limited hospital library, she was not to be outdone. The next day when Dr. Nichols and Dr. Godding went for their daily walk, they discovered on the haw tree a white card on which was written in Miss Dix's familiar hand "Nicoladi Godiana."

It was on one of these visits to St. Elizabeth's that the portrait of Miss Dix which hangs in the chapel arrived. Dr. and Mrs. Godding, Miss Dix, and several of the physicians and attendants gathered around to look at the picture. There was a difference of opinion as to the quality of workmanship and the degree of likeness. Mrs. Godding thought that the portrait greatly flattered Miss

Dix, making her look much younger and more beautiful than she was, but she refrained from making any comment. She did not wish to take any chances on what Miss Dix's reaction might be, recalling that recently she had declared a portrait painted for the McLean Hospital as unsatisfactory and had withdrawn it. Miss Dix alone seemed pleased with the artist's work. "I think it is a good likeness; still if it is not, I shall not accept it." "I neither wish to be flattered nor caricatured." Who would pass the final judgment? No one present cared to take the responsibility. The thought came to Miss Dix of having Dr. Godding's three-year-old daughter, who knew nothing of the portrait, to come in and make the decision. The child would, at least, be honest in her opinion. She was to be called into the room and asked the simple question, "Whose picture?" Inwardly fearing lest the child fail to recognize her friend, Mrs. Godding called her little daughter, "Come and see what we have here." The little girl came into the room and before any one had a chance to ask the question, pointed to the picture and gleefully exclaimed, "Mith Dicth." The little old woman kissed the child and triumphantly announced, "See, it is a good likeness." The discussion ended and the portrait was hung.[17]

Institutions which she had founded regarded her as their especial guardian and friend, and by 1870 six hospitals had already honored her by having life-size portraits of her made in oil.[18] Not one of these portraits had been made from life. Miss Dix always refused to pose, saying she was too busy or did not feel well enough, and the portraits which adorn the walls of various hospitals were all made from a daguerreotype taken many years before, presented to Ann, and then borrowed again and again as each successive artist was commissioned to paint a portrait.[19] Only once was Dorothea Dix induced to pose for a portrait. Late in life, she consented to sit for Rose Lamb, a promising young artist in Boston, and a sister of Horace Lamb, her attorney. This portrait depicted Miss Dix not in her full beauty and prime as did the daguerreotype and the copies in oil, but as a woman long past middle life when age had begun to make inroads on her features. She admitted that the artist had shown rare skill and that the resemblance was good. "But that is not the way I wish to be remembered," she had exclaimed half-petulantly. She bequeathed it to Horace Lamb, requesting that he show it to no one.[20]

It was hard for Miss Dix to admit that she was growing old and that in the near future more of her manifold activities would be curtailed. She tried to keep above the thought of age and its infirmities; again and again the passing of a lifelong friend, however, could not but bring forcibly home the fact that she was no longer a young woman and that soon she too must be going on. Since that Sunday morning thirty-seven years before, when she had gone to the Cambridge jail and the whole trend of her life had been altered, she had given but little thought to death; her energies had been consecrated to abundant living and in ministering to her unfortunate fellow-men.

In 1878, she was startled into consciousness that she had passed her own three score and ten; news came of the death of her brother, Joseph. Then a few months later, while at her desk in the Smithsonian Institute, she picked up a Boston paper for May 8, and read a funeral notice for Ann Heath, who had passed away the evening before in her seventy-ninth year. When Joseph died, she had lost her nearest and dearest of kin, and now her oldest friend was gone. Her brother Charles had died at sea in 1843, the year she presented her first memorial to the legislature of Massachusetts. She had drifted away from her cousins and seldom saw them, but Joseph she had loved and frequently visited in his home. In Dorchester he and his wife had welcomed her and there she rested many times after long and arduous surveys. Dorothea had consoled herself bravely when he died and had tried to comfort her sister-in-law, but with the death of her friend she relived her grief for Joseph.

Dear Annie! Fifty years before, Dorothea had written, "more than a sister's love binds me to thee."

> Oh, Anna, 'tis for thee to smoothe my brow
> And chase the troubler Care away
> And when the storms of sorrow lower
> Ah, thou shall be the brightening ray
> To light my wearied soul to peace.[21]

Half a century had only enhanced their friendship. Ann had not been well for a couple of years, but it did not seem possible that she was gone. Miss Dix now recalled how on her last visit to Ann "infinity was making fast inroads on the vital forces and life was fading for her into deep shadows." "The golden bowl was almost broken," she wrote Abby, "and the light flickering in the socket.[22]

What a procession of years had passed! And what a revolution had been wrought in the care of the poor and afflicted since the day Samuel Gridley Howe had presented her memorial to the legislature of Massachusetts. From thirteen institutions for the mentally ill in 1843, the number had risen to one hundred and twenty-three in 1880, of which seventy-five were state owned, one was federal, and the others were the property of private corporations, churches, counties, and municipalities. In the founding of thirty-two of the seventy-five state hospitals, Dorothea Dix had had an intimate part. Fifteen training schools for feeble-minded had been established. Of the 91,959 mentally ill persons in the United States, 51,913 were provided with institutional care, and of the 78,895 idiots, 3,811 were being cared for in training schools. There was still work to be done, every hospital had its waiting list, but a social conscience had been awakened and a new conception of the responsibility of the state toward its defectives had taken firm root in the minds of the American people.[23]

Special training for nurses that Miss Dix had so long advocated had become a reality. Dr. Marie Zahrewska had begun instructing nurses in the New England Infirmary for Women and Children as early as 1860 but it was not until 1872, after Dr. Susan Dimock returned from Kaiserwerth, that a graded course in nurses' training was instituted in the United States. In 1873, the first class was graduated and these "graduate" nurses in turn became teachers of other nurses. A move to develop special training schools for attendants and nurses in institutions for the mentally ill was successfully inaugurated by Dr. Edward Cowles, Superintendent of the McLean Hospital, at Somerville, Massachusetts, in 1882.[24] Before Miss Dix's death, three states were to establish training schools for nurses in connection with their hospitals for mental diseases.[25]

The years that followed were to witness steady improvement in the training of nurses and in the care of the patients. Medical schools were to recognize psychiatry not as a mere handmaiden of medicine but as a "legitimate daughter," a science worthy of a special place in the curriculum. Scandals of mismanagement, overcrowding, and incidents of neglect and maltreatment were to recur

from time to time, but the humanitarian impulse had been quickened, and there had been launched a philanthropy that promised
to endure.[26]

Wearied with fatigue and exhausted by a long journey through
New England and New York state, inspecting almshouses, prisons,
and hospitals, Miss Dix went to the hospital at Trenton to rest in
October 1881, and never left its walls again. She was very ill. She
might live for days, weeks, even months, but she would never be
able to travel again. When the managers of the institution learned
that Miss Dix was seriously ill in the hospital and would probably
never be able to leave it, they hurriedly called a meeting and by
unanimous vote tendered her an invitation to remain under the
roof of the institution that she had founded and to spend the rest
of her life there as its beloved and honored guest. She was given
an apartment under the pediment of the Greek portico which
formed the facade of the main building, and from which she had
an excellent view of the grounds, the broad countryside and the
Delaware River. For more than five years she lingered on in this
home of her "first-born child." She had ample funds with which
to provide nurses and attendants in some private home, but with
grateful heart she accepted the invitation of the directors of the New
Jersey Hospital to remain as their guest.

For more than fifty years she had known no home. The institutions that she founded were her only "children." She had loved
and cared for them most tenderly in their youth and now that she
was old and unable to perform further service for them, it was only
fitting that one of them in filial gratitude should throw open its
doors to her and care for her to the end of her days. The funds
that she had conserved to take care of her in old age might now be
properly diverted to charitable objects.

Her health rallied somewhat in the spring, and she was able to
take up her correspondence and daily reading again, but the pain
never completely ceased. She was slowly dying from ossification
of the arterial membrane and the doctors could offer her no relief.
She found confinement within four walls hard indeed, but she
seldom complained, saying, "It is all right, it should be so; it is
God's will." She took refuge in the Scriptures which had comforted her all through life, and she turned once more to hymns and
religious verse for consolation. She again composed bits of poetry,

repeating the lines over and over until she was able to copy them or to recite them to Miss Kirby, her faithful nurse and amanuensis.

Letters from her friends were an unfailing source of happiness; especially was she pleased to have letters from John Greenleaf Whittier, and Tom and Etta Eliot. Thomas Lamb Eliot, the son of her old friend, William Greenleaf Eliot of St. Louis, was the pastor of the First Unitarian Church in Portland, Oregon, and it was in his home that she had stayed while inspecting the hospitals and prisons in Portland. His great ambition and his frail health coupled with responsibility for his growing family caused Miss Dix much anxiety and she was ever advising him not to overwork but to have a "thought for tomorrow." She delighted in hearing from Henrietta about the children, especially the little "Dora" that had been named in her honor. Miss Dix always had a keen affection for her name and she had many namesakes. "Dorothea" to her was a beautiful name for it meant "gift of God." From Maine to Georgia and from New England to the Pacific may be found silver thimbles and tiny china teapots which she gave to little girls bearing her given name, "Dorothea," or any of its diminutives, Dorothy, Dora, Doris, Eldora, Theodosia, Theodora, or Dolly. At no time in her life, save in those early teaching days in Orange Court, did Dorothea Dix display more of a love for children than during those last years in Trenton. To the Eliot children and to the Godding children, Mary and Rena and Alvah, she frequently sent picture cards and inexpensive gifts of bean bags, statuettes, needle-cases, and books. She was always wanting to make someone a gift regardless of whether the things she had on hand were suitable. In one of the very last letters that she wrote, dated October 31, 1886, she enclosed a little paper of pins which she thought Etta might find useful. She wanted to give the children something too. "What can I send them, and how many have you?" she asked. "Will another five dollars get anything for Thanksgiving or Christmas, a small gift?"[27]

For many years she had exchanged letters with the Quaker poet, John Greenleaf Whittier. He sent her many of his poems before they were ever published. It was she who had written him the dramatic incident of Barbara Frietchie which he immortalized in verse. They shared a common love for moral heroism, obedience to conscience, and faith in the beautiful and good. It was to Whittier that she had appealed for an inscription for the watering fountain which she had presented to the city of Boston in 1879. He could not recall the Arabic inscription to which she had referred and had written another himself:

. . . taking it for granted that the fountain is to be thy gift though thee did not say so. Such a gift would not be inappropriate for one who all her life has been opening fountains in the desert of human suffering, who, to use a Scripture phrase, has "passed over the dry valley of Baca, making it a well."

> Stranger and traveler
> Drink freely and bestow
> A kindly thought on her
> Who bade this fountain flow
> Yet hath for it no claim
> Save as a minister
> Of blessing in God's name.[28]

He too "had known the pains and limitations of age and infirmities." A visit in 1882 to Haverhill Academy, where he had gone to school fifty-six years before, found that the trees which had stood young and green in front of it then, were now like himself, "old, feeble, and decaying." The faces that he had known then were now nearly all gone. When he learned that she was ill in the hospital at Trenton, he wrote:

I am glad that thou art with kind friends. Thou hast done so much for others, that it is right for thee now, in age and illness to be kindly ministered to. He who has led thee in thy great work of benevolence will not forsake thee. With a feeling of almost painful unworthiness I read thy overkind words as regards myself. I wish I could feel that I deserved them. But compared to such a life as thine, my own seems poor and inadequate. But none the less do I thank thee for thy generous appreciation.[29]

When she was able to write, she spoke again of her regard for his friendship.

How well I remember with comfort and cheer . . . your calls when I was at Danville. You did not suspect the good you were doing me; your presence bringing to recollection so much you had written inciting to a deeper hope and trust in Divine Providence, a more profound reverence for the Great Creator and a deeper conviction of the truths of the gospel of our Lord and Savior, Jesus, the Christ. I do not think, Mr. Whittier, you have ever realized the wide reaching blessing of your published works, . . . In saying this I am both earnest and honest.[30]

During those first years in the New Jersey Hospital, many visitors came softly up the stairs to Miss Dix's room. How happy it made her feel to know that though her activities were ended, she was not forgotten by her friends. Former students came bringing their grandchildren; medical superintendents, civil war nurses, humanitarians, statesmen asked to be directed to her room. George Emerson, to whom she had entrusted her charity school nearly sixty years before, and Henry Bellows stopped one. day on their way back from California. Hack 'Tuke, visiting America to obtain material for his book, *The Insane in the United States and Canada,* made a special trip to Trenton to see her. Tom Eliot came by on his way to Boston, and his father sent a poem.

Dear Sister, in thy lonely hours of suffering and pain,
Take comfort! The ten thousand prayers can not ascend in vain
From hearts which thou hast comforted and homes which thou hast
    cheered,
And children, saved from ignorance, whose pathway thou hast cleared,
From loyal hearts and homes, wherever they are found
In palaces and cottages with peace and honor crowned.
Dear Sister, thou art not alone, God's angels hover near,
His presence is thy sure defense, then what hast thou to fear?
The "good fight" thou hast nobly fought and truly "kept the faith;"
The crown awaits thee, Sister dear, the "victory over death;"
Take courage then, dear friend! The "prize" is almost won.
Hark! 'Tis the Saviour's voice we hear, "Servant of God, well done!"
                          Your brother-friend
                          W. G. Eliot.[81]

Tributes of love and veneration from many parts of the world helped to brighten the days when paroxysms of pain threatened to break her very spirit. Her afflictions were many. She became extremely deaf; her sight became impaired, and her memory on which she had drawn so much for comfort and entertainment failed. It distressed her not to be able to recall a name or a face. Friends tried to help her, but in vain. "Try to put this tube in my ear so as not to pain and yet allow me to hear what you have to say." Often she reminisced of Greenbank, Orange Court, Ann in Brookline, and Dr. Channing. In her last letter to Matilda Lieber, and perhaps the very last that she wrote unaided, her mind wandered back over forty-five years to Dr. Channing's home in Boston, and instead of giving her address as the New Jersey Hospital, she absently wrote across the margin, "85 Mount Vernon Street."[82]

About her room were mementoes of her long career; especially noteworthy was a large box of highly polished wood, inlaid on the top with the metallic inscription, "To Miss D. L. D. from the American Club of Bohemian Ladies." It was sent to her in 1868 as a token of affection and admiration from a group of women in Prague who were interested in elevating the status of women and the poorer classes in Bohemia. It contained a biographical sketch of Miss Dix in the Bohemian language, translations of Bohemian poems, and an album of historical scenes and another of distinguished Bohemian women and statesmen. Among the numerous papers in the little desk were testimonials from the British Government, and the distinguished Japanese ambassador, Jugio Arinori Mori, who had met her in Washington and been inspired to do something for the mentally ill when he returned to his own country. Two hospitals there now bore noble testimony to his endeavors.

At last, unable to receive many callers or to talk for any length of time, she spent hours gazing across the landscape communing in spirit with those she would never see again. For a month she had been growing steadily weaker. She realized the time of her departure was not far distant. She asked Dr. Ward not to give her anything that would cause her to lose consciousness and to tell her when the last hour had come. On the evening of July 18, 1887, as he sat in his apartment, a nurse came hurrying down the hall. "Miss Dix is sinking, sir." As he opened the door she breathed a quiet sigh.

Under her pillow was found a well-worn manuscript copy of Whittier's "At Last." It was read at the burial service held a few days later in Mount Auburn Cemetery, near Boston. Her funeral was marked by the simplicity that she loved. Dr. John Ward, Dr. Charles Nichols, Horace Lamb, and a few other friends stood by as the scriptural text and the commitment were read.

I was an hungered and ye gave me meat; I was thirsty and ye gave me drink; I was a stranger and ye took me in; naked and ye clothed me; I was sick and ye visited me; I was in prison and ye came unto me.

Today the American flag, together with the standard of the Corps of Army Nurses, flies over the grave of this forgotten samaritan. The marble marker, erected by Horace Lamb, bears neither epitaph nor date, only "Dorothea L. Dix."

NOTES

CHAPTER I

1. William D. Williamson, *History of Maine*, II, 566.

2. The *Worcester Vital Records*, 1894, p. 74, gives the children of Dr. Elijah Dix and Dorothy Lynde Dix as follows: William, born August 2, 1772; Joseph, born February 6, 1774; Mary, born April 14, 1776; Joseph, born March 29, 1778; Clarendon, born September 26, 1779; John, born April 1, 1781; Alexander, born August 18, 1782. An eighth child, Henry Elijah, also born in Worcester, on February 6, 1793, does not appear on the Worcester Records. The first Joseph, for whom Dorothea's father was named, died on October 18, 1775.

3. Alfred S. Roe, *Dorothea Lynde Dix*, pp. 1 ff. Mr. Roe credits this information to the Rev. Mr. Francis Tiffany who was then at work on his *Life of Dorothea Lynde Dix*. Mr. Tiffany made no use of this datum in his work which was written according to Miss Dix's wishes and under the supervision of her executor, Mr. Horace Lamb, of Boston. Miss Dix's aversion to discussing her family or her age was a well known idiosyncrasy.

4. From an old handbill in the Library of Congress.

5. A letter from Elizabeth L. Bond, a relative of Dorothea Dix, to the author, November 1931.

6. Francis Tiffany, *Life of Dorothea Lynde Dix*, p. 5.

7. Letter from Mrs. H. S. Hayward, Boston, September 28, 1836, to Dorothea Dix, Liverpool, on the occasion of the death of Mary Bigelow Dix. Quoted in Tiffany, *op. cit.*, p. 48.

8. The date of the birth of Charles Wesley Dix is not known. It was perhaps in 1808. He died at sea in 1843.

9. Williamson, *op. cit.*, II, 566.

10. William Dix, eldest son of Dr. Elijah Dix and Mary Lynde Dix, died in Dominique, West Indies, 1799; Alexander, sixth son, was killed in Canada, March 23, 1809; Clarendon, fourth son, lost his life in Kentucky, September 1, 1811.

11. Caroline A. Kennard, *Dorothea L. Dix and Her Work*, Brookline, 1887, p. 1.

12. This portrait is now in the possession of Madam Dix's descendants through her daughter, Mary Dix Harris, at present living in Cambridge, Massachusetts. See illustration facing p. 24 in the present work.

13. Dorothea Lynde Dix, *Meditations for Private Hours,* p. 21. "She [religion] tells thee that though thou hast no certain trust, no enduring home, One has gone to prepare for thee a mansion in thy Father's House, where thou wilt have rest. There will He prepare a place for thee and thou shalt not call theyself an orphan, one is thy parent, even God."

14. Roe, *op. cit.*, p. 135.

15. Letter from Elizabeth Bond to Helen Marshall, November 1931. Marshall Papers.

16. The dates of Dorothea Dix's sojourn in Worcester are not known. It is not probable that she remained there more than three years, if that long.

17. Roe, *op. cit.*, p. 136.

18. Anne Bancroft became the wife of Dr. Charles Ingalls, of Jacksonville College, Louisiana.

19. Roe, *op. cit.*, p. 135.

CHAPTER II

1. Charles Shaw, *A Typographical and Historical Description of Boston*, p. 202.

2. Sarah D. Locke Stow, "Higher Education for Women," in George Gary Bush, ed., *History of Education in Massachusetts*, p. 395.

3. *Ibid.*, pp. 277-78. Subscribers to the circulating libraries paid $7.00 a year and were entitled to take out three or four volumes at a time which had to be returned within limits that restricted relending. Non-subscribers paid six cents a week for duodecimo volumes and twelve and one-half cents for octavos.

4. Percy H. Epler, *Master Minds at the Commonwealth's Heart*, p. 126.

5. Arthur Wellington Brayley, *Schools and Schoolboys of Old Boston*, p. 102.

6. *Ibid.*, pp. 185-86. In one Boston school the early thirties were known as the "reign of terror." There was much flogging; children were "whipped into intelligence." Teachers in whipping often repeated the formula, "And this I do to keep you from the gallows."

7. Kennard, *op. cit.*, p. 1.

8. Dorothea Dix to Ann Heath, undated. Dix-Heath MSS.

9. *Ibid.*

10. Brayley, *op. cit.*, p. 49.

11. Dorothea Dix to her grandmother, Madam Dorothy Lynde Dix, undated. Quoted in Tiffany, *op. cit.*, p. 16.

12. Charles A. Harris, *Rapid Survey of the Massachusetts Educational System*, p. 89.

13. Dorothea Dix to Ann Heath, undated. Dix-Heath MSS.

14. Dorothea Dix to Ann Heath. Sunday evening, undated. Dix-Heath MSS

15. *Ibid.* Attached are two quotations from Lord Thames, on inconstancy in love, and envy and the conditions in life which breed envy.

16. Dorothea Dix to Ann Heath, 1823. Dix-Heath MSS.

17. Thomas Wyse, *Publications of the Central Society of Education*, II, London, 1838. (*Old South Leaflets*, VI, 306-11.) Boston, 1843.

18. Dorothea Dix to Ann Heath, undated. Dix-Heath MSS.

19. Vernon Louis Parrington, *Main Currents in American Thought*, II, 327.

20. William E. Channing, *The Works of William E. Channing*, pp. 5-7.

21. *Ibid.*, "Sermon on the Ordination of Jared Sparks, Baltimore, 1819," pp. 381-82.

22. These conclusions are the product of a careful study of Dorothea Dix's early letters to Ann Heath and her later correspondence with George Emerson, John Greenleaf Whittier, Matilda Lieber, and the Eliots in Portland, Oregon, and of the fact that although she frequently tried to serve as matchmaker herself, she always resented any attempt of friends to perform those "good offices" in her own behalf. For a while the youthful Dorothea and Ann made much of the calls and conversations with Ezra Stiles Gannett, newly appointed assistant to Dr. Channing; but time proved that his attentions were only those of an earnest young pastor who was more concerned with the souls than with the hearts of his lady parishioners.

23. Channing, "The Perfecting Power of Religion," *op. cit.*, p. 984.

24. The Fragment Society was incorporated in November, 1816, for the relief of women and children in destitute circumstances.

25. Dorothea Dix to Ann Heath, undated. Dix-Heath MSS.

26. Dorothea Dix to Ann Heath, 1825. Dix-Heath MSS.

27. Kennard, *op. cit.*, p. 2.

28. Dorothea Dix to Ann Heath, undated. Dix-Heath MSS.

29. Dorothea Dix to Ann Heath, 1825. Dix-Heath MSS.

30. Excerpt quoted by Munroe and Francis, Publishers, in the back of Dorothea Lynde Dix's *Hymns for Children.*

31. Dorothea Lynde Dix, *Conversations on Common Things.* Preface to the third edition, 1828. Copy in the Athenaeum, Boston.

32. Dorothea Dix to Ann Heath, undated. Dix-Heath MSS.

33. Dix, *Hymns for Children,* Preface.

34. *Ibid.,* p. 8.

35. Dorothea Dix to Ann Heath. Sunday evening, undated. Dix-Heath MSS.

36. *Ibid.*

37. Dorothea Lynde Dix, *Evening Hours.* No copies are extant. It is probable that *Meditations for Private Hours* published in 1828 was an enlargement of this work and that only one edition was brought out.

38. This was especially true in later years. Many of these verses were written in honor of a birthday or other anniversary.

39. Dorothea Dix to Ann Heath, January 1826. Dix-Heath MSS.

40. William Ellery Channing to Dorothea Dix. Quoted in Tiffany, *op. cit.,* p. 22.

41. Mary Channing Eustis to Francis Tiffany. *Ibid.,* p. 34.

42. Clarence L. F. Gohdes, *Periodicals of American Transcendentalism,* p. 145.

43. Dorothea Dix to Ann Heath, June 23, 1827. Dix-Heath MSS.

44. Dorothea Lynde Dix, *American Moral Tales for Young Persons,* p. 59. Contents: John Williams or the Sailor Boy; Little Agnes and Blind Mary; Robert Woodard or the Heedless Boy; James Coleman or the Reward of Perseverance; The Dainty Boy; Alice and Ruth; Marrion Wilder, the Passionate Little Girl; Sequel to Marrion Wilder; George Mills; the Storm.

45. *Ibid.,* p. 266.

46. *Ibid.,* p. 161.

47. *Ibid.,* p. 167.

48. Dix, *Meditations for Private Hours.*

49. *Ibid.,* p. 13.

50. Dorothea Lynde Dix, *The Pearl or Affection's Gift: A Christmas and New Year's Present,* Philadelphia, 1829. There are no known copies extant.

51. Dorothea Lynde Dix, *Garland of Flora.* This work indicates Miss Dix's familiarity with the best of English literature.

52. Dorothea Dix to Ann Heath, May 31, probably 1827. Dix-Heath MSS. The "Miss Frances" referred to was probably Lydia Maria Francis who married Mr. Child. She became a prominent writer and feminist.

53. Tiffany, *op. cit.,* p. 33.

54. *Ibid.,* p. 29.

55. Brayley, *op. cit.,* p. 103.

56. Harris, *op. cit.,* pp. 25 ff.

57. In the Library of Congress there is a broadside which was circulated by Mr. Bailey. It gives light on the curricula of the girls school of the period. It included the three R's, English grammar, and geography. The tuition per quarter was $15 for juniors, and $20 for seniors.

58. Ednah D. Cheyney, "Women of Boston," in Justin Winsor, ed., *Memorial History of Boston,* IV, 343-44.

59. Seth Curtis Beach, *Daughters of the Puritans,* p. 137.

60. Kennard, *op. cit.,* p. 2.

61. Dix, *Hymns for Children,* Dedication.

62. Margaret J. W. Merrill to Francis Tiffany. Quoted in Tiffany, *op. cit.,* p. 41.

63. *Ibid.,* p. 38.   64. *Ibid.,* p. 40.   65. *Ibid.*

CHAPTER III

1. Dorothea Dix to Ann Heath, March 5, 1826. Dix-Heath MSS.

2. Chamberlain Autographs, a collection containing Dorothea Dix's letters to George Barrell Emerson, Boston Public Library. This poem was enclosed in a letter dated March 1836.

3. Edward H. Jenkins, "George Barrell Emerson," *Dictionary of American Biography*, VI, 127.

4. *Suffolk County Court Records*, Boston, Massachusetts. Will of Elijah Dix, Case No. 23353. Certain estate in Maine was bequeathed to the grandchildren of the deceased, excepting the children of his son, Henry. Dorothy Dix, the granddaughter, was to receive $100 annually from his unappropriated estate until the date of her marriage.

5. Dorothea Dix to G. B. Emerson, April 9, 1836. Chamberlain Autographs.

6. *Ibid.*, April 3, 1836.

7. Rev. J. H. Thom (1808-94) was a Unitarian preacher in Liverpool who later married a daughter of Mr. Rathbone. This sermon greatly impressed William Rathbone, V, who later became a wealthy merchant, shipowner, and member of Parliament. Before he was thirty he was giving one tenth of his income to public objects, and he increased his gifts in proportion to his income until he was giving away one-half of all that he earned.

8. Mrs. H. S. Hayward to Dorothea Dix, September 28, 1836. Quoted in Tiffany, *op. cit.*, p. 48.

9. Dorothea Dix to Ann Heath, January 25, 1837. Dix-Heath MSS.

10. The group of transcendentalists who later edited *The Dial*.

11. Harriet Bailey, *Nursing Mental Diseases*, pp. 23-24.

12. Dorothea Dix to Ann Heath, Liverpool, November 12, 1836. Dix-Heath MSS.

13. Thaddeus Mason Harris, "Notes on the Character of Madam Dorothy Dix, 1746-1837" (Unpublished Manuscript in the Harris Papers).

"Rigorous as she was in judging herself, she used much lenity in judging the conduct and character of others. . . . In the common intercourse of life it was uniformly her object no less to avoid giving pain than to study to give pleasure, and withal to promote the improvement and to contribute to the benefit, temporal and spiritual, of all around her. . . . Her disposition was affectionate and benevolent. The poor, the sick and the afflicted found in her a compassionate and bountiful benefactress."

14. Tiffany, *op. cit.*, p. 51. Dorothea was never popular with Mrs. Harris' daughters who resented that she had remained in England while her grandmother lay dying and asking for her. Upon her return the breach widened and in later years they became practically estranged. Although living within a dozen miles of her, some of Miss Dix's second cousins never met her.

15. *Ibid.*

16. Roe, *op. cit.*, p. 12.

17. *Suffolk County Court Records*, Boston, Massachusetts. Will of Mrs. Dorothy Dix, Case No. 31557.

18. In 1923 Mr. Horace A. Lamb, of Boston, the executor of Miss Dix's estate, turned over to Simmons College, $50,000.00 the last residue from royalties and sundry sources of income that could not be liquidated immediately upon her decease, to be used as a loan and trust fund to assist worthy young women through college. Much of this money accrued from royalties on the Rev. Mr. Francis Tiffany's *Life of Dorothea Lynde Dix*, and as Miss Dix directed, was now to be applied

to a worthy cause identified with her interests. A portion of the fund also came from royalties on Miss Dix's own writings, and from gifts of friends who wished to honor her memory.

19. Clinton J. Furness, *The Genteel Female*, p. 3.

20. Edward Dillingham Bangs was born in Worcester, Massachusetts, on April 24, 1790, and died there on April 2, 1838. He was secretary of state for the Commonwealth of Massachusetts from 1824 to 1836. On April 12, 1824, he was married to Mary Grosvenor, of Worcester.

21. Dorothea Dix to Ann Heath, Washington, D. C., February 24, 1838. Dix-Heath MSS.

22. Dorothea Dix to Ann Heath, Washington, D. C., March 3, 1838. Dix-Heath MSS.

23. Ralph Waldo Emerson to Margaret Fuller. Quoted in George Willis Cooke's Introduction to the Rowfant edition of *The Dial* (Cleveland, 1902), I, 92.

24. Dr. T. G. Nichols was for many years pastor at Saco, Maine.

25. B. O. Flowers, "Treatment of the Insane Poor in Massachusetts Sixty Years Ago; or How a Woman Wrought a Revolution in Human Progress," *Arena*, XXXII (1904), 535-42.

26. Charles Sumner to Samuel Gridley Howe. Quoted in Tiffany, *op. cit.*, p. 75.

CHAPTER IV

1. *Sixth Census of the United States, Population*, 1840, p. 475. The special census report and investigation of statistics on the insane, 1904, declare the census of 1840 to be unreliable and the number of mentally ill underestimated. No attempt was made by the Census to distinguish between idiocy and psychosis before 1850.

2. Charles D. Lee, *Report on Insanity*.

3. Pierre Janet, "Neurosis and Psychoses," in *A Psychiatric Milestone*, p. 123.

4. Jacob Goldberg, *Social Aspects in the Treatment of the Insane*, p. 15; Robert Howland Chase, *The Ungeared Mind*, p. 3; James J. Walsh, "Some Chapters in the History of Care for the Insane," *Medical Life*, Series No. 139 (April, 1932), pp. 208-20.

5. Smith Ely Jelliffe, "Some Random Notes on the History of Psychiatry in the Middle Ages," *American Journal of Psychiatry*, II (September, 1930), 276; Emil Kraepelin, *Hundert Jahre Psychiatrie*, pp. 10 ff.

6. Daniel Hack Tuke, *Chapters in the History of the Insane in the British Isles.*

7. William P. Letchworth, *The Insane in Foreign Countries*, p. 2.

8. W. A. F. Browne, *Insanity and Asylums for the Insane*, p. 100.

9. *Ibid.*, p. 102.

10. Smith Ely Jelliffe, "Some Random Notes on the History of Psychiatry in the Middle Ages," *American Journal of Psychiatry*, II (September, 1930), 275.

11. J. C. Prichard, et al., "Insanity and Insane Hospitals," *North American Review*, XLIV (1837), 91-121.

12. *Minutes of Evidence Taken Before the Select Committee of the House of Commons, 1815*, p. 95. Quoted in Tuke, *The Insane in the United States and Canada*, p. 21.

13. Doctor Cabanes, "La Centenaire d'un Médecin Philanthrope: Pinel, Libérateur des Aliénés," *L'Illustration*, LXXXIV (October 23, 1926), pt. 2, p. 453.

14. Frank B. Sanborn, "Belgian System of Family Care," *Charities Review*, IX (1899), 182.

15. J. Colombier and F. Doublet, *Instruction sur la Maniere de Gouverner les Insenses et de Travailler a leur Guerison dans les Asyles qui lieur sont Destines.*

16. Vincienzi Chiarugi, 1759-1821, learned Italian physician, like Pinel, maintained courageously the need for fundamental reform in the system of providing for the indigent mentally ill and in the methods of medical treatment. Arturo Castiglioni, *Storia della Medicina*, pp. 644-45.

17. In 1803 Pinel published his *Traite sur l'Alienation Mentale*, which received commendation in England. See Professor Henry Reeve's review, "Pinel, Traite sur l'Alienation Mentale," *Edinburgh Review*, II (April 1803), 161.

18. Napoleon in 1803 sent neglected mentally diseased soldiers to Gheel where the Brussels physician, Dr. Parigot, was in charge.

19. M. J. Esquirol, *Des Etablissimens consacres aux Alienes en France et des Moyens de les Ameliorer*, pp. 14 ff.

20. Lucy H. Hooper, "Maniacs and Madhouses of Paris," *Lippincott's Magazine*, XXI (1878), 763; J. R. G., "Notes on French Asylums for the Insane under the Religious," *The Month*, VIII (1868), 148.

21. York Lunatic Asylum was founded in 1772. At that time there were only four other hospitals for the reception of lunatics in the kingdom, one being located at Newcastle, another in Manchester, and two, Bethlehem and St. Luke's in London.

22. Tuke, *Chapters in the History of the Insane in the British Isles*, pp. 112 ff.

23. Daniel Hack Tuke, "Legislation for the Insane," *Contemporary Review*, XXX (1877), 743.

24. *See* Anthony Ashley Cooper, Earl of Shaftesbury, *Speeches of the Earl of Shaftesbury Upon Subjects Having Relation Chiefly to the Claims and Interests of the Labouring Class*, pp. 169 ff.

25. Tuke, "Legislation for the Insane," *Contemporary Review*, XXX (1877), 743.

26. The Committee Report of 1829 showed the total number of hours spent by patients in restraint was 20,423; by 1838 the number was reduced to 0.

27. Sir James Clark, "A Memoir of John Conolly," *Edinburgh Review*, CXXXI (April 1870), 418.

28. Robert Gardiner Hill, *A Concise History of the Entire Abolition of Mechanical Restraint in the Treatment of the Insane; and of the Introduction, Success, and Final Triumph of the Non-Restraint System*, pp. 52 ff.

29. James Galt was keeper, 1773-1801; upon his death a relative, William T. Galt, succeeded him. Dr. Minson Galt, of the same family, was visiting physician, 1795-1809; his son, Dr. Alexander Galt (1777-1840) a pupil of Sir Ashley Cooper, was physician to the hospital, 1800-1840, and a grandson, Dr. John M. Galt, Jr. (1814-1862), was superintendent of the hospital, 1841-1861. Thus four generations served in the hospital at Williamsburg. Esther Garland Iglehart, "Brief History of the Eastern State Hospital" (unpublished Master's thesis, William and Mary College, Williamsburg, Virginia, 1930).

30. Henry Mills Hurd, *Institutional Care of the Insane in the United States and Canada*, I, 408.

31. *American Journal of Insanity*, VII (July 1850), pp. 64-65; Elizabeth Wisner, *Public Welfare Administration in Louisiana*, p. 85.

32. *Records of Savannah, Georgia*, Minutes of the Council from October 1817 to March 1822, p. 221.

33. Joseph McFarland, "History of Nursing, Blockley Asylum," *Medical Life*, Series No. 146, XXXIX (November 1932), 632.

34. "Historical Sketch of the New Orleans Charity Hospital," *New Orleans Medical Journal*, I (May 1844), 72-77. Women prisoners detailed for sick room duty frequently drank the stimulants provided for the patients.

35. Cotton Mather expressed this viewpoint in his "The Life of Mr. William Thompson," the devout pastor of Braintree, who became afflicted with a "black melancholy." Note the case of David and Saul, I Sam. 16: 16. See Dr. Amariah Brigham, "Moral Treatment of Insanity," *American Journal of Insanity*, IV (1847-1848), 1, 2.

36. Hurd, *op. cit.*, I, 82.

37. *Ibid.*, p. 89.

38. *Laws of New York*, 1800, Chapter III entitled, "An Act to pardon John Pastano." The governor did not have the authority to pardon under such conditions. Goldberg, *op. cit.*, p. 18.

39. Goldberg, *op. cit.*, pp. 18-19.

40. Richard H. Shryock, "Public Relations of the Medical Profession in Great Britain and the United States, 1800-1870: A Chapter in the Social History of Medicine," *Annals of Medical History*, n. s. II (May 1930), 308-39.

41. Isaac Woodbridge Riley, *American Thought from Puritanism to Pragmatism*, p. 104; Tuke, *The Insane in the United States and Canada*, p. 7; Francis R. Packard, *History of Medicine in the United States*, I, 114 ff.

42. Benjamin Rush, *Medical Inquiries and Observations*, p. 38.

43. *Ibid.*

44. Carter Atkinson, "Notes from Benjamin Rush's lectures on 'The Institutes and Practices of Medicine'," University of Pennsylvania, 1800. Manuscript in Duke University Library.

45. Rush, *Medical Inquiries and Observations*, p. 178.

46. Dr. Rush was facetiously called the "old ten in ten" because of his invariable prescription of ten grains of calomel and ten grains of jalap.

47. The gyrator was a chair in which the patient was strapped; it was spun rapidly by a mechanical device. The rotary motion was intended to "give a centrifugal direction of the blood toward the brain" and thus cure the patient. Chase, *op. cit.*, p. 239.

48. Francis T. Stribling, "Medical Treatment of the Insane in Virginia," *The American Journal of Medical Science*, VI (1843), 145. In 1857 Dr. Pliny Earle complained bitterly that Rush's theories were annually consigning hundreds prematurely to the grave and hundreds more to premature mental illness; and that this influence would continue as long as his book was to be found in more libraries than all other books on the same subject. See Franklin B. Sanborn, *Memoirs of Pliny Earle*, p. 145.

49. Tuke, *The Insane in the United States and Canada*, p. 35.

50. Robert W. Kelso, *History of Public Poor Relief in Massachusetts*, pp. 133 ff.

51. The New York General Hospital received its charter from the royal governor, Dunmore, but owing to a fire and the American Revolution it was not ready for occupancy until 1791.

52. By 1844 New York had appropriated $550,000 to enable the governors of the New York Hospital to care for mentally ill patients. Amariah Brigham, "Brief Notice of the New York State Lunatic Asylum, Utica, New York," *American Journal of Insanity*, I (July 1844), 3.

53. Wisner, *op. cit.*, p. 85. 53a. Drewry, "Care and Treatment of the Defectives in the South," *The South in the Building of the Nation*, X, 597-602.

54. Dr. Nehemiah Cutter, of Pepperel, Massachusetts, began in 1822 to take mentally ill persons into his home, and kept a private institution until it burned in 1853. Hurd, *op. cit.*, IV, 384.

55. *Ibid.*, II, 70; Charles Whitney Page, "Dr. Eli Todd and the Hartford Retreat," *American Journal of Insanity*, LXIX (April, 1913), 761.

56. Hurd, *op. cit.*, II, 70; also Tuke, *The Insane in the United States and Canada*, p. 24. Dr. Wyman, first physician and superintendent of McLean Hospital, although not very widely known as a medical writer, was a man of superior qualifications and performed admirable work in organizing the hospital. He objected to bleeding, purging, and low diet.

57. "Insane Asylums of the United States," *American Journal of Insanity*, II (July, 1845), 54.

58. Iglehart, *op. cit.*, p. 45.

59. *History of the Maryland Hospital for the Insane*, pp. 5 ff.

CHAPTER V

1. George Allen Hubbell, *Horace Mann, Educator, Patriot, and Reformer*, pp. 66; F. B. Sanborn, *Report of the Public Charities of Massachusetts, during the century ending January 1, 1876*, pp. 25 ff.

2. Hubbell, *op. cit.*, p. 61.

3. Hurd, *op. cit.*, II, 584.

4. *Ibid.*, p. 586.

5. Robert Cassie Waterston, *The Condition of the Insane in Massachusetts*, pp. 9-10.

6. Mary Tyler Mann, *Life of Horace Mann, by His Wife*, p. 56.

7. Horace Mann to Charles Sumner, April 29, 1837. Quoted in *ibid.*, p. 57.

8. According to the revised statute of 1836, the several counties of the commonwealth were required to provide for the paupers within their limits who being mentally ill or idiotic, were unsafe to go at large and who could not be admitted to the hospital at Worcester either because of their condition or the crowded state of the institution.

Hurd, *op. cit.*, II, 59; also, Kelso, *op. cit.*, p. 127.

9. Excerpt from the Inaugural Speech of Mayor Samuel Eliot, 1837. Reprint from *The Christian Examiner*, January 1843.

10. The Boston Prison Discipline Society founded 1824, disbanded in 1844.

11. The control of the Boston Lunatic Asylum was transferred to the state, December 1, 1908. It is now known as the Boston State Hospital. Hurd, *op. cit.*, II, 591.

12. Queenie Bilbo, "Elizabeth Peabody, Transcendentalist" (unpublished Ph.D. Thesis, Columbia University, 1932).

13. Dorothea Lynde Dix, *Memorial to the Legislature of Massachusetts (Old South Leaflets*, Vol. VI, No. 148), p. 2.

14. *Ibid.*, p. 5.

15. *Ibid.*, p. 4.

16. *Ibid.*, p. 6.

17. *Ibid.*, pp. 15-16.

18. *Ibid.*, pp. 22-23.

19. *Ibid.*, p. 2.

20. Samuel Gridley Howe to Dorothea Dix. Quoted in Tiffany, *op. cit.*, p. 89.

21. See conclusion of Dix, *Memorial to the Legislature of Massachusetts*.

22. J. T. Buckingham, editorial in the *Boston Courier*, January 19, 1843.

23. B. O. Flowers, editorial, "Treatment of the Insane Poor in Massachusetts Sixty Years Ago; or How a Woman Wrought a Revolution for Human Progress," *Arena*, XXXII (November 1904), 536-42.

24. Compare J. T. Buckingham's editorials in the *Boston Courier* for January 19, 1843 and February 22, 1843.

25. Editorial, *Boston Courier*, February 23, 1843.

26. *Boston Daily Advertiser*, February 23, 1843.

27. *Ibid.*, February 27, 1843.

28. Samuel Gridley Howe to Dorothea Dix. Quoted in Tiffany, *op. cit.*, p. 90.

29. Public Letter, Charles Sumner to the Editor, *Boston Courier*, February 25, 1843.

30. Tiffany, *op. cit.*, pp. 87-88.

31. *Boston Daily Advertiser*, January 23, 1843.

CHAPTER VI

1. *New York Tribune*, January 24, 1844; *ibid.*, March 19, 1844; J. L. Bigelow, "Miss Dix and What She Has Done," *Galaxy*, III (1867), pp. 668 ff.

2. Dorothea Dix to Mrs. William Rathbone, 1845. Rathbone MSS.

3. The hospitals referred to are (1) the Butler Hospital, Providence, R. I., reorganized and refounded; (2) the hospital at Trenton, N. J., the first hospital created outright by Miss Dix's efforts, and spoken of by her as her "first-born child"; (3) the "Asylum" at Harrisburg, Pennsylvania; (4) State Hospital, Utica, N. Y., doubled in size; (5) hospital at Toronto, Canada. In 1843 Miss Dix had aided leading physicians in their efforts to secure a hospital by presenting a memorial to the Provincial Parliament of East and West Canada. Tiffany, *op. cit.*, p. 132.

4. Edward Field, *State of Rhode Island and Providence Plantations at the End of the Century*, III, 390.

5. Tiffany, *op. cit.*, p. 96.

6. Beach, *op. cit.*, p. 190.

7. The *Providence Journal*, April 10, 1844.

8. Codicil to the will of Nicholas Brown, dated March 3, 1841. Quoted in Hurd, *op. cit.*, III, 554.

9. Sanborn, *Memoirs of Pliny Earle*, p. 367.

10. *Ibid.*, p. 96.

11. Dorothea Dix to G. B. Emerson, Newport, May 11, 1844. Chamberlain Autographs.

12. *Ibid.*

13. Hurd, *op. cit.*, III, 59.

14. Harry Elmer Barnes, *A History of the Penal, Reformatory, and Corrective Institutions of the State of New Jersey*.

15. Dorothea Lynde Dix, *Memorial Soliciting a State Hospital for the Insane*, submitted to the Legislature of New Jersey, January 2, 1845.

16. Tiffany, *op. cit.*, p. 116.

17. Dorothea Dix to Mrs. Hare, Trenton, N. J., February 1845. Quoted in *ibid.*, pp. 114-15.

18. Dorothea Dix to G. B. Emerson, November 13, 1843. Chamberlain Autographs.

19. Tiffany, *op. cit.*, p. 105.

20. Dorothea Lynde Dix, *Memorial Soliciting a State Hospital for the Insane of Pennsylvania*, February 3, 1845. Harry Elmer Barnes, *Repression of Crime*, New York, 1921, p. 250.

21. Marion Hathway, "Dorothea Dix and Social Reform in Western Pennsylvania, 1845-1875," *Western Pennsylvania Historical Magazine*, XVII (December, 1934), 249.

22. *Ibid.*   23. *Ibid.*, p. 250.   24. *Ibid.*, p. 251.

25. In 1786 Pennsylvania acted upon the demand of the Society for Alleviating the Miseries of Public Prisons, and the convicts were separated as to sex and type. Solitary confinement was also instituted. Harry Elmer Barnes, *Repression of Crime*, p. 124; see also, E. C. Wines, *The State of Prisons and Child-Saving Institutions in the Civilized World*, I, 22.

26. Mann, *op. cit.*, p. 188.

27. Dorothea Lynde Dix, *Remarks on Prisons and Prison Discipline*, p. 21.

28. Dorothea Dix to Ann Heath, Jackson, Mississippi, November 16, 1846. Dix-Heath MSS.

29. Dorothea Dix to G. B. Emerson, Nashville, Tennessee, December 10, 1845. Chamberlain Autographs.

30. Miss Dix probably over-estimated facilities in New Orleans as she never visited the city during the fever season when all the wards of the hospitals were full, and the insane patients were shifted from their quarters to make room for fever patients. In 1843 there were 5,023 patients admitted to Charity Hospital. Of this number one-fifth died. See Beach, *op. cit.*, p. 154; O. T. Powell, "A Sketch of Psychiatry in the Southern States," *American Journal of Insanity*, LIV (July, 1897), 21-36.

31. Dorothea Dix to George Emerson, Charleston, South Carolina, April 1846. Chamberlain Autographs.

32. In 1821, South Carolina passed an act creating the state hospital at Columbia, but it was not opened until December 1828. The Georgia State Sanatorium, established by the legislature in 1837, was opened in December 1842. Virginia's second institution for the insane was opened at Staunton in 1828.

According to C. B. Hayden, "On the Distribution of Insanity," *Southern Literary Messenger*, X (March 1844), the ratio of insane in the non-slaveholding states was one white to 1,635, one black to 153, and in the slaveholding states, one white to 1,740, and one black to 1,722.

33. Dorothea Dix to Ann Heath, Cincinnati, Ohio, November 16, 1846. Dix-Heath MSS.

34. Dorothea Lynde Dix, *Memorial to the General Assembly of North Carolina*.

35. A special room was fitted up by the trustees as a home for Miss Dix to occupy when she chose to visit the institution. *History of Tennessee*, p. 291.

36. This and subsequent memorials to Congress will be discussed in a separate chapter.

37. William K. Boyd, *The Federal Period*, p. 251.

38. Nothing was done for the blind in North Carolina until 1852, when the Institution for the Deaf, Dumb, and Blind was established.

39. See Dix, *Memorial to the General Assembly of North Carolina*, pp. 2 ff.

40. Samuel A. Ashe, ed., *Biographical History of North Carolina*, VI, 209.

41. *Ibid.*, pp. 208 ff.

42. *Greensboro* (N. C.) *Patriot*, December 2, 1848.

43. R. D. W. Connor, *Makers of North Carolina History*, p. 186.

44. This incident was related to the author by Colonel Fred Olds, a nephew of the surgeon. Raleigh, North Carolina, April, 1932.

45. Dorothea Lynde Dix, *Memorial Soliciting a State Hospital for the Insane*, *submitted to the Legislature of Alabama*, November 15, 1849.

46. Miss Dix's work was entirely lost. In 1851 the hospital question was revived. A bill passed the legislature and was approved by the governor on February 9, 1852. Owing to the difficulty in securing materials, the construction of the main

building continued over a period of eight years. It was opened for the reception of patients in October 1860. The building, four stories with three wings, was modeled after the Kirkbride plan. The hospital is now known as Bryce Hospital in honor of Dr. Peter Bryce, who was its superintendent from the time of its opening until his death in August 1892.

47. Hurd, *op. cit.*, I, 451, 482-87.

48. Dorothea Dix to Ann Heath, Jackson, Mississippi, February 1, 1850. Dix-Heath MSS.

49. Mann, *op. cit.*, p. 57.

50. *Greensboro Patriot*, February 10, 1849.

51. Dorothea Dix to Ann Heath, Jackson, Mississippi, February 18, 1850. Dix-Heath MSS.

52. *Ibid.*

53. Anna E. Heath to D. L. Dix, January 15, 1849. Dix-Heath MSS.

54. The legislature in 1852 appointed a commission to select a site. In 1853 work was begun on the new buildings at Spring Grove, near Catonsville, Maryland. The general assemblies of 1856, 1859, and 1860 made liberal appropriations, but it was not until 1872 that the patients were transferred to the new quarters.

55. Dorothea Dix to Ann Heath, St. Johns, Newfoundland, June 1853. Dix-Heath MSS.

56. These figures are taken from an article in *Harper's New Monthly Magazine* for December, 1866, and quoted in Tiffany, *op. cit.*, p. 210.

57. Tiffany, *op. cit.*, p. 216.

58. The "Victoria of Boston," for the use of Sable Island, was a gift to Miss Dix for that purpose from Abbott Lawrence, Jonathan Philipps, Colonel T. H. Perkins, William Appleton, R. C. Harper, R. B. Forbes, and G. N. Upton, of Boston.

59. Dorothea Dix to Sir George Seymour, New York, November 29, 1853. Tiffany, *op. cit.*, pp. 218-19.

60. Francis George Shaw, "Review of Dorothea Dix Memorial on Prisons and Prison Discipline," *The Harbinger*, I (November 8, 1845), 346-47.

61. Dorothea Dix to Mrs. William Rathbone, June 1850. Rathbone MSS.

CHAPTER VII

1. *Niles' Weekly Register*, September 13, 1848.

2. John A. Dix and Dorothea Dix were not related. They were very good friends. Miss Dix often visited in the Dix home in New York and so many people thought they were related that the senator frequently addressed her as "sister."

3. John A. Dix, *Congressional Globe*, 30th Cong., 1st Sess., June 27, 1848, XIX, 875.

4. *New York Courier*. Quoted in *Niles' Weekly Register*, September 13, 1848.

5. Dorothea Dix to Mrs. Robert Hare, Washington, D. C., July 5, 1848. Quoted in Tiffany, *op. cit.*, pp. 172-73.

6. Dorothea Dix, *Memorial to the United States Congress*, June 27, 1848.

7. *Ibid.*

8. *Ibid.* The ratio given by Miss Dix is considerably higher than the figures given by the census of 1840 and that of 1850. In view of subsequent corrections, Miss Dix's estimate is probably more reliable.

9. Dix, *Memorial to Congress*, June 27, 1848.

10. Dorothea Dix to Mrs. Hare, Washington, D. C., July 5, 1848. Quoted in Tiffany, *op. cit.*, p. 172.

11. *Ibid.*, p. 173.

12. *Ibid.*

13. Kennard, *op. cit.*, p. 10.

14. Dorothea Dix to Ann Heath, Washington, D. C., January 29, 1850. Dix-Heath MSS.

15. The first meeting of medical superintendents grew out of a casual conversation between Dr. S. B. Woodward, of the Worcester State Hospital, and Dr. F. T. Stribling, of the Western State Hospital, Staunton, Virginia. A meeting was called at the James Hotel, Philadelphia, for October 16, 1844. Thirteen were present; six of these were in charge of state institutions, four represented endowed institutions under public control, two were from private hospitals, and one was in charge of a municipal institution. Hurd, *op. cit.*, I, 1.

16. The first issue of the *American Journal of Insanity*, adopted as the organ of the Association of Medical Superintendents, was published by Dr. Amariah Brigham, in July 1844. It was the first medical periodical in English which was devoted solely to the study of mental diseases. In the same year German alienists founded the *Allegemeine Zeitschrift fur Psychiatrie;* the French had founded their *Annales Medico Psycholigiques* in 1843. The English journal did not appear until 1853. Tuke, *Chapters in the History of the Insane in the British Isles,* p. 446.

17. Dr. Brigham died in 1849.

18. Luther V. Bell to Dorothea Dix, McLean Hospital, Somerville, Massachusetts, December 29, 1848. Tiffany, *op. cit.*, p. 177.

19. Dorothea Dix to Joseph Dix, Washington, D. C., January 30, 1849. Tiffany, *op. cit.*, p. 178.

20. See James A. Pearce's speech, *Congressional Globe,* 31st Cong., 1st Sess., Vol. XXI, pt. 2, p. 1290.

21. Hurd, *op. cit.*, I, 20.

22. Dorothea Dix to Ann Heath, Washington, D. C., August 28, 1850. Dix-Heath MSS.

23. Mann, *op. cit.*, p. 330.

24. Horace Mann to S. J. May, Washington, D. C., September 25, 1850. Mann, *op. cit.*, p. 334.

25. Dorothea Dix to Ann Heath, Washington, D. C., September 27, 1850. Dix-Heath MSS.

26. Dorothea Dix to Ann Heath, Washington, D. C., February 11, 1851. Dix-Heath MSS.

27. Fredrika Bremer, *Homes of the New World,* II, 108.

28. *Ibid.*, pp. 106-8.

29. *Ibid.*, p. 107.

30. *Ibid.*, p. 108.

31. Fredrika Bremer to Dorothea Dix, Cincinnati, Ohio, November 2, 1850. Tiffany, *op. cit.*, p. 163.

32. Bremer, *op. cit.*, III, 290; Amariah Brigham, "Lunatic Asylums in the United States," *American Journal of Insanity,* I (July, 1844), 81-88.

33. *Journal of Insanity,* I (July, 1844), 87; also *Niles' Weekly Register,* March 11, 1843; February 3, 1844, and February 11, 1844.

34. Horace Mann to S. Downer, Washington, D. C., August 17, 1852. Mann, *op. cit.*, p. 380; also, William A. White, "Government Hospital for the Insane," in Hurd, *op. cit.*, II, 144-45.

35. Horace Mann to his wife, Mary Peabody Mann, Washington, D. C., February 24, 1853. Mann, *op. cit.*, p. 389.

36. Dorothea Dix to Ann Heath, Washington, D. C., March 9, 1854. Dix-Heath MSS.

37. Dr. Thomas Kirkbride to Dorothea Dix. Quoted in Tiffany, *op. cit.*, p. 190.

38. *Ibid.*, p. 191.

39. Ann Heath to Dorothea Dix, Brookline, Massachusetts, April 22, 1854. Dix-Heath MSS.

40. Dorothea Dix to Ann Heath, Washington, D. C., April 28, 1854. Dix-Heath MSS.

41. Dorothea Dix to Ann Heath, Washington, D. C., May 2, 1854. Dix-Heath MSS.

42. Franklin Pierce, "Veto Message." Quoted in Tiffany, *op. cit.*, p. 195.

43. William Darlington to Dorothea Dix, 1854. *Ibid.*, pp. 193-94.

44. Albert G. Brown, *Congressional Globe*, 33rd Cong., 1st Sess., n. s. Vol. XXXI, Appendix, p. 642.

45. S. Foot, *Congressional Globe*, 33rd Cong., 1st Sess., May 3, 1854, Appendix, p. 550.

46. William H. Seward, *ibid.*, June 19, 1854, p. 59.

47. R. M. T. Hunter, *ibid.*, May 3, 1854, p. 798.

48. C. C. Clay, *ibid.*, June 20, 1854, p. 969.

49. Lewis Cass, *ibid.*, June 13, 1854, p. 979.

50. Broadhead, *ibid.*, July 5, 1854, pp. 1068-69.

51. Solomon Foot, *ibid.*, May 31, 1854, p. 804.

52. Dorothea Dix to Ann Heath, Washington, D. C., May 18, 1854. Dix-Heath MSS.

CHAPTER VIII

1. Dorothea Dix to Ann Heath, Harrisburg, Pennsylvania, February 25, 1854. Dix-Heath MSS.

2. Pliny Earle, "Institutions for the Insane in Prussia, Austria, and Germany," *American Journal of Insanity*, IX (October 1852), 106; also, Sanborn, *Memoirs of Pliny Earle*, p. 308.

3. Eleanor F. Rathbone, *William Rathbone: A Memoir*, pp. 39-51.

4. *New York Daily Tribune*, September 15, 1854; also *Raleigh Weekly Register*, September 20, 1854.

5. A careful search of the records at the New Jersey Hospital fails to reveal that the sum was ever paid to the institution. The author doubts if Miss Dix's health at the time would have warranted the risk on the part of the insurance company. The incident, however, was given wide circulation.

6. *New York Daily Tribune*, September 15, 1854.

7. Dorothea Dix to Ann Heath, Steamship *Arctic*, September 11, 1854. Dix-Heath MSS.

8. *Ibid.*

9. Dorothea Dix to Ann Heath, Liverpool, September 22, 1854. Dix-Heath MSS.

10. Dorothea Dix to Ann Heath, November 16, 1854. Dix-Heath MSS.

11. Dorothea Dix to Mrs. William Rathbone, Ballinsaloe, Ireland, October 25, 1854. Tiffany, *op. cit.*, p. 206.

12. Letter from Captain M. D. McKenna, Superintendent of the Relief Station at Sable Island, to Hugh Bell, Chairman of the Board of Works, Halifax; dated Sable Island, December 6, 1854. *Ibid.*, p. 223.

13. Hugh Bell to Dorothea Dix. *Ibid.*, p. 222.

14. *Ibid.*, p. 227.

15. Dorothea Dix to Ann Heath, Liverpool, November 16, 1854. Dix-Heath MSS.

16. *Ibid.*

17. Dorothea Dix to Ann Heath, Liverpool, December 8, 1854. Dix-Heath MSS.

18. Dorothea Dix to Ann Heath, Edinburgh, February 26, 1855. Dix-Heath MSS.

19. *Ibid.*

20. Dorothea Dix to Mrs. William Rathbone, February 1855. Tiffany, *op. cit.*, pp. 232-33.

21. Dorothea Dix to Mrs. William Rathbone, Edinburgh, February 20, 1855. *Ibid.*, pp. 233-34.

22. Tuke, *Chapters in the History of the Insane in the British Isles*, pp. 330 ff.

23. 35 *George* III, c 89.

24. Tuke, *Chapters in the History of the Insane in the British Isles*, p. 323.

25. T. S. Clouston, "Lunacy Administration of Scotland, 1857-1892, Commitment, Detention, Care and Treatment of the Insane," sec. 4, International Congress of Charities, Correction and Philanthropy, Chicago, June 1893. Published Baltimore 1894.

26. Dumfries, Marston, Glasgow, Perth, Dundee, Aberdeen, Edinburgh.

27. Dorothea Dix to Ann Heath, London, March 8, 1855. Dix-Heath MSS.

28. D. H. Tuke to Francis Tiffany, Hanwell, England, August 1888. Tiffany, *op. cit.*, p. 243.

29. Dorothea Dix to Mrs. Samuel Torrey of Boston, 18 Gloucester Square, London, March 8, 1855. *Ibid.*, p. 245.

30. Tuke, *Chapters in the History of the Insane in the British Isles*, pp. 340-41. Statistics on the insane in Scotland, 1855: Private patients, 2,732; paupers, 4,642; criminals, 29; total, 7,403. (Curable, 768; incurable, 4,032; congenital idiots and imbeciles, 2,603.) The 2,732 private patients were distributed as follows: chartered asylums, 652; licensed houses, 231; poorhouses, 9; reported houses, 10; school for idiots, 12; with relatives, 1,453; unlicensed houses, 18; with strangers, 297; no care, 50.

31. Dorothea Dix to Mrs. William Rathbone, London, February 28, 1855. Tiffany, *op. cit.*, p. 250.

32. The act passed in 1845 made it incumbent upon the justice of every county and borough within three years to obtain or provide necessary accommodation for their insane. They were allowed to make this provision either separately or jointly with other counties or boroughs; however, by 1852 only four boroughs had provided for their insane and in 1853 stricter laws relative to the insane were passed in England. Letchworth, *op. cit.*, pp. 23-24.

33. Dorothea Dix to Mrs. Torrey, London, March 8, 1855. Tiffany, *op. cit.*, p. 249.

34. Members of the commission were William Gaskell, Fellow of the Royal College of Surgeons, William George Campbell, Advocate Sheriff of the Shire of Fife, Alexander Earle Monteith, Barrister-at-law, and James Coxe, Doctor of Medicine.

35. Dorothea Dix to Dr. H. A. Buttolph, York, May 16, 1855. *Ibid.*, pp. 259-60.

36. D. H. Van Leuven to D. H. Tuke, Jersey, May 8, 1855. *Ibid.*, pp. 260-61.

37. Dorothea Dix to Ann Heath, York, June 1, 1855. Dix-Heath MSS.

38. William Rathbone to Dorothea Dix, Greenbank, July 8, 1855. Tiffany, *op. cit.*, pp. 272-73.

39. *Ibid.*, p. 268.

40. *Ibid.*, pp. 268 ff.

41. Dorothea Dix to Mrs. William Rathbone, 8 Queen's Terrace, St. Helliers, July 1855. *Ibid.*, p. 270.

42. Dorothea Dix to Dr. H. A. Buttolph, Island of Jersey, July 18, 1855. *Ibid.*
43. D. H. Tuke to Dorothea Dix. *Ibid.*, p. 271.
44. *Transactions of the American Association of Medical Superintendents,* Summer 1855. Dix-Heath MSS. See also J. H. Nichols to Dorothea Dix, 1855.
45. Dorothea Dix to Mrs. Rathbone, Summer 1855. Rathbone MSS.
46. Dorothea Dix to Mrs. Torrey, Paris, November 1855. Tiffany, *op. cit.*, p. 282.
47. Dorothea Dix to Ann Heath, Genoa, March 7, 1856. Dix-Heath MSS.
48. Dorothea Dix to Mrs. Samuel Torrey, Genoa, March 6, 1856. Tiffany, *op. cit.*, p. 284.
49. Dorothea Dix to Mrs. William Rathbone, Turin, Italy, March 7, 1856. *Ibid.*, p. 285.
50. Dorothea Dix to Dr. H. A. Buttolph, Florence, Italy, 1856. *Ibid.*, p. 286.
51. *Ibid.*
52. Dorothea Dix to Dr. Buttolph, Island of Corfu, March 27, 1856. *Ibid.*, p. 295.
53. Dorothea Dix to William Rathbone, Island of Corfu, March 27, 1856. *Ibid.*
54. Dorothea Dix to Mrs. William Rathbone, Piraeus, Greece, April 2, 1856. Rathbone MSS.
55. Dorothea Dix to Mrs. William Rathbone, Constantinople, April 10, 1856. Rathbone MSS.
56. Cyrus Hamlin to Francis Tiffany, Lexington, Massachusetts, August 7, 1889. Tiffany, *op. cit.*, pp. 301-3.
57. Dorothea Dix to Mrs. William Rathbone, Constantinople, April 29, 1856. *Ibid.*, pp. 299-300.
58. In Constantinople, Miss Dix was well received and made the impression, said Dr. Hamlin, "of a person of culture, judgment, self-possession, absolute fearlessness in the path of duty, and yet a woman of refinement and true Christian philanthropy. . . . She was equally worthy with Elizabeth Fry to be called the female Howard." *Ibid.*, pp. 300-1.
59. Dorothea Dix to Ann Heath, Assoria, Hungaria, May 1, 1856. Dix-Heath MSS.
60. Dorothea Dix to Ann Heath, London, August 14, 1856. Dix-Heath MSS.

CHAPTER IX

1. Dorothea Dix to Ann Heath, Assoria, Hungary, May 1, 1856. Dix-Heath MSS.
2. Dorothea Dix to Ann Heath, December 26, 1856. Quoted in Kennard, *op. cit.*, p. 12.
3. Dorothea Dix to Ann Heath, December 30, 1856, Toronto, Canada. Dix-Heath MSS.
4. Dorothea Dix to Ann Heath, March 24, 1857. Dix-Heath MSS.
5. "Report of the Scotch Lunacy Commission," *North British Review,* XXVII (Edinburgh, 1857), 114-15.
6. D. H. Tuke to Dorothea Dix, September 14, 1856. Tiffany, *op. cit.*, pp. 307-8.
7. J. Conolly to Dorothea Dix, Hanwell, England, August 14, 1856. *Ibid.*, p. 308.
8. Dorothea Dix to Mrs. William Rathbone, Washington, D. C., 1862. *Ibid.*, p. 280.
9. Thomas Blagden to Dorothea Dix, Washington, November 13, 1852. *Ibid.*, p. 155.
10. Dorothea Dix to Mrs. William Rathbone, Zelienople, Pennsylvania, August 10, 1857. *Ibid.*, p. 316.

11. Dorothea Dix to Mrs. William Rathbone, Conshohocken, Pennsylvania, April 20, 1858. Rathbone MSS.

12. Dorothea Dix to Mrs. William Rathbone, Lancaster, Pennsylvania, March 30, 1857. Rathbone MSS.

13. Dorothea Dix to Mrs. William Rathbone, March 31, 1858. Rathbone MSS.

14. Dorothea Dix to Ann Heath, Nashville, Tennessee, July 16, 1858. Dix-Heath MSS.

15. Dorothea Dix to Ann Heath, New Orleans, Louisiana, April 11, 1859. Dix-Heath MSS.

16. Dorothea Dix to Mrs. Hare of Philadelphia, Austin, Texas, March 28, 1859. Tiffany, *op. cit.*, pp. 318-19.

17. Dorothea Dix to Mrs. Samuel Torrey, Baton Rouge, Louisiana, April 7, 1859. Ibid., pp. 319-20.

18. *Ibid.*, p. 320.

19. Dorothea Dix to Ann Heath, April 11, 1859, New Orleans, Louisiana. Dix-Heath MSS.

20. Dorothea Dix to Mrs. William Rathbone, Harrisburg, Pennsylvania, March 18, 1860. Tiffany, *op. cit.*, p. 327.

21. The census of 1850 revealed 17,365 insane and idiotic out of a population of 23,191,876, while the forthcoming census of 1860 was to show 23,999 out of 31,443,321. Both of these reports have been declared inaccurate. The number of insane persons in the United States greatly exceeded the number given in the census. W. J. Harris, Bureau of Census, Department of Commerce, in a Brochure on Insane and Feeble-minded Institutions, 1910, gives figures for the mentally ill in institutions in 1850 as 15,610 or 97 to every 100,000 population, and in 1860 a total of 24,042 persons in institutions or 76.5 to every 100,000 population.

22. "Reports of American Asylums," *American Journal of Insanity*, XVI (October, 1859), 259.

23. *Ibid.*, p. 219.

24. Dorothea Dix to Ann Heath, Philadelphia, April 9, 1860. Dix-Heath MSS.

25. Hathway, *op. cit.*, pp. 247-57.

26. The appropriation was to be distributed as follows: $60,000 for the support of the hospital for which she had labored, 1852-1858, $5,000 for repairs, $10,000 for expenses in arrears and $90,000 for the construction of new wings.

27. Dorothea Dix to Mrs. William Rathbone, Columbia, South Carolina, December 19, 1860. Tiffany, *op. cit.*, p. 329.

28. Dorothea Dix to Ann Heath, Washington, December 23, 1860. Dix-Heath MSS.

29. Samuel Felton to Francis Tiffany, Philadelphia, May 8, 1888. Tiffany, *op. cit.*, pp. 333-34.

30. Repeatedly Mr. Felton tried to obtain Miss Dix's permission to make public the part that she had played in warning the railroad of the conspiracy to attack Washington and circumvent Lincoln's inauguration but she always gave point-blank refusal to have any use made of her name; however, some years later Mr. Felton did relate the incident to Mr. Sibley who was then librarian at Harvard University.

31. Dorothea Dix to Ann Heath, begun State Library, Springfield, Illinois, February 21, 1861, finished at State Hospital, Jacksonville, Illinois, February 24, 1861. Dix-Heath MSS.

32. Dorothea Dix to Ann Heath, Frankfort, Kentucky, March 1861. Dix-Heath MSS.

CHAPTER X

1. Dorothea Dix to Ann Heath, Washington, D. C., April 20, 1861. Dix-Heath MSS.

2. Diary of John Hay. Quoted in Helen Nicolay, *Our Capital on the Potomac*, p. 364.

3. Letters of John Nicolay. *Ibid.*

4. *Ibid.*

5. Dorothea Dix to Ann Heath, Washington, D. C., April 20, 1861. Dix-Heath MSS.

6. Harvey E. Brown, *The Medical Department of the United States Army, 1775-1873*, p. 219.

7. R. C. Wood to Dorothea Dix, Surgeon-General's Office, April 23, 1861. Letterbook, 1861, p. 2.

8. R. C. Wood to Dorothea Dix, April 24, 1861. *Ibid.*, p. 5.

9. Charles J. Stillé, *History of the United States Sanitary Commission*, p. 40.

10. Among those present were Mrs. John Dix, wife of General Dix, Mrs. Hamilton Fish, Mrs. William Cullen Bryant, Mrs. M. Grinnell, Mrs. Charles Butler, Mrs. Parke Godwin, Mrs. George Curtis, Mrs. H. W. Bellows, Mrs. S. F. B. Morse, Mrs. Alonzo Potter, Mrs. W. B. Astor, Sr., Mrs. Peter Cooper, and Miss Louisa Lee Schuyler.

11. *Boston Transcript*, May 4, 1861.

12. Havelocks were duck caps designed to protect soldiers from sunstroke and were copied from the British soldiers in India. American soldiers refused to wear them. Thousands were destroyed.

13. The New England Hospital for Women and Children was the first hospital in America to inaugurate such a nursing curriculum. Miss Linda Richards, the first "trained nurse" in America, was awarded her diploma in 1873.

14. Mary A. Holland, *Our Army Nurses*. Quoted in Julia C. Stimson and Ethel C. S. Thompson, "Women Nurses with the Union Forces," *Military Surgeon* (February, 1928), p. 29.

15. Tiffany, *op. cit.*, p. 339.

16. Lavinia Dock and Isabel Maitland Stewart, *Short History of Nursing*, pp. 147-49.

17. *Boston Transcript*, June 6, 1861.

18. *The Liberator*, May 31, 1861.

19. Adjutant-General's Office, General Orders, 1861, No. 31, pp. 2-3.

20. Acting Surgeon-General to Miss D. L. Dix, Surgeon-General's Office, Letterbook, 1861, pp. 24-25.

21. John Hay's Diary, Nicolay, *op. cit.*, p. 366.

22. Samuel Gridley Howe, "Sanitary Conditions and New England Troops," *Boston Evening Transcript*, May 30, 1861.

23. United States War Department, *Surgeon-General's Medical and Surgical History of the War of the Rebellion*, Pt. III, I, 897.
The Trinity churches of Georgetown and Washington, the Dumbarton Street Hospital, Waters' Warehouse, Georgetown College, Gaspari's Hotel, Island Hall, Old Fellows Hall, Grace Church, Church of the Epiphany, Ryland Chapel, Union Chapel, the Baptist Church on E near Sixth Street, the Unitarian on Sixth and D, the Church of the Ascension, the Presbyterian Church on H near Ninth, and the Eighth Street Methodist Church were in turn converted into hospitals.

24. Jane C. Hoge, *The Boys in Blue*, p. 110.

25. Dorothea Dix to Ann Heath, Washington, May 26, 1861. Dix-Heath MSS.

26. Dr. Harris' hobby was preventive medicine. Dr. Van Buren was for five years attached to the staff of the Medical Bureau.

27. Elisha Harris, "The Sanitary Commission," *North American Review*, XCVIII (1864), 161.

28. Katherine P. Wormeley, *The United States Sanitary Commission*, p. 16.

29. Compare, Stillé, *op. cit.;* Brown, *op. cit.;* Wormeley, *op. cit.;* Louis C. Duncan, *The Medical Department of the United States Army in the Civil War*.

30. Olmsted reported "that a complete system of drains, so essential to the health of the men, did not exist in any of the camps, that the tents were so crowded at night that the men were poisoned by the vitiated atmosphere, that the sinks were unnecessarily and disgustingly offensive, that personal cleanliness among the men was wholly unattended to, that the clothing was of bad material and almost always filthy to the last degree, and that there was scarcely a pretence of performing the ordinary police duties of a military camp." Quoted in Stillé, *op. cit.*, p. 85.

31. Duncan, *op. cit.*, p. 4.

32. Before the advent of the American Red Cross, the United States army hospitals were designated by the use of yellow flags. For general hospitals there were yellow flags nine feet by five with a twenty-four inch letter "H" in green bunting in the center. Post and field hospitals bore a similar flag six feet by four. For ambulances and for guidons to mark the way to a field hospital there were small yellow flags fourteen by twenty-eight inches with a one inch border of green. Brown, *op. cit.*

33. Duncan, *op. cit.*, p. 11. By this time the prisoners had been taken to Richmond.

34. Stimson and Thompson, *op. cit.*, p. 9.

35. *Surgeon General's Medical and Surgical History of the War of the Rebellion*, Pt. III, I, 897.

36. Louisa May Alcott, *Hospital Sketches*, pp. 5 ff.

37. Stimson and Thompson, *op. cit.*, p. 13.

38. Ednah D. Cheyney, *Louisa May Alcott, Her Life, Letters and Journals*, pp. 143-44.

39. Alcott, *op. cit.*, pp. 5 ff.

40. Dorothea L. Dix, Circular Orders, No. 8, July 14, 1862. Circular, Surgeon-General's Office, 1862-63, p. 56.

41. William A. Hammond, Circular Orders, No. 10, July 23, 1862. Circular, Surgeon-General's Office, 1862-63, p. 62.

42. The duties of male nurses included not only caring for the sick and wounded of the army in hospitals, but in cooking and other work in connection with the sick, to which the medical officers might assign them. They were divided into squads of eleven, one of whom was held responsible for the efficiency of the others. One squad was assigned to every hundred patients. Male nurses wore the undress uniform of a private soldier with a green half chevron on the left forearm but there was no prescribed uniform for women nurses.

43. Assistant Surgeon J. R. Smith to Miss D. L. Dix, July 9, 1862. Letterbook, 1862, p. 393.

44. Lavinia Dock, *History of Red Cross Nursing*, p. 7.

45. *Ibid.*

46. Compare, Mary Livermore, *My Story of the War*, p. 247; Surgeon-General's Letterbook, 1862-63, p. 179; Stillé, *op. cit.;* Charles B. Johnson, *Muskets and Medicine*, p. 46.

47. Roe, *op. cit.*, pp. 142-43.

48. Dorothea Dix to Mrs. William Rathbone, Washington, D. C., June 20, 1862. Rathbone MSS.

49. Carbolic acid and other disinfectants were not in use at the time of the Civil War. Wounds were first treated with cold water dressings, and as soon as they began to supperate, they were coated with simple cerate consisting of two parts of fresh lard and one of white wax. Pus in bullet wounds was not considered as especially dangerous, as it was instrumental in the elimination of such foreign objects as cloth and leather, first struck by the missile and driven into the flesh. In warm weather, wounds often became infested with maggots. This looked terrible, but it was not regarded as detrimental. Johnson, *op. cit.*, p. 104.

50. The Union Army numbered 2,335,949 men. 59,860 were killed in battle, and 280,240 wounded, of whom 49,205 died. 25 per cent of the amputation cases died. There were 2,642 cases of gangrene; 201,769 died from disease, 285,545 were discharged because of disability from disease. There were 1,163,814 cases of malaria, and 49,871 cases of typho-malaria fever. 4,059 died from malaria. *Ibid.*, p. 250.

51. Charlotte C. Eliot, *William Greenleaf Eliot, Minister, Educator, and Philanthropist*, p. 217.

52. Roe, *op. cit.*, p. 241.

53. Stimson and Thompson, *op. cit.*, p. 8.

54. Dorothea Dix to Ann Heath, Washington, D. C., March 16, 1863. Dix-Heath MSS.

55. Dorothea Dix to Ann Heath, Washington, D. C., April 24, 1863. Dix-Heath MSS.

56. Adjutant-General's Office, Washington, October 29, 1863. General Orders No. 351.

57. Tiffany in his life of Miss Dix devoted but eight pages to the melancholy period of the Civil War.

58. C. H. Crane to Miss D. L. Dix, Surgeon-General's Office, Letterbook, 1864, p. 441.　　　　　　　　　　　　59. Brown, *op. cit.*

60. Mrs. Wittenmyer had worked as the unofficial agent of various aid societies organized in Iowa, and later served with the Christian Commission.

61. Ruth A. Gallaher, "Annie Turner Wittenmyer," *Iowa Journal of History and Politics*, XIX (October 1931), 520.

62. C. H. Crane to Miss D. L. Dix, Surgeon-General's Office, September 11, 1865, Letterbook, 1865, p. 562.

63. Dorothea Dix to Ann Heath, Washington, D. C., September 11, 1865. Dix-Heath MSS.

64. Tiffany, *op. cit.*, p. 342.

65. Dorothea Dix to General E. D. Townsend, January 25, 1867. *Ibid.*, p. 343.

66. Dorothea Dix to Edwin M. Stanton, January 25, 1867. *Ibid.*

CHAPTER XI

1. Poem by John S. Dwight, Kennard, *op. cit.*, p. 17.

2. Dorothea Dix to Mrs. William Rathbone, Washington, D. C., August 18, 1868. Tiffany, *op. cit.*, p. 346.

3. *Ibid.*, p. 347.

4. Charles Lee, *Report on Insanity* (Reprint from *Transactions of the American Medical Association*), pp. 5 ff.

5. Tuke, *The Insane in the United States and Canada*, p. 44.

6. Benjamin Silliman to Dorothea Dix, New Haven, Connecticut, May 6, 1868. Tiffany, *op. cit.*, p. 353.

7. Dorothea Dix to Ann Heath, Trenton, New Jersey, April 21, 1869. Dix-Heath MSS.

8. Alfred Huger to Dorothea Dix, Charleston, South Carolina, January 31, 1870. Tiffany, *op. cit.*, pp. 350-51.

9. Dorothea Dix to Ann Heath, Raleigh, North Carolina, January 2, 1871. Dix-Heath MSS.

10. Dorothea Dix to Mrs. Torrey. Tiffany, *op. cit.*, p. 353.

11. Dorothea Dix to Mrs. William Rathbone, Boston, Massachusetts, November 24, 1870. Rathbone MSS.

12. Dorothea Dix to Ann Heath, St. Elizabeth's Hospital, Washington, D. C., February 27, 1871. Dix-Heath MSS.

13. Beach, *op. cit.*, p. 161.

14. Dorothea Dix to Abby Heath Barnett, January 4, 1873. Dix-Heath MSS.

15. *Ibid.*

16. Tiffany, *op. cit.*, pp. 354-55.

17. Incident related by Alvah Godding, son of Supt. Godding, to the author, Washington, D. C., July, 1932.

18. Dorothea Dix to Ann Heath, Washington, D. C., February 6, 1870. Dix-Heath MSS.

19. The portrait of Miss Dix which is used as a frontispiece was taken from a copy in oil of the original daguerreotype. Courtesy of Dr. Robert Stone, New Jersey State Hospital, Trenton, New Jersey.

20. Incident related to the author by Mrs. Horace Lamb, Boston, Massachusetts, December 1931.

21. Dorothea Dix to Ann Heath, about 1825. Dix-Heath MSS.

22. Dorothea Dix to Abby Heath Barnett, May 1878. Dix-Heath MSS.

23. Distribution of the insane, 1880: In hospitals and asylums 40,942 or 44.42%; other institutions 235 or .26%; in almshouses 9,302 or 10.12%; jails 397 or 4.8%; at home or in private families 41,083 or 44.68%; total, 91,959. U. S. Census, 1880. Tuke, *The Insane in the United States and Canada*, pp. 51-52, 96, Appendix F.

24. In 1874, Bellevue Hospital, New York City, instituted a training school for nurses, and in 1883, Blockley.

25. In 1884, a training school was established at the State Hospital, Buffalo, New York; in 1886, at the Illinois Eastern Hospital, Kankakee, Illinois; and in 1887, at the Willard State Hospital, New York.

26. C. B. Burr, "What Improvements Have Been Wrought in the Care of the Insane by Means of Training Schools," *Congress of Charities*, Fourth Session, Chicago, 1893, p. 124.

27. Dorothea Dix to Mrs. Thomas Lamb Eliot, Trenton, New Jersey, October 31, 1886. Dix-Eliot MSS.

28. John G. Whittier to Dorothea Dix, 28 day 7 month, 1879. Samuel T. Pickard, *Life and Letters of John Greenleaf Whittier*, II, 650.

29. *Ibid.*, II, 679.

30. Dorothea Dix to John G. Whittier, *ibid.*, p. 686.

31. Tiffany, *op. cit.*, pp. 367-68.

32. Dorothea Dix to Matilda Lieber, September (?), 1886. Lieber Papers.

BIBLIOGRAPHY

A. Primary Sources

I. MANUSCRIPTS

Atkinson, Carter, "Notes from Benjamin Rush's lectures on 'The Institutes and Practices of Medicine'," University of Pennsylvania, 1800. Manuscript in Duke University Library.

Chamberlain Autographs. Letters from Dorothea Dix to George Barrell Emerson. Boston Public Library, Boston, Massachusetts.

Circular Orders. Surgeon-General's Office, 1861-1865, Archives of the Surgeon-General, Washington, D. C.

Clay Manuscripts. Letters from Sue (Withers) Battle to Susanna Claiborne (Withers) Clay regarding Dorothea Dix, March 24, 1848, Duke University Library.

Dix, Dorothy (Lynde). Fragmentary. Included in Miscellaneous Collection, Boston Public Library, Boston, Massachusetts.

Dix-Eliot Manuscripts. Correspondence of Dorothea Dix and members of the Thomas Lamb Eliot family. Private collection, Portland, Oregon.

Dix-Heath Manuscripts. Correspondence of Dorothea Dix and Ann Heath, covers period 1825-1878. Private collection, Wellesley Hills, Massachusetts.

Dobbin Papers. Papers of James E. Dobbin. North Carolina Historical Commission, Raleigh, North Carolina.

Dorothea Dix Papers. Fragmentary. Most notable is copy of a letter to the Boys' Department, State School for Deaf Mutes, Jacksonville, Illinois, April 6, 1852. Library of Congress, Washington, D. C.

General Orders, 1861-1865. Office of the Adjutant-General, United States Army, Washington, D. C.

Harper Papers. John L. Harper papers. Western Pennsylvania Historical Association, Pittsburgh, Pennsylvania.

Harris Papers. Thaddeus Mason Harris, "Notes on Character of Madam Dorothea Dix, 1746-1837." Private collection, Cambridge, Massachusetts.

Letterbooks. Surgeon-General United States Army, 1861-1865. Office of the Surgeon-General, Washington, D. C.

Lieber Papers. Henry E. Huntington Memorial Library, San Marino, California.

Marshall Papers. Miscellaneous correspondence relating to Dorothea Dix and various phases of movement for reform in care and treatment of mental diseases. Helen E. Marshall, Normal, Illinois.

North Carolina Governor's Letterbook, 1848. North Carolina Historical Commission, Raleigh, North Carolina.

North Carolina Legislative Papers. North Carolina Historical Commission, Raleigh, North Carolina.

Rathbone Manuscripts. Papers of William Rathbone V. Letters of Dorothea L. Dix to Mr. and Mrs. William Rathbone, 1837-1875. Greenbank, Liverpool, England.

Sever Papers. Letter from Dorothea Lynde Dix to Hon. Benjamin Sever, October 25, 1864 (?). Massachusetts Historical Society Library, Boston, Massachusetts.

Swain Papers. Letters of D. L. Swain regarding Miss Dix's work in North Carolina. North Carolina Historical Commission, Raleigh, North Carolina.

II. PRINTED SOURCES

1. Official Documents

Documents of the United States Christian Commission, 1861-1865. Adjutant's Archives, War Department, Washington, D. C.

Memorials of Dorothea Lynde Dix to various legislatures, and published as separate documents:

"Memorial for an Insane Hospital in Nova Scotia," in Henry M. Hurd, *Institutional Care of the Insane in the United States and Canada*, vol. I, Baltimore, 1916.

Memorial to the General Assembly in the Behalf of the Insane of the State of Maryland, February 25, 1852, Annapolis, 1852.

Memorial to the General Assembly of North Carolina, November, 1848. Raleigh, 1848.

Memorial to the Honorable Legislature of New York. Albany, 1844.

Memorial to the Illinois General Assembly, January, 1847. Springfield, 1847.

Memorial to the Legislature of Massachusetts (Old South Leaflets, vol. VI, no. 148), Boston, 1843.

Memorial to the United States Congress Praying a Grant of Land for the Relief and Support of the Indigent Curable and Incurable Insane in the United States, June 27, 1848. Washington, 1848. Senate Document No. 150.

Memorial Soliciting Adequate Appropriations for the Construction of a State Hospital for the Insane in the State of Mississippi, February, 1850. Jackson, 1850.

Memorial Soliciting a State Hospital for the Insane, Submitted to the Legislature of Alabama, November 15, 1849. Montgomery, 1849.

✓*Memorial Soliciting a State Hospital for the Insane, Submitted to the Legislature of New Jersey,* February 2, 1845. Trenton, 1845.

✓*Memorial Soliciting a State Hospital for the Insane of Pennsylvania,* February 3, 1845. Harrisburg, 1845.

✓*A Review of the Present Conditions of the State Penitentiary of Kentucky, with Brief Notices and Remarks upon Jails and Poorhouses in Some of the Most Populous Counties.* Written by request, Frankfort, 1845.

Report on Gaols and Houses of Correction in the Commonwealth of Massachusetts, made by the committee appointed by the House of Representatives, 1833. Boston, 1833.

Report, Minority Committee of the Boston Prison Discipline Society, May 27, 1845. Boston, 1845.

Reports, Boston Society for Prison Discipline and Philanthropy. Nos. 8, 9, 11, 12, 13, 14 are especially helpful.

Reports, House of Commons. First Annual report on madhouses. Made by a select committee appointed by the House of Commons to inquire and consider provisions being made for the better regulation of public and private madhouses in England. London, 1816.

Semi-Annual Report of the Condition of Primary Schools in the City of Boston, for the half year ending October, 1837.

Sixth Census of the United States, Population, 1840. Washingtón, 1840.

The War of the Rebellion: A Compilation of the Official Records of the Union and Confederate Armies. Published under the direction of the Secretary of War. 130 vols., Washington, 1880-1901.

2. Newspapers

✝*Baltimore American,* 1861
✝*Baltimore Clipper,* 1861
Baltimore Daily Advertiser, 1861
Baltimore Evening Picayune, 1861
Baltimore Sun, 1852, 1861-1865
Baltimore Weekly Sun, 1861-1865
Boston Beacon, 1887
Boston Courier, 1841-1843
Boston Daily Advertiser, 1841-1843, 1865
Boston Transcript, 1841-1843, 1860-1865, 1887
Congressional Globe for various dates.
Greensboro (North Carolina) *Patriot,* 1848, 1852
Knoxville Standard, 1847

The Liberator, edited in Boston, by William Lloyd Garrison, 1843, 1861

Nashville National Union, 1846

Nashville Tri-Weekly Union, 1848

New Orleans Daily Picayune, 1847

Newport Mercury, 1844

New York Times, 1861-1865, 1887

New York Tribune, 1855, 1861-1865, 1887

Niles' Weekly Register, published in Baltimore, by Hezekiah Niles, 1848

Providence Journal, 1844

Quincy Patriot, 1841

Raleigh Weekly Register, 1854

3. Works of Dorothea Lynde Dix

American Moral Tales for Young Persons, Boston, 1832.

Conversations on Common Things, Boston, 1824.

Evening Hours, Boston, 1825.

Garland of Flora, Boston, 1829.

Hymns for Children, Boston, 1825.

Letter to the Convicts in the Western State Penitentiary of Pennsylvania, Alleghaney, Washington, 1848.

Meditations for Private Hours, Boston, 1828.

Remarks on Prisons and Prison Discipline, Boston, 1845.

4. Collections

Brady's Collection of Official Photographs of the Civil War. Library of Congress, Washington, D. C.

Materials for a History of Boston. Hundreds of pamphlets and broadsides dealing with education, development of the city of Boston, leading citizens, churches, etc. Library of Congress, Washington, D. C.

B. SECONDARY WORKS

I. PAMPHLETS

Beedy, Helen Coffin, *Dorothea Lynde Dix,* a brief sketch of her life work, Bangor, 1901.

Borland, John R., *Progress of a Century in the Theory and Practice of Medicine,* Philadelphia, 1877.

Bush, George Gary, *History of Education in Massachusetts,* Washington, 1891.

Earle, Pliny, *Institutions for the Insane in Prussia, Austria, and Germany,* Utica, 1853.

Eddy, Thomas, *Communication* to the Board of Governors, New York, April, 1815, "Hints for Introducing an improved mode of treating the insane in asylums," Reprint, Bloomingtondale Hospital Press, 1916; also, Appendix III, *A Psychiatric Milestone,* New York, 1921.

Ellis, W. C., *Letter to Thomas Thompson, M. P., containing certain considerations on the necessity of proper places being provided by the legislature for the reception of the insane, and on some of the abuses which have been found to exist in madhouses with a plan to remedy them,* Hull, 1815.

Esquirol, J. A., *Des Etablissimens consacres aux Alienes en France et Des Moyens de les Ameliorer, Memoire presente au ministre de l'Interieur, en Septembre, 1818,* Paris, 1838.

History of the Maryland Hospital for the Insane, Catonsville, Maryland, 1897.

Kinnicutt, Lincoln, *Forty Immortals of Worcester and its County.* Brochure issued by the Worcester Bank and Trust Co., 1920.

Sprague, John Francis, "Dorothea Lynde Dix." Reprint from *Sprague's Journal of Maine History,* Bangor, 1901.

———, *Maine's Joan of Arc,* Address before the Kennebec Historical Society, January 8, 1924. Kennebec Historical Society Brochures, Ser. I, No. 2.

Tuke, Samuel, *A Letter on Public Lunatic Asylums,* New York, 1815.

Waterson, Robert Cassie, *The Condition of the Insane in Massachusetts,* Boston, 1843. Reprint from the *Christian Examiner,* January, 1843.

II. PERIODICALS

Allis, T., "Comparative Number of Insane in the Society of Friends," *Lancet,* I (London, 1839), 52-55.

"American Hospitals for the Insane," *North American Review,* LXXIX (1854), 67-90.

Anderson, M. B., and Devereux, J. C., "Report relating to hospitals for the sick and insane, to which is appended a report relating to the management of the insane in Great Britain, by H. B. Wilbur," *Report of the Board of Charities of New York,* IX (1875).

"Spiritual Pathology; or, The Autobiography of the Insane," *Living Age,* XLIII (1854), 51-66.

Beard, George M., "Who of Us are Insane?" *Putnam's,* XII (1869), 513.

Beck, T. R., "An account of some of the Lunatic Asylums in the United States," *New York Medical and Physicians Journal,* VII (1828), 251.

"The Star of Bethlehem," *Living Age,* LV (1857), 297-302.

"Bicetre Asylum," *Chambers' Edinburgh Journal,* VII (Edinburgh, 1847), 668.

Bigelow, J. L., "Miss Dix and What She Has Done," *Galaxy*, III (1867), 668.

Brigham, Amariah, "Brief Notice of the New York State Lunatic Asylum, Utica, New York," *American Journal of Insanity*, I (July, 1844), 3.

———, "Lunatic Asylums of the United States," *American Journal of Insanity*, I (July, 1844), 81-88.

———, "Moral Treatment of Insanity," *American Journal of Insanity*, IV (1847-1848), 1 ff.

Brockett, L. P., "Sketches from Humane Institutions; Asylums for the Insane," *National Magazine*, XI (1857), 315.

Browne, W. A. F., "Cottage Asylums," *Medical Critic and Psychological Journal*, I (London, 1861), 213, 449.

Bucknill, John Charles, "Abolition of Proprietary Madhouse," *Nineteenth Century*, XVII (1885).

Burr, C. B., "What Improvements have been Wrought in the Care of the Insane by means of Training Schools," *Report* of the Fourth Section of the International Congress of Charities, Correction and Philanthropy, Chicago, June 1893. Published in Baltimore, 1894.

Burrows, et al, "Insanity," *Monthly Review*, CXVIII (London, 1829), 102.

Buttolph, H. A., "Historical and Descriptive Account of the New Jersey Insane Asylum at Trenton," *American Journal of Insanity*, VI (1849-1850), 185.

Cabanes, Docteur, "Le Centenaire d'un Medecin Philanthrope: Pinel, Libérateur des Aliénés," *L'Illustration*, LXXXIV (Paris, October 23, 1926), pt. 2, 453.

Carlton, Frank T., "Humanitarianism Past and Present," *International Journal of Ethics*, XVII, 48.

Chance, Burton, "Needed Reforms in the Care of the Insane," *Outlook*, LXXVIII (1904), 1031.

Child, Lydia Maria, "The Missionary of Prisons," *The Present*, I (December 5, 1843).

Clark, Sir James, "A Memoir of John Conolly," *Edinburgh Review*, CXXXI (April, 1870), 418.

Clouston, T. S., "Lunacy Administration of Scotland, 1857-1892: Commitment, Detention, Care and Treatment of the Insane," *Report* of the Fourth Section of the International Congress of Charities, Correction and Philanthropy, Chicago, June 1893. Published in Baltimore, 1894.

Cookson, W. D., "Treatment of the Insane in the Lincoln Lunatic Asylum," *Lancet*, II (London, 1840-1841), 337-39.

Cotton, H. A., "A Review of the Progress of Modern Psychiatry," *Journal of the Medical Society of New Jersey*, V (1908-1909), 74-78.

Curwen, J., "The Organization of Hospitals for the Insane," *Alienist and Neurologist*, 1881, pp. 67, 208.

"Dorothea Lynde Dix," *Lend a Hand*, V (November, 1890), 743.

Earle, Pliny, "Institutions for the Insane in Prussia, Austria, and Germany," *American Journal of Insanity*, IX (October, 1852), 106.

———, "The Psychopathic Hospital of the Future," *American Journal of Insanity*, XXIV (1867-1868), 117-30.

———, "A Visit to Gheel," *American Journal of Insanity*, VIII (1851-1852), 67.

Eaton, Dorman B., "Despotism in Lunatic Asylums," *North American Review*, CXXXII (1881), 263-75.

Eliot, William Greenleaf, "Loyal Work in Missouri," *North American Review*, XCVIII (1864), 519-30.

Flowers, B. O., "Treatment of the Insane Poor in Massachusetts Sixty Years Ago; or How a Woman Wrought a Revolution for Human Progress," *Arena*, XXXII (November, 1904), 535-42.

Gallaher, Ruth A., "Annie Turner Wittenmyer," *Iowa Journal of History and Politics*, XIX (October, 1931), 520.

Galt, J. M., "On the Propriety of Admitting the Insane of the Two Sexes into the same Lunatic Asylum," X (1854-1855), 224-30.

Girdner, John H., "Theology and Insanity," *North American Review*, CLXVIII (1899), 77-83.

Gordon, D. A., "Insanity and Physical States," *National Quarterly*, XXXIX (1879), 1 ff.

Granville, George, "Increase in Insanity," *North British Review*, L (Edinburgh, 1869), 123.

Hale, Edward Everett, "The United States Sanitary Commission," *Atlantic*, XIX (April, 1867), 416-29.

Hammond, W. A., "Society vs. Insanity," *Putnam's*, XVI (1870), 326.

Harris, Elisha, "The Sanitary Commission," *North American Review*, XCVIII (1864), 153-94.

Hathway, Marion, "Dorothea Dix and Social Reform in Western Pennsylvania, 1845-1875," *Western Pennsylvania Historical Magazine*, XVII (December, 1934), 247-57.

Hayden, C. B., "On the Distribution of Insanity," *Southern Literary Messenger*, X (March, 1844), 179-81.

Higgins, J. M., "The Necessity of a Resident Medical Superintendent in an Institution for the Insane," *American Journal of Insanity*, VII (July, 1850), 64-65.

Hill, Robert Gardiner, "Cure of Insanity," *Eclectic Review*, XXI, 39.

———, "Lunacy, Past and Present," *Edinburgh Review*, CXXXI (April, 1870), 418.

"Historical Sketch of the New Orleans Charity Hospital," *New Orleans Medical Journal*, I (May, 1844), 72-77.

"History of Ameliorations in Treatment of the Insane," *Westminister Magazine*, LXXXV, 331.

Hooper, Lucy H., "Maniacs and Madhouses of Paris," *Lippincott's Magazine*, XXI (1878), 761-63.

Hopkins, Ellice, "Moral Insane," *Fraser*, XCV (London, 1877), 425.

"Humane Treatment of the Insane," *Westminister Magazine*, LXVII, 284.

"Iniquitous Insane Asylums," *Cornhill's Magazine*, XIX, 699.

"Insane Asylums," *Penny Magazine*, X (London, 1841), 22.

"Insane Asylums of the United States," *American Journal of Insanity*, II (July, 1845), 54.

"Insanity, Disease, and Religion," *London Quarterly*, VIII (1857), 145.

"Insanity and Genius," *Nation*, XXXIX (1884), 315.

"Insanity and Madhouses," *Museum of Foreign Literature*, XXXVII (1839), 514.

"Insanity and Madhouses," *Tait's Magazine*, VI (Edinburgh, 1839), 746.

Jarvis, Edward, "Causes of Mental Disease," *North American Review*, LXXXIX (1859), 316-39.

———, "Insanity in Massachusetts," *North American Review*, LVI (1843), 171-91.

Jelliffe, Smith Ely, "Some Random notes on the History of Psychiatry in the Middle Ages," *American Journal of Psychiatry*, II (1930), 275-86.

J. R. G., "Notes on French Asylums for the Insane under the Religious," *The Month*, VIII (London, 1868), 148.

Kinnaird, J. B., "Footprints of our Medical Predecessors in Kentucky," *Kentucky Medical Journal*, XVIII (1920), 359.

Lawney, E. M., "Supervision of the Insane," *Penn Monthly*, X (1879), 431.

Lewis, W. A., "History of Medicine in the South," *Virginia Medical Monthly*, XLVIII (1922), 655-700.

Lowder, William Lane, "Pioneer Physicians of Charleston, South Carolina during the Colonial Period," *Journal of the South Carolina Medical Association*, XV (1919), 451-53.

McCarthy, F. A., "Life of Dorothea Lynde Dix," *Institution Quarterly*, VI (1915), 32-35.

McFarland, Joseph, "History of Nursing, Blockley Asylum," *Medical Life*, Series No. 146, XXXIX (November, 1932), p. 632.

McNair, Rush, "Ante-Revolutionary American Graduates of the University of Edinburgh," *Medical Age*, XXI (1903), 561-63.

Massey, G. Belton, "Organization and Management of State Hospitals for the Insane," *Penn Monthly*, X (1879), 835.

Maudsley, Fr. Henry, "Juries, Judges, Insanity," *Popular Science Monthly*, I (1872), 440.

Mayo, Thomas, "On the Moral Phenomena of Insanity and Eccentricity," *Living Age*, LXX (1861), 216-21.

"Medical Jurisprudence and Insanity," *Monthly Review*, CL (1839), 147.

Meredith, E. A., "Miss Dix, Philanthropist and Asylum Reformer," *American Journal of Politics*, III (1893), 252.

"Mr. Moss's 'Christian Commission,'" *The Nation*, VI (March 12, 1868), 214-15.

"Moral Insanity" (review of Ray's "Medical Jurisprudence"), *Nation*, XII (1871), 322-23.

Morton, W. J., "Town of Gheel in Belgium and its Insane, or Occupation and Reasonable Liberty for Lunatics," *Journal of Mental and Nervous Diseases*, VI (1881), 102-23.

Page, Charles Whitney, "Dr. Eli Todd and the Hartford Retreat," *American Journal of Insanity*, LXIX (April, 1913), 761.

Parigot, J., "Asylums and Psychiatric Administrations in France and England," *American Journal of Insanity*, XX (1863-1864), 186-200.

———, "The Gheel Question: from an American Point of View," *American Journal of Insanity*, XX (1862-1863), 332-54.

———, "Psychological Literature," *American Journal of Insanity*, XIX (1862), 3.

Pearce, F. S., "A Brief Historical Sketch of Medicine and Nursing the Insane," *Trained Nurse*, XXIX (1902), 71-75.

Powell, O. T., "A Sketch of Psychiatry in the Southern States," *American Journal of Insanity*, LIV (July, 1897), 21-36.

Prichard, J. C., Neville, W. B., and Lee, Edwin, "Insanity and Insane Hospitals," *North American Review*, XLIV (1837), 91-121.

Ray, Isaac, "Hereditary Insanity," *North American Review*, CIX (1869), 1-29. This is a translation of an article by I. Moreau.

———, "Insanity," *Monthly Review*, CL (London, 1839), 147.

———, "A Treatise on the Medical Jurisprudence of Insanity," *North American Review*, LXXIX (1852), 327-43.

———, "The Popular Feeling toward Hospitals for the Insane," *American Journal of Insanity*, IX (1852), 36-65.

———, "Statistics of Insanity in Massachusetts," *North American Review*, LXXXII (1856), 78-100.

Reeve, Henry, "Pinel, Traite sur l'Alienation Mentale," *Edinburgh Review*, II (April, 1803), 160-73.

Reid, John, "Insanity," *Eclectic Review*, XXIV (London, 1816), 183.

"Report of the Scotch Lunacy Commission," *North British Review*, XXVII (Edinburgh, 1857), 114-15.

"Reports of American Asylums," *American Journal of Insanity*, XVI (October, 1859), 219-59.

"Review, Dr. Conolly's Inquiry Concerning the Indications of Insanity," *Eclectic Review*, LIII (London, 1831), 149.

Reynolds, G., "A Fortnight with the Sanitary," *Atlantic*, XV (1865), 233-48.

Robertson, A., "Notes of a Visit to American Asylums," *Journal of Mental Science*, XV (London, 1869-1870), 49-89.

Robinson, Mary S., "Dorothea Dix," *Century Magazine*, November, 1892, p. 468.

Rush, William, "Thoughts on Insanity," *Knickerbocker*, VII (1836).

Sanborn, Frank B., "Belgian System of Family Care," *Charities Review*, IX (1899), 182.

Sears, E. I., "Treatment of the Insane," *National Magazine*, XII (1858), 25.

Shaw, Francis George, "Review of Dorothea Dix Memorial on Prisons and Prison Discipline," *The Harbinger*, I (November 8, 1845), 346-47.

Sheppard, J., "Connection between Insanity and Diseases of the Blood," *Journal of Psychological Medicine*, I (London, 1848), 541-57.

Shryock, Richard H., "Public Relations of the Medical Profession in Great Britain and the United States, 1800-1870: A Chapter in the Social History of Medicine," *Annals of Medical History*, n. s., II (May, 1930), 308-39.

Smith, Sydney, "Tuke's Asylum, York," *Edinburgh Review*, XXIII, 189.

Stimson, Julia C., and Thompson, Ethel C. S., "Women Nurses with the Union Forces," *Military Surgeon*, Reprint, February, 1928.

Stribling, Francis T., "Medical Treatment of the Insane in Virginia," *The American Journal of Medical Science*, VI (1843), 145.

Tarbell, Ida M., "The American Woman and How She Met the Experience of the War," *American Magazine*, LXIX (April, 1910), 802-7.

"Treatment of the Insane," *Tait's Magazine*, VI (Edinburgh), 246.

Tuke, Daniel Hack, "Broadmoor and Our Criminal Lunatics," *Macmillan*, XXXVIII (London, 1878), 137.

———, "Idiots," *Living Age*, XXXVIII (1853), 218-22.

———, "Legislation for the Insane," *Contemporary Review*, XXX (1877), 743.

———, "Modern Life and Insanity," *Living Age*, CXXXVI (1878) 178-86.

Van der Warker, Ely, "Government Supervision of the Insane," *Penn Monthly*, X (1879), 254.

———, "Insane Asylum Management," *Penn Monthly*, VIII (1877) 618.

Walsh, James J., "Some Chapters in the History of Care for the Insane," *Medical Life*, Series No. 139 (April, 1932), 208-20.

Wilkinson, W. C., "The United States Christian Commission," *Baptist Quarterly*, April, 1868, p. 194.

Willard, Frances E., "Dorothea Dix," *Chautauqua*, X (1890), 61.

Winslow, Forbes, "Plea of Insanity in Criminal Cases," *Southern Literary Messenger*, X (1844), 667.

III. BOOKS

Adams, James Truslow, *The March of Democracy*, 2 vols., New York, 1932-1933.

Alcott, Louisa May, *Hospital Sketches*, Boston, 1863.

———, *Hospital Sketches, and Camp and Fireside Stories*, Boston, 1872.

Ashe, Samuel A'Court, ed., *Biographical History of North Carolina*, 8 vols., Greensboro, 1905-1917.

———, *History of North Carolina*, 2 vols.: vol. I, Greensboro, 1908; vol. II, Raleigh, 1925.

Bacon, Corrine, *Prison Reform*, New York, 1917.

Bailey, Harriet, *Nursing Mental Diseases*, New York, 1920.

Barlow, John, *On Man's Power Over Himself to Prevent or Control Insanity*, Philadelphia, 1846.

Barnard, Henry, ed., *Memoirs of Eminent Teachers and Educators*, New York, 1859.

Barnes, Harry Elmer, *Evolution of Penology in Pennsylvania: A Study in American Social History*, Indianapolis, 1927.

———, *History of the Penal, Reformatory, and Correctional Institutions of the State of New Jersey*, Trenton, 1918.

———, *The Repression of Crime*, New York, 1926.

Beach, Seth Curtis, *Daughters of the Puritans*, Boston, 1905.

Bilbo, Queenie, "Elizabeth Peabody, Transcendentalist" (Unpublished Ph.D. Thesis, Columbia University, 1932).

Blanton, Wyndham B., *Medicine in Virginia in the Eighteenth Century*, Richmond, 1931.

———, *Medicine in Virginia in the Nineteenth Century*, Richmond, 1933.

——, *Medicine in Virginia in the Seventeenth Century*, Richmond, 1930.

Bolton, Sarah Knowles, *Famous Types of Womanhood*, New York, 1892. "Dorothea Dix," pp. 241-73.

Bowers, Claude G., *The Tragic Era*, Cambridge, Massachusetts, 1929.

Boyd, William K., *The Federal Period* (vol. II, Connor R. D. W., Boyd, W. K., and Hamilton, J. G. deR., *History of North Carolina*, 6 vols., Chicago and New York, 1919), Chicago, 1919.

Brayley, Arthur Wellington, *Schools and Schoolboys of Old Boston*, Boston, 1894.

Breckenridge, Sophronia P., *Public Welfare Administration in the United States*, Chicago, 1927.

Bremer, Fredrika, *Homes of the New World: Impressions of America*, 3 vols. Translated by Mary Howitt, London, 1853.

Brockett, L. P., and Vaughan, Mary C., *Our Army Nurses.* Compiled by Mary H. Gardner, 1895.

——, *Woman's Work in the Civil War*, Philadelphia, 1867.

Brown, Harvey E., *The Medical Department of the United States Army, 1775-1873*, Washington, 1873.

Brown, William Garrott, *History of Alabama*, New York, 1900.

Browne, W. A. F., *Insanity and Asylums for the Insane*, Edinburgh, 1837.

——, *What Asylums Were, Are, and Ought To Be*, Edinburgh, 1837.

Bush, George Gary, *History of Education in Massachusetts*, Washington, 1891.

Castiglioni, Arturo, *Storia della Medicina*, Milan, 1927.

Channing, William E., *Memoir of William Ellery Channing*, 3 vols., Boston, 1851.

——, *The Works of William E. Channing*, Boston, 1891.

Chase, Robert Howland, *The Ungeared Mind*, Philadelphia, 1918.

Cheney, Ednah D., *Louisa May Alcott, Her Life, Letters and Journals*, Boston, 1889.

——, "Women of Boston," in Justin Winsor, ed., *Memorial History of Boston*, 4 vols., Boston, 1880-1881.

Clarke, James Freeman, *Autobiography, Diary, and Correspondence*, ed. by E. E. Hale, Boston, 1891.

Clouston, T. S., *Unsoundness of Mind*, London, 1911.

Coleman, Emily Holmes, *The Shutter of Snow*, New York, 1930.

Collis, Septima M., *A Woman's War Record*, New York, 1889.

Colombier, J., and Doublet, F., *Instruction sur la Maniere de Gouverner les Insenses et de travailler a leur Guerison dans les Asyles qui leur sont Destines*, Paris, 1785.

Connor, R. D. W., *Makers of North Carolina History*, Raleigh, 1917.

Cooke, George Willis, *Introduction to Rowfant edition of "The Dial,"* vol. I, Cleveland, 1902.

Dictionary of American Biography, 18 vols., New York, 1928-1935.

Dock, Lavinia, *History of Red Cross Nursing,* New York, 1922.

——, and Stewart, Isabel Maitland, *Short History of Nursing,* New York, 1931.

Drewry, William F., "Care and Treatment of the Defectives in the South," *The South in the Building of the Nation,* X, 597-602, Richmond, 1909.

Duncan, Louis C., *Medical Department of the United States Army in the Civil War,* Washington, 1913.

Earle, Pliny, *A Visit to Thirteen Asylums for the Insane in Europe; to which are added a brief notice of similar institutions in transatlantic countries and in the United States,* Philadelphia, 1841.

Edmonds, S. Emma E., *Nurse and Spy in the Union Army,* Hartford, 1865.

Eliot, Charlotte C., *William Greenleaf Eliot, Minister, Educator, and Philanthropist,* Boston, 1904.

Emerson, George Barrell, *Reminiscences of an Old Teacher,* Boston, 1878.

Epler, Percy H., *Master Minds at the Commonwealth's Heart,* Worcester, 1909.

Farmer, W. S., "Care of the Insane in Tennessee," in *Centennial History of the Tennessee State Medical Association,* edited by Philip May Hamer, Nashville, 1930.

Field, Edward, *State of Rhode Island and Providence Plantations at the End of the Century,* 3 vols., Boston, 1902.

Fish, Carl Russell, *Rise of the Common Man,* New York, 1927.

Furness, Clifton Joseph, *The Genteel Female,* New York, 1931.

Galt, John M., *Essays on Asylums for Persons of Unsound Mind,* Richmond, 1850.

——, *Treatment of Insanity,* New York, 1846.

Gohdes, Clarence L. F., *Periodicals of American Transcendentalism,* Durham, 1931.

Goldberg, Jacob A., *Social Aspects in the Treatment of the Insane* (Columbia University Studies in History, Economics, and Public Law, No. CCXXI), New York, 1921.

Gooch, R., *What are the grounds of the prevailing doctrine that mental derangement is a moral disease?* (vol. VI, Transactions of the College of Physicians), London, 1820.

Goodwin, E. J., *History of Medicine in Missouri,* St. Louis, 1905.

Hale, George Silsbee, "Charities of Boston," *Memorial History of Boston,* Boston, 1881.

Hale, Sara Josepha (Buell), *Woman's Record or Sketches of all Distinguished Women from the Creation to A. D. 1868*, New York, 1870.

Harris, Charles A., *Rapid Survey of the Massachusetts Educational System*, [Holliston, 1910].

Hart, Bernard, *Psychopathology, Its Development and Its Place in Medicine*, Cambridge, England, 1927.

Hill, Robert Gardiner, *A Concise History of the Entire Abolition of Mechanical Restraint in the Treatment of the Insane, and of the Introduction, Success, and Final Triumph of the Non-Restraint System*, London, 1857.

History of Tennessee from the Earliest Time to the Present, Nashville, 1886. Published by The Goodspeed Publishing Company.

Hoge, Jane C., *The Boys in Blue; or, Heroes of the Rank and File*, New York, 1867.

Holstein, Anna Morris, *Three Years in Field Hospitals of the Army of the Potomac*, Philadelphia, 1867.

Horton, Edward A., *Noble Lives and Noble Deeds*, Boston, 1893.

Howe, Samuel Gridley, *Letters and Journals*. Edited by Laura E. Richards, 2 vols., Boston, 1906-1909.

Hubbell, George Allen, *Horace Mann, Educator, Patriot, and Reformer*, Philadelphia, 1910.

Hurd, Henry M., et. al., eds., *Institutional Care of the Insane in the United States and Canada*, 4 vols., Baltimore, 1916-1917.

Iglehart, Esther Garland, "A Brief History of the Eastern State Hospital" (Unpublished Master's Thesis, William and Mary College, Williamsburg, Virginia, 1930).

Jacobi, Maxmilian, *On the Construction and Management of Hospitals for the Insane*. Translated by John Kitching, London, 1841.

Janet, Pierre, "Neuroses and Psychoses," in *A Psychiatric Milestone* (Centenary of the Bloomingtondale Hospital, New York), New York, 1921.

Johnson, Charles Beneulyn, *Muskets and Medicine*, Philadelphia, 1917.

Kelso, Robert W., *History of Public Poor Relief in Massachusetts, 1620-1920*, Boston, 1922.

Kennard, Caroline A., *Dorothea L. Dix and Her Work*, Brookline, 1887.

Kirkbride, Thomas S., *On the Construction, Organization, and General Arrangements of Hospitals for the Insane, with some Remarks on Insanity and Its Treatment*, Philadelphia, 1880.

Koren, John, *Summaries of State Laws Relating to the Insane*. Revised by S. W. Hamilton and Roy Haber, New York, 1917.

Kraepelin, Emil, *Hundert Jahre Psychiatrie*, Berlin, 1918.

Lee, Charles A., *Report on Insanity*. Reprint from the *Transactions of the American Medical Association*, Philadelphia, 1868.

Letchworth, William P., *The Insane in Foreign Countries*, New York, 1889.

Livermore, Mary Ashton, *My Story of the War; A Woman's Narrative of Four Years' Personal Experience, as Nurse in the Union Army, and in Relief Work at Home, in Hospitals, Camps, and at the Front*, Hartford, 1888.

Mann, Mary Tyler, *Life of Horace Mann, by His Wife*, Boston, 1891.

Martineau, Harriet, *Society in America*, 3 vols., London, 1837.

Mather, Cotton, "The Life of Mr. William Thompson," in *Ecclesiastical History of New England*, book 3, chapter 17. In the edition of 1855, Boston, I, 438-40.

Memorable Unitarians. A series of biographical sketches published by the British and Foreign Unitarian Association, London, 1906.

Mesick, Jane L., *The English Traveller in America, 1735-1835*, New York, 1922.

Meyer, Adolph, "Psychiatry and Life Problems," in *A Psychiatric Milestone* (Centenary of the Bloomingtondale Hospital, New York), New York, 1921.

Miller, Francis Trevelyan, *Photographic History of the Civil War*, 10 vols., New York, 1911.

Millingen, J. D., *Aphorisms on the Treatment and Management of the Insane*, London, 1840.

Moon, Robert O., *Relation of Medicine to Philosophy*, New York, 1909.

National Cyclopedia of American Biography, The, 12 vols., New York, 1893-1921.

Nevins, Allan, *The Emergence of Modern America, 1865-1878*, New York, 1927.

Nicolay, Helen, *Our Capital on the Potomac*, New York, 1924.

Osler, William, *A Concise History of Medicine*, Baltimore, 1919.

Packard, Francis R., *History of Medicine in the United States*, 2 vols., New York, 1931.

Parrington, Vernon Louis, *Main Currents in American Thought*, 3 vols., New York, 1927-1930.

Peabody, Elizabeth, *Old Boston for Young Eyes, a letter from Grandmama to the Little Folks*, Boston, 1880.

Perry, Martha D., *Letters from a Surgeon in the Civil War*, Boston, 1906.

Pickard, Samuel T., *Life and Letters of John Greenleaf Whittier*, 2 vols., Boston, 1894.

Pinel, Philippe, *Traité médico-philosophique sur l'aliénation mentale*, Paris, 1802.

Pinel, Scipion, *Traité complet du Régime Sanitaire des Aliénés ou Manuel des Etablissemens qui leur sont consacrés*, Paris, 1836.

Ramsay, David, *History of South Carolina, 1670-1803*, 2 vols., Charleston, 1809.

Rathbone, Eleanor F., *William Rathbone: A Memoir*, New York, 1905.

Richards, Linda Ann J., *Reminiscences of Linda Richards, America's First Trained Nurse*, Boston, 1911.

Riley, Isaac Woodbridge, *American Thought from Puritanism to Pragmatism*, New York, 1915.

Robinson, Nicholas, *A New System of the Spleen, Vapours, and Hypochrondiak Melancholy*, London, 1729.

Roe, Alfred S., *Dorothea Lynde Dix*, Worcester, 1889.

Rush, Benjamin, *Medical Inquiries and Observations*, Philadelphia, 1809.

———, *Medical Inquiries and Observations, upon the diseases of the Mind*, Philadelphia, 1818.

Russell, William, ed., *A Psychiatric Milestone* (Centenary of the Bloomingtondale Hospital, New York), New York, 1921.

Sanborn, Edwin W., *Social Changes in New England in the Past Fifty Years*. Reprint, Report of the Proceedings of the American Social Science Association for 1900, Boston, 1901.

Sanborn, Franklin B., *Memoirs of Pliny Earle*, Boston, 1898.

———, *Report of the Public Charities of Massachusetts during the Century Ending January 1, 1876*, Boston, 1876.

Sanders, William H., *History, Philosophy, and Fruits of Medical Organization in Alabama*, [Montgomery, 1914].

Seldes, Gilbert V., *The Stammering Century*, New York, 1928.

Shaftesbury, Anthony Ashley Cooper, Earl of, *Speeches of the Earl of Shaftesbury Upon Subjects Having Relation Chiefly to the Claims and Interests of the Labouring Class*, London, 1868.

Shaw, Charles, *A Topographical and Historical Description of Boston*, Boston, 1817.

Souchon, Edmond, *Original Contribution of Louisiana to Medical Science*, New Orleans, 1915.

Spurzheim, J. G., *Observations on the Deranged Manifestations of the Mind, or Insanity*, Boston, 1833.

Stillé, Charles J., *History of the United States Sanitary Commission*, New York, 1868.

Stow, Sarah D. Locke, "Higher Education for Women," in George Gary Bush, ed., *History of Education in Massachusetts*, Washington, 1891.

Thayer, William Makepeace, *Women Who Win or Making Things Happen*, London, 1885.

Tiffany, Francis, *Life of Dorothea Lynde Dix*, Boston, 1890.

Tuke, Daniel Hack, *Chapters in the History of the Insane in the British Isles*, London, 1882.

———, *The Insane in the United States and Canada*, London, 1885.

————, *Insanity in Ancient and Modern Life*, London, 1878.

————, *Past and Present Provision for the Insane Poor in Yorkshire, with suggestions for the future provision of this class*, London, 1889.

United States War Department, *Surgeon-General's Medical and Surgical History of the War of the Rebellion, 1861-1865*, 8 vols., Washington, 1870.

Warner, Amos Griswold, *American Charities*. Revised by Mary Roberts Coolidge, New York, 1908.

————, *Evolution of Charities and Charitable Institutions*, New York, 1893.

White, William A., *Introduction to the Study of the Mind*, Washington, 1924.

Williamson, William D., *History of the State of Maine*, 2 vols., Hollowell, 1832.

Wilson, Francis L., *The Aristocracy of Boston for the Last Forty Years*, Boston, 1848.

Wines, E. C., *The State of Prisons and Child-Saving Institutions in the Civilized World*, Cambridge, 1880.

————, and Dwight, Theodore W., *Report on the Prisons and Reformatories of the United States and Canada, made for the Legislature of New York*, Albany, 1867.

Wisner, Elizabeth, *Public Welfare Administration in Louisiana*, Chicago, 1930.

Wittenmyer, Mrs. Annie, *Under the Guns; A Woman's Reminiscence of the Civil War*, Boston, 1895.

Woolsey, Jane Stuart, *Hospital Days*, New York, 1870.

Wormeley, Katherine P., *The United States Sanitary Commission*, Boston, 1863.

Wyse, Thomas, *Publications of the Central Society of Education*, II, London, 1838 (*Old South Leaflets*, VI, 306-11, Boston, 1843).

INDEX